Teaching
Mathematics
in Primary Schools

D. Pa

Oxford Univer

Preface

During the last twenty-five years there has been a worldwide movement towards making the content of mathematical courses in schools, colleges, and universities more appropriate to present needs. At the same time — and perhaps more importantly — much thought, time, and energy have been given to investigating ways in which children and students can be better helped to understand mathematical ideas and become more proficient in using the associated techniques.

New mathematics has now been introduced at all levels and there has been a positive move from 'telling' children to encouraging them to build up mathematical ideas through their own activities and experiences.

It is easy, however, to be too enthusiastic about changing all that has gone before. It always has to be remembered that children in primary schools still need to be competent in dealing with topics essential for everyday living. They still need a sound basis for the topics introduced in their later mathematical education.

This book has been written with these objectives in mind. To help teachers themselves, it looks again at the ideas and techniques which underlie much of what is taught. It suggests enlightened ways in which children can build up mathematical ideas through their own activities. It stresses the need for practice, through a variety of activities, in memorizing number facts. It indicates how the work can be arranged in suitable steps and how the topics can be interwoven into a coherent course. It aims at making mathematics an enjoyable subject.

It is my hope that the book will, in its own way, make a contribution towards the improvement of mathematical teaching in primary schools.

Note:

1   In this book, sterling is used whenever reference is made to money. As most countries use a decimal money system, then the local names of coins and banknotes can be substituted for pence and pounds.

2   The various pieces of apparatus detailed in the book may have to be modified at times according to availability of local materials.

D. Paling

Contents

Chapter 1
Mathematics in primary schools

What is mathematics? Why children study mathematics. Helping children to progress in mathematics. The content of the primary school mathematics course.

What is mathematics?

In primary schools throughout the world much time and effort is given to the study of mathematics. Why is this so? Why is mathematics considered to be such an important subject? When we try to answer these questions we quickly find that they lead to another: What is mathematics? Until we have an answer to this question we cannot start to discuss the place of mathematics in primary schools. Neither can we begin to consider ways of helping children to progress in the subject.

When we begin to think about 'What is mathematics?' we find that it is not easy to give one simple straightforward answer. Our idea of mathematics depends so much upon our own experiences and our own knowledge of the subject. Some of us may think only of calculations involving addition, subtraction, multiplication, and division. Some may want to include topics such as algebra, geometry, and trigonometry. Many may feel that mathematics involves some kind of logical thinking. There are many views on the subject.

However, it is likely that most of us would agree that mathematics is used in finding the answers to questions and problems which arise in everyday life and in trades and professions. Some examples of these are given below.

1 I have three pounds. I want to buy a book and a pen. Have I enough money?

2 How much petrol will I need for my car to drive from Paris to Berlin?

3 How many concrete blocks will I need to build a wall?

4 I want to make a regular hexagon from a sheet of metal. How can I mark out the hexagon?

5 A trader sells shoes. How does he decide how many of each size to order?

6 A printer is working out how much paper he will need for 5000 books. Each page is 18 cm by 24 cm and there are 96 pages in a book. The paper is in rolls, of width 100 cm. How much paper will he need?

7 A man wishes to tile a floor using various different shapes of tiles which

fit together without leaving gaps. What shapes can he use so as to form a repeating pattern?

We could go on and on listing questions of this kind. We could then start to list more difficult problems which arise in science, industry, technology, government, education, and economics.

When we try to find the answer to any of these problems we make use of:

a) the information we are given;

b) our knowledge of numbers, shapes, and measures;

c) our ability to calculate.

There is one other essential requirement. We must be able to recognize and use relationships. For example, using the questions listed earlier:

in (2), to calculate how much petrol I need, I have to use the relationship between the distance from Paris to Berlin and the number of kilometres my car goes on one litre of petrol.

in (3), to calculate the number of blocks I need, I have to use the relationships between the length and height of a block and the length and height of the wall.

in (7), to decide what shapes he can use, the man who is tiling the floor has to make use of the relationship between the angles of various regular polygons and the ways in which they can be fitted together to make 360°.

We can now give a *first* answer to "What is mathematics?". We see it as a way of finding answers to problems; a way in which we use information, use our knowledge of shapes and measures, use our ability to calculate, and – most important – think for ourselves in seeing and using relationships. This view of mathematics is sufficient to enable us to go on to consider why we think children should study mathematics and how we can best help them to progress in their studies.

Why children study mathematics

In our everyday life we all need:

a) to be able to count and make simple calculations with numbers;

b) to know about money and be able to make simple calculations;

c) to be able to measure and make simple calculations;

d) to be able to recognize shapes and know some of their properties.

It is also helpful if we are able to deal with ordinary fractions, decimal fractions, and percentages and able to read and understand graphs in their various forms.

Side by side with satisfying these needs it is necessary that we should develop as far as possible our ability to use our knowledge in dealing with specific problems. There is no point in acquiring knowledge if we cannot use it. "

Some of these needs arise at an early age. So it is necessary to provide for them throughout the whole age range of the primary school. For this reason mathematics is considered to be an essential subject in primary schools throughout the world.

There is, however, more to it than this. In the modern world, mathematics is being increasingly used in science, technology, industry, government, education, and economics. If a country wishes to produce men and women able to cope with the subject at these higher levels, then it must make sure that the proper foundations are provided in the primary school. This need highlights the necessity for children not only to acquire a body of knowledge but also to think for themselves in seeing and using relationships. For at the higher levels the latter becomes all important.

Helping children to progress in mathematics

From the start our approach in the classroom must be based on two interwoven objectives:

a) the need to pass on to the children a body of mathematical knowledge and skills,

b) the need to develop as far as possible the ability of each child to think for himself or herself in acquiring and using this knowledge.

Linked with these two objectives is the need to remember how a child builds up a mathematical idea or fact. Using $2 + 2 = 4$ as an example:

a) A young child finds that if he has two beans and puts with them two more beans, he has four beans altogether.

b) He then finds that if he uses other objects (pencils, oranges, bottle-tops, etc.) he always gets the same total (four).

c) From these many practical activities he generalizes the result as $2 + 2 = 4$.

This is a very simplified example but it does illustrate the kind of progression which we should have in mind when we are thinking about introducing new ideas to children. The starting-point is very important. As far as possible it should involve some practical activity by each child — handling objects, drawing, sorting, measuring, etc. — with a simple clear question to answer. The children can then go on to other similar activities and, in time, begin to see the general result which emerges from all of these practical activities. Discussion will, of course, play an important part in helping the children to see the generalized result.

3

The importance of discussion cannot be over-stressed. If children are expected to think for themselves they *must* be given the opportunity to ask questions. As adults we all know how essential discussion is in sorting out problems in everyday life. It helps us to know all the facts and then to see the relationships between them. So it should be with children. They should be *encouraged* to ask questions and to discuss problems with each other and with the teacher.

Discussion not only helps the children, but can also be of great help to the teacher. For the questions the children ask often indicate very clearly to the teacher the way in which they are thinking. They can also indicate whether a child really understands some new idea or whether his thinking about it is muddled.

Another important factor to bear in mind when planning the children's work is the need for practice. Understanding must come first, but this in itself is not always enough. For example, a child may understand that 7×5 represents $7 + 7 + 7 + 7 + 7$, without being able to give the result (35) quickly. He will need practice, of the right kind, so that he can memorize $7 \times 5 = 35$, and, whenever necessary, use it without thinking.

There is another kind of practice which is also essential. For example, the division $125 \div 9$, has to be done in various steps. The teacher may think that a child understands these, but it is only after the child has done several of the same type successfully that the teacher can be sure. If the child gets incorrect answers, his written working should be examined carefully to see where he has made mistakes. These may arise from a lack of understanding of the division operation. They may however arise from other factors, such as errors in multiplication or subtraction. Whatever the cause, the mistakes need to be discussed fully. This is the reason for this kind of practice. It is to clarify misunderstandings. It is not to give more practice in something which a child can do successfully. For an able child this can be very tedious and boring.

Above all, in planning our work in mathematics we should aim at making it lively and enjoyable. This can be achieved if each child feels personally involved in and understands the work he is doing, if he sees the relevance of the topics he is studying, if he feels free to ask questions, and if he experiences reasonable success. The pleasure, interest, and desire to work which children feel usually reflect, of course, the attitude of their teacher towards the subject. If a teacher shows these attitudes in his teaching most children will develop them too.

This approach to the teaching of mathematics makes heavy demands on the teacher. It requires skill, insight, dedication, and much hard work and time both in and out of the classroom. In the ideal situation the teacher must be concerned with each child as an individual and must cater for his or her particular abilities and aptitudes. With a class of thirty or more children this is far from easy to organize. Even with a large class, however, there are times — especially in practical activities — when it is possible to arrange the work on an individual basis. There are times, too, when the children can work in small groups, arranged according to the stage they have reached or the abilities they have shown. At other times class teaching is appropriate and desirable.

Most teachers find that children progress best if a mixture of individual, group, and class activities is used. Ways of doing this are discussed in detail in the chapters which follow.

The content of the primary school mathematics course

During recent years much thought has been given to the content of the primary school mathematics course. It was considered that too much time and effort were being spent on meaningless work. Some of the topics which had been traditionally included were out-of-date and no longer relevant to the needs of everyday life or science and industry. Too much emphasis was being placed on rote learning, and many children did not understand what they were doing.

Changes have now been made. New topics have been introduced which are more relevant to the needs of the children and of their country. Greater emphasis is being placed on helping children to think for themselves, to learn through their own activities, and to enjoy what they are doing.

NNS

Thinking about
the first two years

Before a child goes to school he learns much from all that is happening in and about his home, in the streets, and in shops. He learns to listen, to understand, and to speak his language. He has many experiences, some of which are linked with the basic ideas of mathematics (without, of course, using mathematical language). For example:

he uses containers such as cups, bowls, buckets, and jugs;

he handles shapes such as cuboids, cubes, spheres, and cylinders;

he takes part in sorting activities (e.g. sorting beans or beads according to size or colour);

he uses the ideas of *much* and *little, more than* and *less than, big* and *small, full* and *empty*;

he uses the idea of matching (a plate for father, a plate for mother, a plate for John, a plate for Sarah, etc.);

he takes the first steps in learning to count.

These activities involve handling shapes, sorting, comparing, and matching. These are all important aspects of mathematics.

We should remember that most children have had these pre-school experiences. We should extend and develop them during a child's first few weeks at school. This will help very much to form a bridge between everyday life and school.

At the same time as we look backwards at what children have done before they come to school, we must look forwards and plan what they should be doing during their early years at school. For convenience we will start by thinking of the kind of experiences they should have during the first two years, remembering, of course, that any plan may need to be adapted to fit best the needs of a particular school.

During the changeover to more enlightened teaching methods there has been much discussion about the work in the first two years. Now, it is generally agreed that if the topics listed below are covered the children will have a good foundation for the work which follows later in the primary course.

a) Sorting.

b) Comparing two objects (*longer than, heavier than, holds more than*, etc.).

c)   Arranging objects in order (of length, height, value, etc.).

d)   Comparing two sets of objects (*more than, as many as, fewer than*).

e)   Combining two sets of objects.

f)   The idea of a number and a numeral. The cardinal and ordinal aspects of a number.

g)   The idea of place-value.

h)   The first ideas of addition, subtraction, multiplication, and division.

i)   Handling, recognizing, and describing common 2-D and 3-D shapes.

j)   Recognizing and using common coins and bank notes.

k)   Measuring and measures. The use of 'natural' measures (e.g. a stride) and standard measures (e.g. a metre).

l)   Starting to tell the time.

m) The first ideas of graphical representation. Use of an arrowed line for a phrase (e.g. *is longer than*).

n)   The use of the symbols $=, +, -, \times, \div$.

o)   The idea and use of a number line.

p)   The first ideas of a fraction.

   In Chapter 2, the ways in which the pre-school experiences can be extended and developed are discussed. In the chapters which follow the topics listed above are discussed in detail.

Chapter 2
The first few weeks

Handling shapes. Sorting sets. Comparing the members of a set. Matching the members of two sets.

In 'Thinking about the first two years' it was suggested that in the first few weeks we should try to form a bridge between a child's pre-school activities and the mathematical activities of the first year. One way of doing this is to provide activities which involve:

a) *handling shapes*. These link the pre-school activities with the need to develop a child's awareness of shapes and their names and properties.

b) *sorting sets of objects*. These give more experience of sorting, which is an essential part of much of the mathematics which follows.

c) *comparing the members of a set of objects*. These introduce the idea and use of phrases such as *is longer than, is shorter than, holds more than,* etc. Again these are important mathematical ideas.

d) *matching the members of two sets of objects*. These lead to the idea and use of *more than, fewer than, as many as*. The idea of *as many as* leads to the idea of the number of a set.

Some helpful activities which can be used for this stage of the work are given below. The apparatus needed is first described. Some items may need to be modified according to local availability of materials.

Sorting

Apparatus

1 Beads   Where clay is available, beads can be made by the children.
For some activities, each bead needs to have a hole through its centre. This can be done at the time the bead is made, by putting the bead on a bicycle spoke or thin twig to make the hole, and leaving it there to dry. The beads may later be coloured by soaking them in dye or paint.

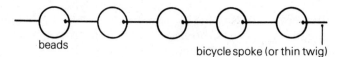

beads   bicycle spoke (or thin twig)

2 Seeds These can be collected by the children and, if necessary, can be coloured by soaking in dye or covering with paint.

3 Bottle-tops, buttons, pebbles These can be collected by the children.

4 Set boxes Empty cigarette packets (or other suitable small cartons) can be collected by the children. In each the teacher puts a selection of different objects. Each child can then be provided with a 'set of objects'. The packets should be collected at the end of the lesson and kept by the teacher.

5 Sorting frames Cornstalks, canes, string, etc. are laid on a table or desk to make a sorting frame. The children use the spaces for sorting objects.

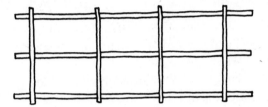

6 Sorting trays A shallow, rectangular carton is divided into sections by using cardboard strips, cornstalks, sticks, or canes. The sections are used for sorting objects.

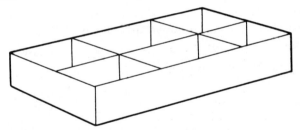

For use with a set of larger objects, large stones can be used to make a sorting tray on the floor of the classroom.

stones

Activities

1 The children regularly tidy up the classroom — this a sorting activity. They put the pencils, crayons, books, etc. in their proper places. The rubbish is put in a separate container.

2   Each child is given a set of objects (as described in item 4 of the apparatus). He puts them all together on the desk and then sorts them (beads, seeds, etc.). He can show the sorting by:

a)   using a sorting frame;

b)   using a sorting tray;

c)   drawing a loop with chalk round each set of objects;

d)   putting a loop of string round each set of objects.

When sorting is completed the children describe the objects in each set.

3   The children sort their set of objects, as in Activity 2, but now use other properties. For example, they sort:

a)   by colour (red, green, brown, etc.);

b)   by material (metal, fabric, stone, etc.);

c)   by use (for writing, for growing, for clothing, etc.).

4   During or after a Physical Education lesson the children sort the apparatus into sets of balls, hoops, ropes, etc. They can enclose each set in a loop of rope on the floor, or in a chalked loop drawn on the floor.

5   The children in a class sort themselves in various ways. For example:

a)   boys; girls;

b)   children with brothers; children without brothers;

c)   children with sisters; children without sisters;

d)   children who live in the same village or district;

e)   children who are taller than a particular boy or girl; children who are shorter than the boy or girl.

6   Four different fruits are used (e.g. banana, orange, pineapple, and apple) and one is placed in each of the four corners of the room. Each child then decides which of the four fruits he or she likes best and goes quietly to the corner in which this fruit has been placed.

7   The children repeat Activity 6 but, instead of four fruits, pictures of four animals are used, and then four differently coloured pieces of material.

8   Each child is given a set of cardboard shapes (e.g. circles, squares, triangles, and rectangles). The set should contain large circles and small circles, large squares and small squares, etc., and different colours should be used (e.g. large red circles, small red circles, large blue circles, small blue circles, etc.). The children sort the set of shapes in various ways. For example:

a)   circles; triangles; squares; rectangles;

b)   red shapes; blue shapes; etc.;

c) large shapes; small shapes;

d) shapes with straight edges; shapes with curved edges.

The children show their sortings by using a sorting frame, a sorting tray, or chalked loops on their desks.

9 For this activity a good supply of wooden cubes of various colours (e.g. some red, some blue, some yellow, and some green) is needed. If these are not available painted cartons (e.g. cigarette packets) can be used. In turn, each child chooses a cube (or packet) of the colour he or she best likes. As they choose they put the cubes (or packets) of the same colour on top of each other, as shown below.

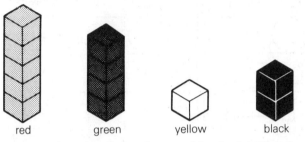

red   green   yellow   black

The children discuss what they have done and by looking at the various completed towers of cubes decide which colour is most popular and which is least popular. This activity can be thought of as a first introduction to the idea of a block graph.

10 The children bring empty matchboxes to school. In some of these the teacher puts a pebble, in some a bead, in some an imitation coin, in some a bean. The boxes are then all put on a table and each child chooses a box. In turn, each child says what is in his box. They then make piles of boxes containing the same kind of article, as shown below. This activity is another introduction to the idea of a block graph.

The children say which pile has most boxes and which has least.

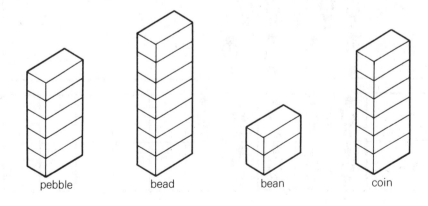

pebble   bead   bean   coin

11 A large sheet of plain paper with a grid of squares drawn on it is fastened to the blackboard. The rows of the grid are labelled with the names of simple shapes, as shown.

Each child has a piece of gummed paper (a little smaller than a square on the grid). On this he draws one of the four shapes. In turn the children then stick their pieces of gummed paper onto the grid (starting at the left of the row corresponding to the shape they have drawn).

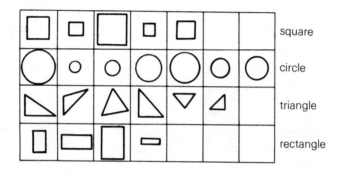

The children then discuss which row has most shapes and which has least.

12 The children work in groups. Each group makes a drawing to show the boys and girls in the group. There are two examples of such drawings below. Which do you think is the more useful?

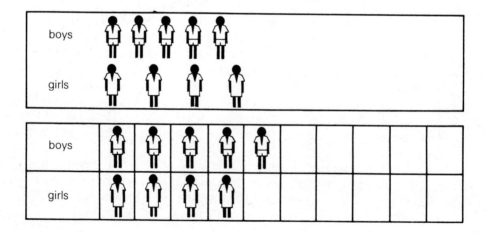

A grid, as in the second drawing, should always be used for activities like this. This helps to show how the first set matches the second set.

A drawing of this kind is often called a picto-graph. It is sometimes called an iso-type.

Many sorting activities can be represented by simple drawings in this way. For example, sorting beads by colour, sorting containers (cups, tins, bowls, buckets, etc.), sorting children by age or by the size of their shoes, etc.

Comparing

We compare two or more objects by looking for differences and similarities. Where possible, we should use all our senses — sight, hearing, touch, smell, and taste to find out these differences and similarities. To express the differences and similarities we may use the ideas of length, mass, capacity, etc. These will introduce the use of phrases such as *is longer than, is heavier than*, holds *as much as*, etc.

If the children have not reached the stage of being able to write a sentence such as 'Peter is taller than Kaye' to record an activity, then the idea of using an arrowed line (called an *arrow* in a shorter form) to record an activity can be introduced and discussed. Using this idea the sentence is recorded by a simple drawing such as:

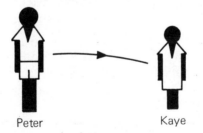

Peter   Kaye

It is very important that the children understand that the arrow stands for *is taller than* and that they should have practice in reading and saying the sentence shown as 'Peter *is taller than* Kaye'.

This kind of arrow can be used whenever necessary for many other phrases such as *holds more than, is shorter than*, etc. Each time it is used, however, it is essential that the children say what it stands for and read the complete sentence shown by their recording. If they do not do this they might easily become confused.

A recording in which an arrow is used is called an *arrow graph*. An arrow graph is very useful in later work in showing relationships between several members of a set or between the members of two sets. An example of each of these uses is shown on the next page.

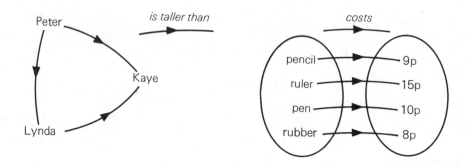

It will be noticed that the phrase for which the arrow stands is written above an arrow on the arrow graph. This is essential if other people are to be able to read and understand the graph. As soon as children can write the phrases the teacher should insist that they show what the arrow stands for in this way.

Activities

Note: In Activities 1 to 7 the children are looking for the member of the set which *is different from* the others.

In Activities 8 to 15 the children are *comparing* two members of a set.

1   Five boys (or five girls) stand in front of the class. Four have their hands by their sides. One has his hands on his head. Ask the class to say which child is different and in what way he is different. (The children may, of course, notice other differences. Discuss these with them.)

2   Repeat Activity 1, using differences such as: one child has a book in his hand; one child is sitting down; one child has his eyes closed; etc.

3   Put a set of five tins on the teacher's desk, so that all the children can see them. Four tins are the same, one is bigger. Ask the children to touch the one which is different. Ask them to say how it is different.

4   Tell the children to close their eyes and listen. Tap on the desk four times and once on a bottle or tin. Ask the children to say which sound is different. (This can be varied in many ways, perhaps using the foot or a drum.)

5   Ask the children to listen carefully while you clap a rhythm with your hands. Clap-clap; clap-clap; clap-clap; clap-clap. (Clap this rhythm several times.) Change the rhythm. Clap-clap; clap-clap; clap-clap; clap. (Clap this rhythm several times.) Ask the children to say what is different.

6   Bring each child in turn to the front of the class. Tell him to hold his hands out in front of him and to close his eyes. Put four objects (e.g. stones) in his hands, one large and the other three small and about the same size. Tell him to show, without looking, which one is different from the others.

He should hold up the largest stone. Ask him to say how it is different, and to say in what way the others are the same as each other. Use other common objects, e.g. three pencils and a pen; three pieces of chalk and a pencil; three stones and a rubber.

7   Use five tins of the same size, four of them full of sand, one empty. Ask a child to come to the front and, with eyes closed, to pick up each tin in turn. He decides which one is different. (You can vary this activity by having the four tins empty and the one tin full.)

8   Ask two children of different heights to stand side-by-side. Using their real names, the other children should make statements such as 'Joey *is taller than* Anna', 'Anna *is shorter than* Joey'.

9   Ask three children to stand in a line and arrange themselves in order of height. The other children can use phrases like *is taller than* and *is shorter than* to make statements about the heights of pairs of children.

10   Use two poles or canes of different lengths to introduce the use of *is longer than* and *is shorter than*.
    Discuss the ways in which the children decide which is longer or shorter.

11   Give a child two large stones of different masses. He should hold each stone in turn and then make a statement using *is heavier than*. He may also decide which *is heavier than* the other by holding one stone in each hand at the same time.

12   Repeat Activity 11, but use two objects made of different materials (e.g. a piece of metal and a bag of flour).

13   Collect containers of different shapes, preferably ones which can be seen through (e.g. squash bottles, Fanta bottles, medicine bottles, jam jars). Ask the children 'Which do you think holds more water, the jam jar or the Fanta bottle?'. If a child says the Fanta bottle holds more than the jam jar, ask him how he would check this. He might decide to fill the bottle with water. Then tell him to pour the water from the bottle into the jam jar.
    Discuss the result of the activity with the children, using phrases such as *more than, less than, as much as*. Repeat this activity for other pairs of containers.

Note: in activities of this kind some children will insist that a tall container holds more than a shorter one. Filling the taller container with water and showing that the water does not fill the shorter container does not always convince them. It has been found that young children often think in this way in the early stages of dealing with capacity. The teacher needs to be patient and to give these children plenty of practical experience to help them to understand that they cannot use height alone in comparing the capacities of containers.

14   Collect other containers of various sizes and shapes, including some which may not hold water (e.g. sugar bags, jugs, matchboxes, cups, tins, large spoons, etc.). Repeat Activity 13 but this time use dry sand instead of water. Make sure that the children understand that they must fill the containers to the same *level*.

15   Let the children work in small groups. Each group should have a bucket or bowl of water or dry sand, and containers of different sizes and shapes. In turn, each child of the group should choose two containers and ask another child a question about them using the phrases *more than, less than*, or *as much as*. The child who asks the question can check the answer he is given by filling one of the containers with either water or dry sand which he then pours into the other, as in Activities 13 and 14 above.

Matching the members of two sets

In these activities the use of the phrases *more than, as many as*, and *fewer than* is introduced. The use of *as many as* brings in the important idea of one-to-one correspondence. An understanding of this type of correspondence is necessary for understanding the idea of a number and much of the work which will follow in both primary and secondary school.

Activities

1   Place five girls where they can be seen by the other children. Arrange four chairs near them. Tell the girls to sit on the chairs, with only one girl on each chair. They find that one girl does not have a chair. There are *more* girls *than* chairs. Repeat for other numbers (e.g. 6 girls and 3 chairs; 2 girls and 4 chairs; 3 girls and 3 chairs; etc.). Depending upon the number of girls and chairs, children will find that there are either *more* girls *than* chairs, or *fewer* girls *than* chairs, or *as many* girls *as* chairs.

2   Repeat Activity 1 for other sets. For example:

a)   a set of boys and a set of books;

b)   a set of boys and a set of girls;

c)   a set of pencils and a set of exercise books.

3   Draw on a large sheet of paper, or on the blackboard, a set of boys and a set of goats, as in the example on the next page.

Ask a child to draw an arrow from each boy to a goat. (The arrow can be thought of as meaning *is joined to* or *has*.)

When the child has drawn the arrows, he finds that for one goat there is no boy. There are *more* goats *than* boys. The children should also compare the goats and the boys by using 'There are *fewer* boys *than* goats'.

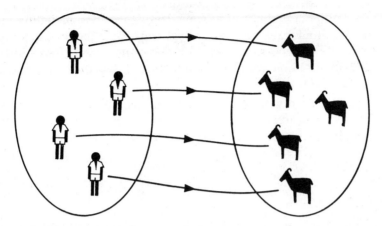

4 Repeat Activity 3 with many other pairs of sets to give practice in the use of *more than, as many as*, and *fewer than*.

5 Draw four circles on the blackboard. Underneath them draw three squares. Ask children in turn to draw a line from each circle to a square. They will find that one of the circles does not have a square. Ask questions such as: 'Are there more squares than circles?'; 'Are there as many squares as circles?'; 'Are there fewer squares than circles?'.

6 Let the children work in pairs. One child in each pair is given a heap of beans. The other is given a heap of bottle-tops. The numbers of beans and bottle-tops in this case are the same. The first child holds up some beans in his hand and the second child must pick up a bottle-top for each bean the first child holds. The second child has *as many* bottle-tops *as* the first child's beans. Repeat for other sets of beans and bottle-tops (i.e. where the number of beans and bottle-tops are not the same).

Summary

From the many activities described in this chapter a child should have made a start in learning how to:

listen to and understand a question

try to find the answer

use simple ways of recording activities

use and understand words and phrases such as: *is longer than, is shorter than, is taller than, is heavier than, more than, less than, as much as, as many as, fewer than*

---

numbers

The idea of a number

We have all used the word *number* for many years, but if we were asked to say exactly what the word means we might not find it easy. Some of us might say 'A number tells us *how many* there are in a set'. But what do we mean by *how many*? To explain this phrase we want to go back and use the word *number*. It can become confusing.

We need to make sure that we ourselves understand the idea of a number. There are two possible approaches we can use. One approach is based on *as many as*. The other uses the idea of *one more*.

1 Using the idea of *as many as*   Look at the sets below. Which of the sets are alike? In what way are they alike? Can you think of a way of sorting them?

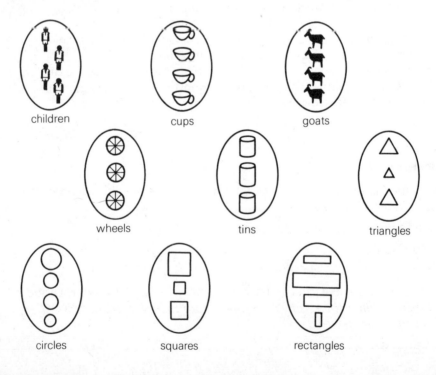

children   cups   goats

wheels   tins   triangles

circles   squares   rectangles

One way of sorting the sets is to use the idea of *as many as*. This method is shown below:

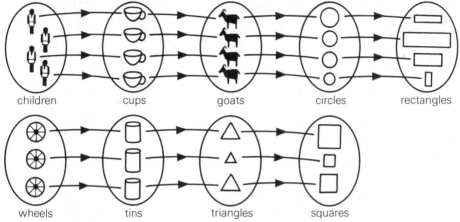

To describe each of these sortings and to distinguish them from each other we introduce the word *number*. We say that all sets which have *as many as* the set of children have the same *number*. In the same way, all sets which have *as many as* the set of wheels also have the same number (but different from the number of the children). To distinguish between the numbers we introduce number names. These names are different depending upon which language is used (e.g. English, Spanish, French). Almost all languages have number names. In English the number name for the set of children (and all other sets with *as many as*) is *four*: in French it is *quatre*; in Spanish it is *quatro*.

The number name for the set of wheels (and all other sets with *as many as*) is *three* in English, *trois* in French, and *tres* in Spanish.

We can go on to use the idea of *as many as* to give number names to all sets.

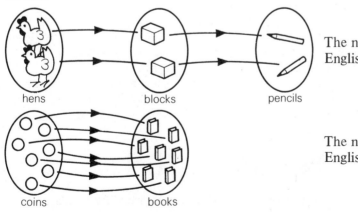

The number name, in English, is *two*.

The number name, in English, is *seven*.

2 Using the idea of *one* and *one more*

The second way in which we can build up the idea of a number starts with a set such as that on the right.
To this set and to all other sets with *as many as* we give the number name *one* (in English).

We then put one more member into the set, as shown. To this new set — and to all other sets with *as many as* — we give the number name *two*.

We then put another member into the set, as shown. To this set — and to all other sets with *as many as* — we give the number name *three*. Going on in this way we can give a number name to all possible sets that we can think of.

Numerals

When men first tried to record numbers they often used pebbles or stones. For example, they used a pebble to show each of their goats. This was not very satisfactory as it was not convenient to carry a heap of pebbles around with them. So they used other ways. For example, they cut notches on a stick, or tied knots in a strip of hide. The early Egyptians made marks on clay or chiselled them in stone.

The Romans used:

I for *one*, II for *two*, III for *three*, V for *five*, X for *ten*, etc.

Nowadays we use:

1 for *one*, 2 for *two*, 3 for *three*, 4 for *four*, etc.

These symbols for number names are called *numerals*. Our present-day numerals are usually referred to as Hindu–Arabic numerals, as they originated in India and were extensively used in the Arab world.

We should not necessarily expect our modern symbols to last forever unchanged. It is interesting to see how our present day numerals have been slightly modified so that they can be 'read' more easily by a computer. For this purpose the numerals used are:

$$0\ 1\ 2\ 3\ 4\ 5\ 6\ 7\ 8\ 9$$

You may have seen numerals like these on cheques issued by banks.

You will notice that the symbol for the number name of an empty set (zero) appears for the first time in this book. This is a very important symbol but its introduction and use should not be hurried with children.

The cardinal and ordinal aspects of numbers

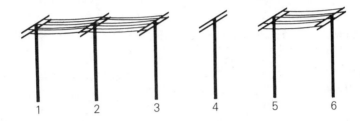

Look at the telegraph poles shown above.

How many are there altogether?

How would you describe the position of the pole with no wires attached to it?

The answer to the first question is 6. It tells us the number of the set of poles.

The answer to the second question is that the pole is the fourth from the left. It is labelled 4.

The answer to the first question uses the *cardinal* aspect of a number. It tells us the *number* of a set.

The answer to the second question uses the *ordinal* aspect of a number. It uses a number to tell us the *position* of a member of a set.

The use of these two aspects of numbers are, of course, very closely interwoven. When, for example, we count the members of a set, we use the ordinal aspect of numbers. We say, *one, two, three, four, . . .* until we have named each member of the set. If, for example, the last name we use is *eight*, then we say that the number of the set is eight. This gives us the cardinal number of the set.

We need to be aware of these two aspects of numbers in our teaching.

Chapter 3
Numbers and numerals: first ideas

Introducing numbers and numerals in three stages: up to five; five to ten; eleven to twenty. Apparatus. Activities.

Before children start school most of them will have used both the cardinal and ordinal aspects of numbers. They will, for example, be able to see that the number of a set is three, and will also be able to count *one, two, three*. Other children, however, may have had little experience of either. We need to make sure that all children build up an understanding of both. In doing this we must remember that if the emphasis is too much on counting, children may ignore the cardinal aspect. (For example, when they are asked to use their fingers to show five, some children show only the fifth finger.) They also need to be introduced to the numerals (the symbols for numbers) and given regular practice in using and writing them.

The numbers and numerals should be introduced in stages. For example:

a) up to five.

b) six to ten.

c) eleven to twenty. (The first ideas of place-value can be introduced at this stage but are not essential.)

d) twenty-one to one hundred. (An understanding of place-value is very helpful at this stage.)

e) over one hundred. (These bring in an extension of the idea and use of place-value.)

The activities for each stage should be spread over a long period of time. The children should be given lots of practice and the work should not be hurried. This is very important when the first ideas of place-value are introduced.

In this chapter, only the first three stages are discussed (i.e. numbers up to twenty). The other stages are dealt with in the section 'Thinking about place-value' and in Chapters 9 and 10. Some suitable activities for the early stages are listed later in this chapter, but first, details are given of some simple, easily made, essential apparatus.

Apparatus

1 Numeral cards (1 to 10)

A set of large cards is needed for the teacher.

Many sets of smaller cards are needed for the children.

These cards can be made from cartons collected by the children. The numeral can be painted with glue and sprinkled with sand (this helps the children to feel the shape of the numeral) or it can be drawn with a coloured marker.

2 Numeral jigsaws

The shapes of the numerals are made from plywood or thick card. Paint each shape a different colour, then cut each one into three or four pieces. This will stop the small pieces getting mixed up.

3 Counting bars

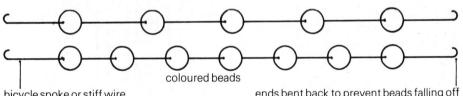

coloured beads

bicycle spoke or stiff wire

ends bent back to prevent beads falling off

These bars can have various numbers of beads on them (from 1 to 10).

4 Counting frames

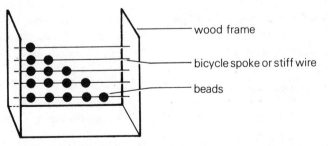

wood frame

bicycle spoke or stiff wire

beads

Some frames should be made for the numbers 1 to 5; others for the numbers 1 to 10.

5 Bead bar

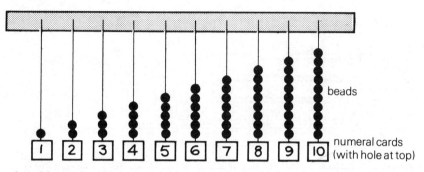

Some bead bars should be made for 1 to 5 and others for 1 to 10. Bottle-tops, with holes punched in them, can be used instead of beads.

6 A number ladder

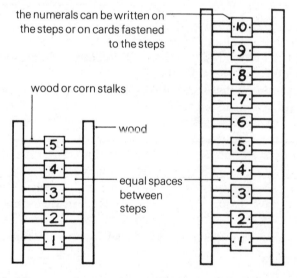

Two number ladders are shown above. Each should be large enough to be placed at the front of the class so that all the children can see it.

7 A string number line

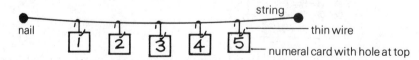

One number line should be made for 1 to 5, and later, another for 1 to 10. The line should be fixed in a position so that all the children can see it and, by standing on a chair, reach it.

8 Coloured number strips

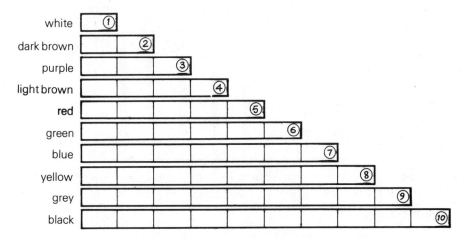

Use strips of card, all the same width (about 2 cm). The various strips should be of different colours (e.g. as indicated).

For a start the strips for 1 to 5 will be needed. Later those for 6 to 10 will also be needed.

If possible a set of strips should be provided for each child. Each set should be carefully kept in a large envelope or plastic bag. This is an important piece of apparatus and will be used throughout the first two years. When the strips for 1 to 5 are used some extra 1-strips and 2-strips are needed (so that, for example, a child can put three 1-strips end-to-end at the side of a 3-strip). Altogether, the set of strips for the numerals 1 to 5 should contain: five 1-strips   two 2-strips   one 3-strip
one 4-strip   one 5-strip.   The set of strips for the numerals 1 to 10 should contain: ten 1-strips   five 2-strips   three 3-strips
two 4-strips   two 5 strips   one each of the 6, 7, 8, 9, and 10-strips.

9 Skittles

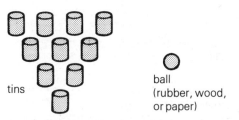

tins

ball
(rubber, wood,
or paper)

A set of skittles can be provided by using ten (or less) empty tins (tall tins are most suitable). The ball can be of rubber or wood. If neither of these is available, then sheets of newspaper can be squeezed into a ball and kept in shape by putting elastic bands tightly round it.

10 Practice numeral sheets

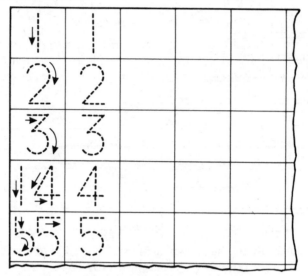

Provide each child with a duplicated sheet, like that above, for the numerals 1 to 5. The first column shows how the numerals are formed. (These drawings need to be discussed in detail.) The second column is for the children to draw over. The other columns are for practice in writing the numerals.

11 A sand tray

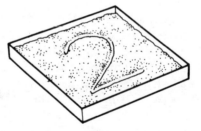

A sand tray helps children to learn to draw numerals correctly. Any large tray or shallow box or box-lid may be used. A depth of 1 cm of sand is enough. After each attempt at drawing the tray is shaken to make the surface of the sand smooth again.

Numbers and numerals up to 5

Activities

1 The children have more practice in the use of: *as many as, fewer than,* and *more than.* For example, the teacher arranges a set of chairs and a set of children in front of the class.

The children are then asked to say whether there are *as many* chairs *as* children, *fewer* chairs *than* children, or *more* chairs *than* children. A child sits on, or stands behind, each chair and the children see, in this example, that for one child there is no chair. There are *more* children *than* chairs. This kind of activity should be repeated many times with various sets of objects.

2   Several sets of objects are drawn on the blackboard.

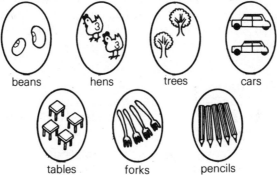

The children draw arrowed lines to show for which pairs of sets they can use *as many as*.

3   From Activity 2, the children pick out sets which have *as many as* the set of beans. For example:

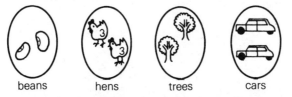

The number name *two* is given to each of these sets. In the same way the number names *three, four, five,* and *one* are introduced.

4   The idea of *one more than* is used to build up sets with 1, 2, 3, 4, and 5 members. For example, each child uses his set of objects.

He puts one on his desk and says *one*.

He puts another on his desk, close to the first, and says *two*.

He puts another on his desk, close to the first two, and says *three*.

He continues in this way for *four* and *five*.

5   The children use a counting frame for 1 to 5, as described on page 23. They count the number of beads in each row.

6   The children work in pairs and are given a set of counting bars, as described on page 23. They count the number of beads on each and check each other's results.

7   A number ladder for 1 to 5, as described on page 24, is used. A child touches the bottom step and says *one*. He then goes up the ladder, step by step, saying the number name as he touches each step.

8   Working in small groups, the children play skittles (with 5 skittles). In turn they each throw the ball and count the number of skittles they knock down. The number name *zero* may have to be used in this game.

   If skittles are not available the children can play the game of *bean bags in a ring*. Each child throws in turn five cotton bags filled with beans into a circle chalked on the floor. He counts the number in the circle (and on the chalk line).

9   The numerals, 1 to 5, are gradually introduced.

a)   The teacher first discusses the numerals for one, two, and three. He draws three sets of objects — with one, two, and three members — on the blackboard and writes the corresponding numeral at the side of each set when he has drawn it.

b)   Each child is given a set of numeral cards for 1, 2, and 3. He puts a numeral card on his desk and then, at its side, puts the corresponding number of objects. This kind of activity is repeated many times.

c)   The teacher shows, on the blackboard, how the numerals 1, 2, and 3, are formed.

The children practise writing these numerals. They find it easier to draw large — rather than small — numerals in the early stages, so provide large sheets of paper or scrap cardboard on which they can practise.

Other activities which help children to recognize and draw the numerals are:

    i)   the use of a sand-tray as described on page 26.

    ii)   the use of *sky-writing*. In this activity each child in a class raises one arm and, with one finger outstretched, writes a numeral (called out by the teacher) in the air. If the teacher stands at the back of the class he can quickly see which children are not forming the numerals correctly.

    iii)   the use of duplicated sheets, as described in (10) on page 26.

    iv)   the use of numeral cards with sanded surfaces, as described on page 23. A child rubs one of his fingers along the numeral (making sure that he has the correct starting-point). From this he gets a feel of how the numeral is formed.

    v)   the use of numeral jig-saws, as described on page 23.

d) The activities (a), (b), and (c) are extended to include the numerals 4 and 5.

10   The coloured number strips, as described on page 25, are used. Each child has a set of strips, for 1 to 5.

He places 1-strips at the side of a 3-strip, as below, and finds that three 1-strips make a 3-strip.

He repeats this activity for the 2-, 4-, and 5-strips. The children may also experiment at this stage to find which strips, placed end-to-end, make up, for example, a 4-strip.

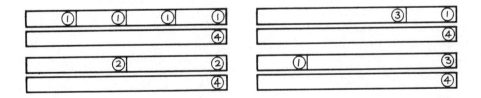

This activity gives practice in fitting together, using the idea of *has the same length as*. Some children may ask whether 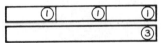 and are the same or different. This should be discussed and the children should be helped to see that, although the same two strips are used, there is a change in the order in which they are placed.

11   A number tray like that shown below is used.

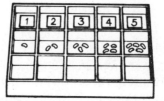

Numeral cards for 1, 2, 3, 4, 5 are put in one section of the tray and the children put sets of beans, etc. in another section of the tray to correspond with the numerals. This activity should be repeated many times.

12   Each child has a piece of string or thread and puts on it a stated number of beads.

13   The children are given sets of beads threaded onto string or thread. For each set they say or write down the number of beads. Alternatively they can tie a numeral card to a set to show the number.

14   The children use real or imitation pennies for counting activities. For example:

a)   The teacher says 'Show me three pennies'. Each child picks up three pennies and holds them in one hand for the teacher to see.

b)   The teacher says 'Show me how many pennies you need to buy an egg' (or other object costing not more than 5 pence).

c)   The teacher writes 5p on the blackboard. The children then write 5p on a piece of paper and on it put the correct number of coins.

15   The teacher draws a long, straight chalk line on the classroom floor. A child stands at one end of the line and is told to take one step along the line. His position on the line is marked, using the numeral 1. He then takes another step and his new position is marked 2. He goes on in this way to 5. The child goes back to the starting-point. Other children in turn, then show where he would be on the line if he took 3 steps, 4 steps, 2 steps, etc. This is an important activity as it introduces the use of a number line which is increasingly used in mathematics throughout the primary school.

16

The teacher puts two sets of the same number of objects (e.g. beans) on a table and asks a child to count each set (e.g. five). He then asks questions such as: 'Are there as many beans in the second set as the first set?'; 'Are there more beans in one set than the other?'. The children will agree that each set has the same number of beans.

Now the beans in the second set are moved further apart, as below.

The questions asked earlier are repeated. Some children will now usually say that there are more beans in the second set than the first. The beans in the second set are moved back to their original positions, and the earlier questions again repeated.

It takes some children a long time to realize that the changing of the positions of a set of objects does not change the number of the set. The conservation of number is an important property of sets and the kind of activity described above should be repeated from time to time to make sure that all the children understand it.

Note: When the children know and understand the numbers from 1 to 5 they can take part in activities which involve the first ideas of addition and subtraction. These are described in detail in Chapter 6.

Numbers and numerals up to 10

When the children are confident in the use of the numbers and numerals from 1 to 5 and understand the idea of zero, they can go on to activities which introduce the numbers and numerals from 6 to 10. Many of the activities will be extensions of those used for the numbers and numerals 1 to 5, but with these new numbers use can begin to be made of pattern, as indicated in the list of activities below.

Activities
1   Activity 4 on page 27 is repeated and extended up to *ten*.
2   Activity 5 on page 27 is repeated with a counting frame for 1 to 10.
3   Activity 6 on page 28 is repeated with counting bars for 1 to 10.
4   Activity 7 on page 28 is repeated with a number ladder for 1 to 10.
5   Activity 8 on page 28 is repeated with 10 skittles.

Note: The idea of showing the results of a group of children by colouring on a grid can be introduced at this stage, as in the example on the next page. A graph drawn in this way is often called a block graph. One essential habit should be introduced, and insisted upon, at this stage. Every graph drawn should have a heading to indicate what information the graph is intended to show. This is a good habit as it not only makes the graph easier to read but also makes the children think carefully about what they are doing. Each axis should, of course, be labelled.

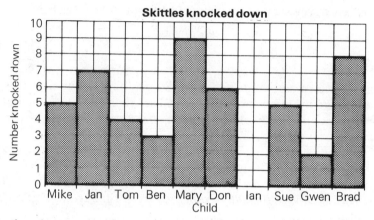

In drawing graphs like this a decision has to be made as to where the numbers on the left should be positioned. Should they be shown as in (a) or as in (b), below?

(a)   (b)

At this stage either can be used. Some teachers, however, may think it is better to use (b) from the beginning as this is the kind of labelling the children will use in their later graphs. This method also has the advantage that a zero can easily be recorded (as in the graph above showing the number of skittles knocked down).

6 Activity 9 on page 28 is repeated for the numerals 6 to 10. The ways in which the numerals are formed are shown below.

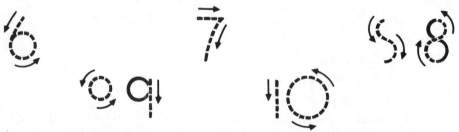

7 Activity 10 on page 29 is repeated with a set of number strips for 1 to 10.

8 Activities 11, 12, 13, and 14 on page 30 are repeated for numbers up to ten.

9 Activity 15 on page 30 is repeated for a number line marked to ten.

10 The children make patterns of dots to represent the numbers one to ten.

Some examples of what individual children might draw are shown below.

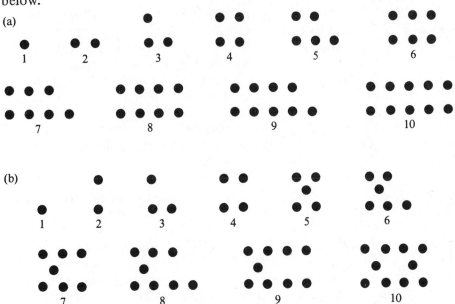

Note: Many of these activities are later linked with addition and subtraction, together with the first ideas of multiplication and division. In particular, the number line, the coloured number strips, and the dot patterns are very important.

Numbers and numerals up to 20

For most children the numeral 10 for ten does not show the idea of place-value. It is simply a symbol used for the number. The numerals 11 to 20 can be thought of in the same way. The children should, however, be gradually introduced to the first ideas of place-value. This is a very important idea and a lack of clear understanding of it is the cause of many difficulties throughout the primary school. It is important therefore that, as part of this extension of number, teachers should lead the children towards a good understanding of this important basic idea in representing numbers. Many of the activities listed below are designed to do this.

Activities

1   The teacher holds up an empty box (matchbox, chalk box, etc.) and the children count aloud as he puts ten matches (sticks of chalk, etc.) into it, one by one. The teacher now takes one more match and puts it on top of the box. He then explains that altogether he has *eleven* matches; ten in the box and one on top of the box. He shows the numeral for eleven (11) on the blackboard.

He then takes the match on top of the box and puts it with the ten inside the box and writes 11 on the box.

The teacher starts again with another empty box and repeats the activity but this time he puts an extra two matches on top of the box, making twelve altogether. He introduces the word *twelve* and the numeral (12), then removes the two matches from the top, puts them with the others in the box, and writes 12 on it.

The teacher continues in this way (using one more match each time) and so introduces the numbers *thirteen* (ten and three), *fourteen* (ten and four), *fifteen* (ten and five).

2   The children use beans, bottle-tops, etc., first to show ten. They then put one more with the ten to show eleven. They write the numeral (11) for the set.

The children add one more bean (bottle-top, etc.) to the set to show twelve (ten and two) and write the numeral (12). They continue in this way to show *thirteen*, then *fourteen*, and then *fifteen*.

3   Instead of putting ten objects into a box or forming a heap of ten to start the activity, the children can use ten small sticks (or pieces of cane) fastened together with cotton, string, or an elastic band.

10

The children then add one more stick to get:

11

They continue in this way to obtain:

12   13   14   15

4   The children work in pairs. First one child holds up his two hands to show 10 fingers.

The other child then puts one of his hands near to the first two held up and shows one finger.

11

34

He then shows two fingers.

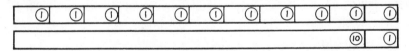

12

The second child goes on to show three fingers (*thirteen* altogether), four fingers (*fourteen*), five fingers (*fifteen*). For each number the children draw a picture (as above) and write the numeral at the side.

5   A set of children (from 10 to 15) stand at the front of the class.

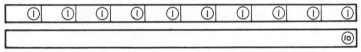

The other children count them and write down the numeral to show the number (e.g. 13). The children at the front of the class now arrange themselves as shown below.

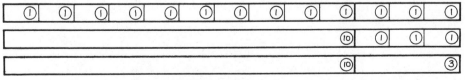

The other children see that there are ten children and three children (i.e. 13 altogether). The children use this arrangement to check their counting.

6   The children use their coloured number strips, as described on page 25. Working in pairs they first put 1-strips at the side of a 10-strip.

①	①	①	①	①	①	①	①	①	①

									⑩

They then put an extra 1-strip at the end of each row.

①	①	①	①	①	①	①	①	①	①

								⑩	①

From this arrangement the children see that eleven 1-strips can be represented by one 10-strip and one 1-strip.

By adding another 1-strip to each row the children see that twelve is the same as ten and two, thirteen is the same as ten and three, etc. The children may then go on to show, for example, thirteen in three ways:

①	①	①	①	①	①	①	①	①	①	①	①	①

									⑩	①	①	①

									⑩			③

They then go on to show 12, 14, and 15 in these three ways.

7

A number line, marked 1 to 15, is drawn on the floor. A child stands on the 10-mark and then moves one space along the line (to 11). He says, 'I started at ten and moved forward one. I am now on eleven.' He goes back and stands on the 10-mark and then moves forward two spaces along the line. ('I started at ten and moved forward two. I am now on twelve.')

In the same way he starts again at the 10-mark and in turn moves on to thirteen, fourteen, and fifteen.

8 When the children are confident in the use of the numbers eleven to fifteen, Activities 1 to 7 above can be repeated and extended to introduce the numbers 16, 17, 18, 19, and 20.

9 Using their coloured number strips the children investigate ways in which a given number strip can be made up from smaller number strips. Six of the ways of making the 14-strip are shown below.

This activity, of course, has a very direct link with addition and subtraction.

Summary

When a child has completed the many activities described in this chapter, he or she should:

understand	the idea of a number
	the idea of a numeral
	the first ideas of place-value
be able to	count up to 20
	write the numerals 0 to 9
	use numerals to write the numbers from 0 to 20

Thinking about
measuring and measures

When we find the *number* of a set of objects we can give an exact answer, e.g. a set of five bottle-tops is exactly *five* bottle-tops. When we try to *measure* something we must do so as exactly as we can, but it is very unlikely that we shall ever be able to give a completely exact answer. For example, if we measure the time that a man takes to run 100 metres the answer that we give depends upon the kind of watch that we use. If it measures only in seconds, we may give the time as 11 seconds. If the watch measures in tenths of a second, then the time may be given as 11.4 seconds. If we have a watch that measures in hundredths of a second, the time may be recorded as 11.43 seconds. If we have a very modern time recorder which measures in thousandths of a second, the time may be given as 11.434 seconds. Going on in this way we see that, however accurate our watch is, there may be an even more accurate watch which would give a time slightly different from ours.

In the same way, when we use a ruler to measure a length we can only give the answer in terms of the smallest unit which is marked on the ruler. We can never be sure that this is an exact answer, especially when we remember that the thickness of the marking lines on the ruler needs to be taken into account.

It is interesting to look at how men developed a system of measures. They started by comparing two quantities, as described in Chapter 2 on pp. 13–16. This led to the use of phrases such as *is taller than, is longer than, is heavier than, holds more than*, etc. For comparing more than two quantities, however — especially when the results had to be recorded — they found it necessary to introduce the use of some simple unit quantity. We still do this ourselves when we are working on the land. For example, we may measure various lengths by our stride or by using a piece of cane. We choose our unit measure from what is readily available around us. And this is what men did when they started to measure. They used what are called *natural measures*. The drawings on the next page show some of the natural units used for measuring lengths.

For longer distances, units such as a *stone-throw*, a *spearcast*, a *furrow long* (or *furlong*), and a *day's journey* were used. In the same way, for measuring capacity, natural units such as a *handful*, a *gourd*, and a *bowl* were used.

For measuring time natural happenings were used, such as the *seasons* (wet and dry), *day* and *night*, the waxing and waning of the *moon, cockcrow,* the *flooding* of the land by the river.

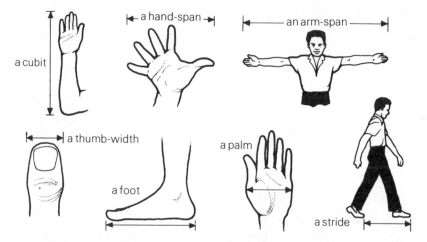

These natural units were, of course, not very accurate. For example, a *stride* depends upon the person doing the striding, and a *bowl-full* depends upon the size of the bowl. This variation caused much argument and disagreement amongst traders, not only when they came from different parts of the country but also when they came from neighbouring villages. So, as commerce and trading developed it became more and more essential to have units which did not vary from village to village, town to town, and country to country. Sets of *standard* units had to be devised and introduced which could be used within a country and between countries.

For a long while it was found that, even within a country, it was far from easy to choose standard units which everyone would accept and use. People did not like to change their habits. They preferred to go on using the old ways of measuring even though these were often unsatisfactory.

The rulers of some countries did try to introduce better units. For example, some used the length of the foot of a particular person as the standard unit of length. 'Thirty-two grains of wheat, dry and taken from the middle of the ear' were used as a unit in weighing. Units of this kind were better than those used previously but they still varied from district to district. Trading remained difficult and inefficient.

Such was the state of affairs in France at the time of the French Revolution in 1789. The efforts of the old government to introduce proper standards had met with little success. There were still many different units in common use. They varied from province to province and even from town to town. Trade was suffering because of the lack of well-defined standard units.

At last, in 1791, a new standard unit of length was agreed upon. It was not like any of the earlier units. It was to be:

'one ten-millionth of a quarter of a circle on the earth, passing through Paris and through the North and South Poles'.

In 1793 the name **metre** was given to this unit of length.

The metre is not, of course, a very convenient or accurate unit for measuring small lengths or long distances, so smaller and larger units – based on the metre – were introduced. These made use of the decimal system: that is, the smaller units were tenths, hundredths, and thousandths of a metre, while the larger units were 10 metres, 100 metres, 1000 metres, etc.

The units for measuring area, volume, and capacity were all based on the metre and so the **metric system** of measure came into being, and is now, more and more, used throughout the world.

Since its introduction two important changes have taken place:

a)   the metre is no longer defined as a distance on the earth's surface. It is now based on the wavelength of the radiation of the Krypton-86 atom. This gives us a much more exact way of recording its length.

b)   *symbols* are now used for the various measures – instead of abbreviations. These are shown below for the measures most frequently used.

	unit	symbol	
Length	metre	m	
(smaller units)	centimetre	cm	(1-hundredth of a metre)
	millimetre	mm	(1-thousandth of a metre)
(larger unit)	kilometre	km	(1000 metres)
Area	square centimetre	cm^2	
	square metre	m^2	(10 000 square centimetres)
	are	a	(100 square metres)
	hectare	ha	(100 ares)
Volume/Capacity	cubic centimetre	cm^3	
	cubic metre	m^3	
	litre	l	(1000 cubic centimetres)
	millilitre	ml	(1 cubic centimetre or 1-thousandth of a litre)

Note: i) the symbols do not require full stops after them;
         ii) no 's' is required for plurals.

There are three other measures which we need to consider in this section. They are measures of time, mass, and value (money).

Time

Throughout the ages people have been very much aware of daylight and darkness, of the changing shape of the moon, of the successive seasons of the year. They have come to realize that there is a regular pattern underlying all these changes. Until the last few centuries, however, no one fully understood the reasons for them. This caused difficulties when people started to try to measure time.

For day-to-day happenings the ideas of 'at cockcrow', 'three moons ago', 'two days' journey', 'during the last rains', etc., were used to give some idea of time. For longer periods of time, however, it was not easy to find a suitable pattern. It was only when it was realized that the earth moves around the sun, the moon moves around the earth, and the earth rotates on its own axis, that it was possible to begin to see how the day, the month, and the year are related to each other.

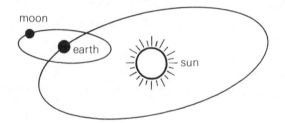

Even then there were problems. This was because it was thought that the moon takes an exact number of days to go through all its phases and that the earth also takes an exact number of days to go through its year. In fact this is not so. The times of the various movements are not constant. For our purposes, however, it is sufficient to say:

a) The time taken for the earth to move around the sun is about 365 days, 5 hours, 48 minutes, 45 seconds.

b) The time taken for the moon to move around the earth varies from 29 days, 7 hours, 20 minutes, to 29 days, 19 hours, 30 minutes.

Note: The time taken for the moon to move around the earth is called a *lunar month*.

Looking at these times we see that it is not possible to have a simple arrangement with an exact number of days in each lunar month and an exact number of lunar months in a year. So, after many attempts we finished up with our present system which has different numbers of days in the various calendar months. We also have 365 days in some years and 366 in others. The reason for this becomes clearer when we remember that the true length of the year is a little more than 365 days. The difference is 5 hours, 48 minutes, and 45 seconds. This is almost a quarter of a day. So we make the adjustment by adding one day to the calendar every four years. A convenient way of doing this is to add an extra day when the number of the last year is exactly divisible by four. This arrangement gives us our *leap year*.

Unfortunately this arrangement is still not completely satisfactory; the calendar year is then too long. It is 365¼ days (365 days, 6 hours) instead of 365 days, 5 hours, 48 minutes, and 45 seconds. There is still a difference of 11 minutes and 15 seconds.

In 400 years this difference would amount to just over three days. To make allowance for this, three *leap days* are omitted from the calendar every 400 years. For convenience, this is done when the centuries change. For example, the years 2100, 2200, 2300 (although divisible by four) will not be leap years. The year 2400 will, however, be a leap year.

There is now only a difference of about 3 hours in 400 years between calendar time and actual time. In our everyday life this will cause us little concern!

Not only do the lunar month and the year vary in length but the day itself — the time of the rotation of the earth — also varies. So none of these is suitable as the unit of time. Some other unit must be chosen. After much discussion it was finally agreed, in 1960, to take a fraction of a particular year as the unit of time. This is now the official **second** (symbol: s).

All other units are based on this second. That is:

1 minute = 60 seconds
1 hour (h) = 60 minutes (3600 seconds)
1 day   = 24 hours   (86 400 seconds)

Months, years, and leap years are as described above.

Mass

In recent years the distinction between mass and weight has been increasingly emphasized and needs to be clearly understood to avoid confusion.

Let us first think of a lump of clay and a piece of iron of the same volume. By handling them we easily recognize that they are different substances.

If, in turn, we hold them in the air and then let them go, they fall to the ground. This is because the earth exerts a pull on them. This pull gets smaller the further the object is from the earth, so that at very great distances the pull is very small indeed. This pull is called the **weight** of the object.

We can compare the weights of the clay and the iron, at a particular place, by hanging each, in turn, on a spring balance and measuring the stretch of the spring. The iron stretches the spring more than the clay. The weight of the iron is greater than the weight of the clay.

If we took the clay and the iron up in the air, further away from the centre of the earth, the pull of the earth on each of them would be smaller. So each of their weights would be smaller than on the surface of the earth.

The amount of clay and the amount of iron, however, would be the same wherever they are. We call this amount of substance its **mass**.

The mass of an object does not change, but its weight can change.

If two objects, at the same place, have the same weight, they also have the same mass. For example, if a large lump of clay and a smaller piece of metal stretch a spring the same distance, then they have the same weight and so the same mass.

If the clay stretches the spring twice as far as the iron then the weight of the clay is twice the weight of the iron. So the mass of the clay is twice the mass of the iron.

The unit of mass is the **kilogram**. It is the mass of a special piece of metal kept in Paris, France. The masses of all other objects are obtained by comparing them with this mass (or copies of it). This can be done by weighing them at the same place.

unit	symbol	
gram	g	
kilogram	kg	(1000 grams)

Value

The value of an object or of services (work of all types) is usually measured nowadays in units of money. There is, unfortunately, no universal system of money at present in use, but there has been a great advance in recent years in that most countries now have a decimal system of units (e.g. £1 = 100p). This makes calculations with money much easier than they used to be (e.g. £12.95 × 67 requires only the ability to multiply 12.95 by 67). This change was accelerated because of the increasing use of calculating machines of all types. For uniformity and efficiency these machines demand a decimal money system. In schools a great advantage of this change is that children do not now have to spend time learning how to calculate with a non-decimal money system, as they had to do in the past.

Chapter 4
Measuring and measures: first ideas

Using natural measures for length, capacity, and mass. Estimation. Putting measurements in order. Telling the time in hours. Buying and selling with 1p coins and a 5p coin.

Before they start school many children will have heard, and perhaps used, phrases such as: Tony *is taller than* Peter; this bottle *holds more than* the tin; his father has a *big* car; the case is very *heavy*; I need two *cup-fulls*; it will take me *two days* to get to Perth. These phrases are concerned mainly with the ideas of length, mass, and time.

Activities which involve comparison of lengths, capacities, and masses have already been suggested in Chapter 2. Children need plenty of experience of this kind before going on to using simple 'natural' measures. It is very important that they should be encouraged to:

a) estimate how many of the unit measures will be needed;

b) use the right kind of unit measure (e.g. a thumb-width is a suitable measure to use for measuring the length of a book but it is not very convenient for measuring the distance between two trees).

Length

Apparatus
Some of the natural units which children can use are listed below.

Parts of the body: foot-length, handspan, thumb-width, stride, distance between the fingertips when the arms are outstretched.

Canes of various lengths.

Pieces of string, rope, or cotton.

Activities
1   The children measure lengths within the classroom. For example: the length of the room; the width of the room; the length of a desk or table; the length and width of a book; the height of a door; the length of a pencil or a stick of chalk; etc. They record the lengths in the natural units they have decided to use and show them on a simple drawing whenever possible. The children should compare their answers with each other, in order to see that, for the same length, they obtain different answers depending upon the

units they use. They will also find that even when they use the same kind of unit (e.g. their stride) they may still obtain different answers. This can be illustrated by drawing a graph for a group of children, as below.

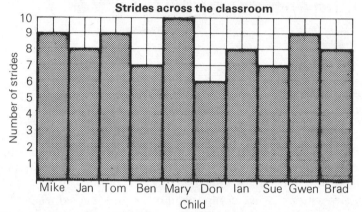

Strides across the classroom

Many of the measurements made will not be an exact number of units. There will often be a bit more or a little less. Do not, at this stage, try to deal with these small amounts. Most of the children will be happy to give the answer in terms of whole units and to ignore any small differences.

Care must be taken, in arranging these measuring activities, that the numbers involved do not go beyond the children's counting abilities. To avoid this happening some guidance may be necessary in deciding which unit is used for the measuring.

2 The children measure lengths outside the classroom. Many of these will be longer lengths than those within the classroom so the children will have to decide upon the type of unit measure to use. For example: a cane length; a stride; the length of a piece of string; etc.

The children should be encouraged to estimate the number of unit lengths involved before actually doing the measuring. Some of these estimates will, of course, be very different from the actual measurement. It will be found, however, that with experience the children will improve and will be very pleased when they begin to give good estimates.

3 By measuring each of three lengths (e.g. the width of the blackboard, the height of a door, the width of a window) using the same unit, the children arrange them in order of size. They can show their results by a drawing. The children show the unit used for measuring on the drawing.

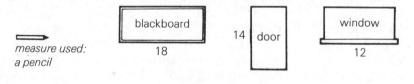

measure used:
a pencil

They could also draw an arrow graph, as below, using the arrow to stand for *is longer than*.

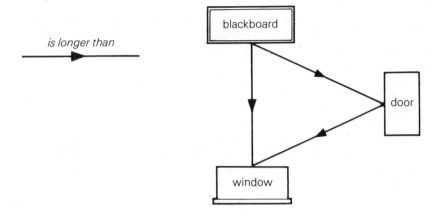

Capacity

Apparatus

For these activities a plentiful supply of water, sand, and containers of all types is essential. If possible, many of the activities should be arranged outside the classroom in order to avoid difficulties arising from the accidental spilling of water.

Activities

1   The children continue to make comparisons. For example, they decide which of two bottles holds more water, by filling one of them to the top with water and then pouring the water into the other one. (Sand can be used if water is scarce.)

2   The children then go on to use a measure, such as a tin-full or a cup-full, to decide which of two containers holds more. They can either start with empty containers and find how many tin-fulls are needed to fill each of them, or they can fill each container with water (or sand) and find how many tins (of the same size) they can fill from each.

Again, estimates should be made before the measuring is done. A variety of measures (small tins, large tins, jugs, bottles, etc.) should be available so that a sufficiently large one can be used to avoid too much repetition of the filling and to make sure that large numbers do not occur.

The children should work in pairs so that one child can keep a record of the number of measures used.

3   The children arrange three containers in order of their capacities. They make a drawing to show their results, as for Activity 3 for length on page 44.

Mass

Apparatus

In Chapter 2 we discussed how children use their ability to feel weight to decide which of two objects is the heavier. Now they go on to use a simple balance for comparing and measuring masses. Several should be available for the children to use.

Activities

1   The children first compare two masses by placing one in each of the two pans of a balance. They tell the teacher which is the heavier or write a simple statement (or make a simple drawing).

2   By comparing the masses of pairs of objects, as in Activity 1, some children may be able to arrange three objects in order.

3   The children are introduced to the idea of *balancing*. They put an object in one pan of a balance and then gradually put sand (or other suitable material) in the other pan until the balance arm is horizontal. At this stage the children can understand only that the object and the sand balance each other. Some children may suggest, however, that since they balance each other they have the same mass (or the same weight). The idea of the pull of the earth on the two masses is too complicated to try to explain at this stage.

4   When the children understand the idea of balancing they can begin to use some readily available units of mass. For example, they balance an object against a number of penny coins, or bottle-tops (or other identical small objects). They should make statements about what they are doing.

Some objects will, of course, not balance an exact number of these small 'weights'. In these cases it may be helpful if the children add a small amount of sand to the 'weight' so as to get some idea of the difference. In their statement, however, they will just use phrases such as 'The stone nearly balances six coins'.

The children should have much practice in this kind of activity, using a variety of 'weights'.

Time

Apparatus

1 **Time charts**   One of the ways in which telling the time can be introduced to children is through the regular happenings at school each day. For example, a set of clock-faces (as shown below) is drawn on a large sheet of white card or paper and is hung where all the children can see it.

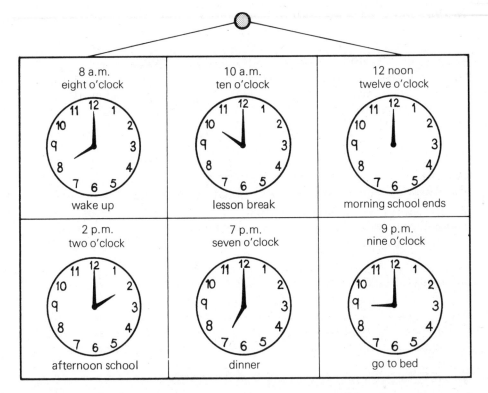

8 a.m. eight o'clock	10 a.m. ten o'clock	12 noon twelve o'clock
wake up	lesson break	morning school ends
2 p.m. two o'clock	7 p.m. seven o'clock	9 p.m. nine o'clock
afternoon school	dinner	go to bed

The clock-faces and the positions of the large and small hands are discussed with the children each day, until they are familiar with them.

For further activities a variety of clock-faces with movable hands is needed. Some suggestions for making these are given below.

2 Classroom clock-faces (large)

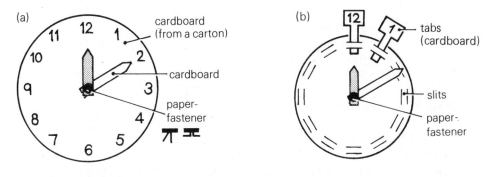

Note: The tabs in (b) are taken out of the slits and the children replace them in the correct order. See Activity 2 on the next page.

3 Clock-faces for the children's use

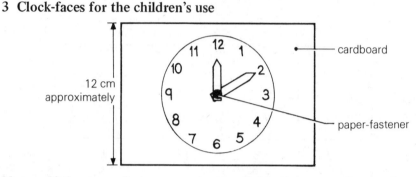

Note: If the paper-fasteners are not available then an ordinary pin can be used. In this case an empty matchbox can be placed at the back of the clock-face to hold the pin more securely and to protect the children from the point of the pin.

A side view of the arrangement is shown on the right.

Note: The bottom of the matchbox and the clock-face should be at the same level so that the 'clock' will stand on a table or desk. (This may involve making the clock-face small enough to fit the matchbox size.)

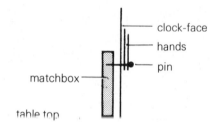

Activities

1   The children show the times of daily happenings by using a large class-room clock-face. In turn, a child shows the time of each of these happenings by moving the hands of the clock to the correct time. This activity should be continued over a long period so that each child has more than one turn in showing the time.

2   The children use the classroom clock-face with the pull-out tabs. The children practise reading the numerals in order and then the tabs are re-moved and put in a heap. The children have to replace the tabs in their correct order. The children should work singly or in pairs for this activity.

3   Depending upon the number of small clock-faces available, the children work as a class or in groups for this activity. The teacher discusses the way in which hours are shown and then asks the children to show 3 o'clock, 6 o'clock, 9 o'clock, etc. on their clocks. This activity may need repeating over several weeks to ensure that all children can show the hours.

4   The teacher discusses the idea of half-past the hour. He demonstrates, on a large clock-face, how the large hand makes a complete turn each hour,

so in half an hour it only makes half a turn and then points to the 6. The children must be aware that, in half an hour, the small hand moves halfway to the next numeral. This may not be easy for some children to understand, so the introduction of 'half-past' should not be hurried.

Money

Apparatus

Before they start school most children have been to the market or to the shops and have seen their mothers obtain goods in exchange for money. So an extension of their 'shopping' activities when they start school will form a natural bridge with pre-school experiences.

In order to participate in classroom 'shopping' activities, the children will need a good supply of coins and some kind of classroom shop. If it is at all possible real coins should be used. If these are not available then it is possible to obtain commercially produced plastic or cardboard imitation coins. If neither of these can be provided then paper 'coins' can be made by the method described below.

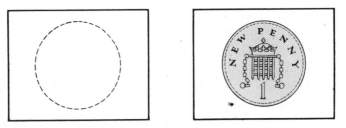

A 1-penny coin is put on a table or desk and a piece of white paper is placed over it. Holding the coin as firmly as possible the paper over the coin itself is rubbed with a pencil or crayon. (Make sure the children do not rub the paper so hard that they tear it.) The markings on the coin gradually appear on the paper. The paper 'coin' can then be cut out and, if desired, can be stuck on to a piece of cardboard of the same size.

Activities

1   The children work in small groups. One child acts as the shopkeeper. Each of the other children in the group has a supply of 1-penny coins (real or imitation). In turn each child chooses and 'buys' *one* article by giving the shopkeeper the necessary number of 1-penny coins.

2   After the children have had plenty of practice in buying one article (up to 10p) they go on to the buying of two articles (the total cost not to be more than 10p).

In the early stages of this activity some children will want to pay for each article in turn. For example, if the two articles cost 3p and 5p, a child might find it easier to give the shopkeeper three 1p coins and then another five 1p coins. Explain to the child that this method would take a long time if he or she were buying several articles. It is quicker to give the shopkeeper the total amount of money needed. So before paying the shopkeeper the child must work out the total cost of the articles. That is, for example, add 3p and 5p.

This can be done in several ways:

a) by putting three 1p coins on the desk and then, by the side, five more 1p coins. By counting, the child finds that there are eight 1p coins altogether.

b) by using the known addition fact, $3 + 5 = 8$.

c) by 'counting on'. That is, starting with three coins, add on, one at a time, five more $(3, 3 + 1 = 4, 4 + 1 = 5, 5 + 1 = 6, 6 + 1 = 7, 7 + 1 = 8)$. Many children do not find this method easy at this stage.

The children can record this kind of activity by drawing each article, putting the price at the side of each, and then writing the total cost underneath.

Give plenty of practice in this activity of buying two articles.

Summary

When a child has completed the many activities in this chapter he or she should:

understand	the idea of units of measurement for length, capacity, and mass
	the idea of estimating
	the idea of buying and selling
be able to	measure lengths, capacities, and masses, using natural units from everyday life
	put lengths, capacities, and masses in order of size
	tell the time in hours
	buy two articles (total not more than 10p) using 1p coins

Thinking about
shapes

In everyday life we can all recognize and name most of the common shapes around us. We may not realize, however, that at times we are not very precise in naming them. For example, we call each of the shapes, shown below, a *triangle*.

The first may be made of rods, the second may be a piece of cardboard.
    In the same way we call each of the shapes, shown below, a *circle*.

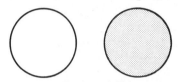

The first may be a hoop used in Physical Education, the second a coin.
    We can have two meanings (the outline or the filled-in shape) for each of these two words in everyday life because we usually have the object in front of us and we know what we are talking about. Mathematicians, however, need to be more definite. They want to be more exact when they use words or phrases to describe a shape.

A line

A *line* is thought of as being made up of a very large number of points. These points can form a straight line or a curved line.
    A *straight line* is thought of as going on and on in both directions. To show this, arrow-heads are sometimes drawn at each end of the line.

←——————————————————————————————————→

If the line is cut at any point to divide it into two parts, then each part is called a *ray*. The point on each ray nearest to the cut is called the end-point of the ray.

←————————————\ /————————————→
                        end-points

If the straight line is cut at two points, as below, then the part of the line between the cuts is called a *line segment*. A line segment has two end-points.

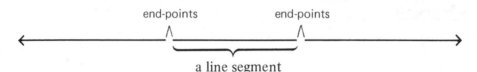

end-points   end-points

a line segment

A circle

A circle is the curved line formed by all the points which are the same distance from a fixed point. A hoop is a circle. But the face of a coin is the surface enclosed by the circle at the coin's edge.

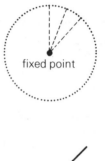

fixed point

An angle

We would all agree that the line shape shown on the right is an angle. But, if we were asked to describe it, some of us would want to start to talk about 'turning' and use right-angles and degrees. What the drawing shows, however, is two line segments (or two rays if we think of the two lines going on and on) with the same end-point. It is only when we need to compare angles and to use some kind of measure that we introduce the idea of 'turning' (and 'units of turn').

A triangle

A triangle is formed by three line segments which intersect (cut) each other, as shown on the right. If we cut along the three lines the paper shape we obtain is the triangle enclosed by the three line segments.

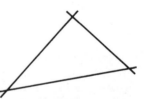

As teachers, we should be aware of these more exact uses of words but the extent to which we introduce them to young children requires discussion.

If, for example, a child uses the phrase 'a straight line' to describe the edge of this page it seems more sensible to let him continue to use this phrase with understanding than to suddenly insist that he should call it a 'line segment'. This may well confuse him. The phrase can be introduced with more understanding at the secondary level if the child continues with his study of mathematics.

Chapter 5
Shapes: first ideas

Handling and naming common 3-D and 2-D shapes. Some properties of the shapes.

Before they start school all children have seen, handled, and used many 3-D shapes. They have also become aware of many 2-D shapes and line shapes. Their pre-school experiences of this aspect of mathematics are much greater than those of any of the other topics which they have to deal with in their years at school. We should make good use of this background experience.

Thinking about these pre-school experiences we see that a first step that we can take is to provide activities which involve handling, sorting, and classifying common 3-D shapes. From these activities the children begin to learn the names of the simple shapes and, at the same time, to build up a knowledge of their properties.

The children can then go on to look at the faces of these shapes. This forms an introduction to the common 2-D shapes. The children learn the names of these shapes and, through suitable activities, find out more about each of them.

Activities

Here are suggestions for activities which have the above objectives in mind.

1   Place a set of everyday objects on a table (the set should include objects which look like a cube, a cuboid, a cylinder, a sphere, a cone). Ask a child to choose one of the objects. Then ask him to describe the object. This leads to some very interesting comments on the part of the child. Much of his description will be concerned with colour, with whether they have one like it at home, with whether it is dirty or clean, with whether it has scratches on it. It may be necessary to lead him to talk about the more mathematical aspects of the objects: for example, whether the faces are flat or curved, whether it has an inside and an outside (that is, whether he can put his hand in it), whether it has any edges, etc.

Repeat this activity with many other children.

2   Continue to use the set of objects provided for Activity 1. Show the children a cube made by the teacher, or use a suitable carton. Get some of the children in turn to describe the cube in their own words. Introduce the word *cube* (write it on the blackboard and let the children copy it). Give

practice in spelling the word. Now ask a child to pick out from the set of objects those which look like a cube. Ask him to say why he has chosen each of these objects. (This will help the teacher to decide whether the child has built up the right idea of a cube.) Other children then say whether they agree or disagree with the child's choice of objects. They may suggest others which the child has not chosen.

Introduce the word *face* and let the children count the faces of a cube.

Introduce the word *edge* and let the children count the edges of a cube.

Introduce the word *vertex* and let the children count the vertices of a cube.

Give practice in saying and writing these words, and in their spelling.

3   Repeat Activity 2 for a *cuboid*, a *sphere*, a *cylinder*, and a *cone*. For some of these shapes, the difference between a straight edge and a curved edge will need to be discussed. This can be illustrated by using a piece of cotton or string. When the cotton is pulled tightly between two hands it is straight.

When the cotton is allowed to sag it forms a curve.

Another easy way of forming a straight edge is to fold neatly a piece of paper, as below.

a straight edge

4   Show a cube to the children and tell them to look at one of its faces. Let them discuss the face in their own words. Introduce the word *square*. The children then look at the other faces. They may suggest that all the six faces are alike (the same as the first face they looked at). Discuss ways in which they can check this, e.g. by placing the cube on a table and drawing a chalk mark around the face on the table, then checking that each of the other faces fits in the chalk mark.

5   Give the children a set of short canes (corn-stalks, sticks, etc.) of various lengths (but with at least four of the same length). Ask a child to make a square outline using some of the canes. This should lead to much interesting discussion. The child will find that he has to place his canes in a special position if they are to form a square, as illustrated below.

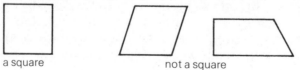

a square   not a square

6 The children look around the classroom and point out any shapes which look like squares and which they can check (e.g. by using a piece of string to measure the four edges).

7 Repeat Activities 4, 5, and 6 for a *rectangle* (one of the faces of a cuboid).

In using canes to make a rectangle the children find that they must use two canes of the same length and another two canes of the same length (but not the same length as the first two).

8 The children look around the classroom to see what shapes they can see which are not squares or rectangles. In most classrooms they will quickly see some *triangles*. Discuss these with the children, emphasizing that a triangle has three edges. The children then make triangles with their canes. They find that with many sets of three canes they can make a triangle. (Most of these will be scalene triangles; some will be isosceles; some will be equilateral; few, if any, will be right-angled. Do *not* introduce these names at this stage.)

To make a right-angled triangle, like many of those around the classroom, a sheet of paper (square or rectangle) can be folded and cut as shown below.

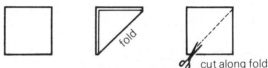

Children may also find it interesting to make triangles by using a loop of rope. Three children hold the loop, at different places, and then pull the rope so that it forms three straight lines, as shown below.

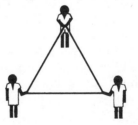

The shape of the triangle can be varied by letting one of the children change his position.

9 Introduce the *circle* to the children. Most of them will have seen many circles before they come to school and will be familiar with the shape. They may not, however, be familiar with the name so give practice in saying and writing the word and in learning its spelling. (It is very important that the correct spelling of all of these shape words should be learned as soon as the children meet them.) The children can obtain circles by drawing around a circular tin lid. They can also make attractive patterns by drawing a set of circles and colouring them.

10 a) Provide the children with a set of identical cartons (cubes or cuboids) and let them experiment in fitting them together in different ways. Some examples are given below.

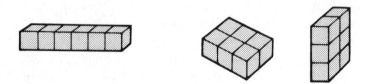

They will find that they can do this without leaving any gaps between the cartons. This is a first experience of the fitting together of shapes, as used when finding volumes.

b) Repeat (a) but now use identical tins. The children find that they cannot always fit them together without leaving gaps between them. Let the children experiment in fitting them together in many different ways. Some examples are shown below.

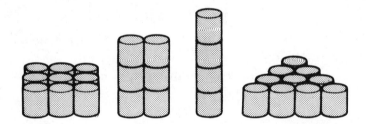

11 By cutting along some of its edges, open out a carton so that it will lie flat on a table. Get the children to do this in as many different ways as possible. Use cartons which are cubes, cuboids, and cylinders. This activity of course must be at a very simple level, but it does give the children their first idea of the net of a shape.

12 Give more activities like Activity 8, on page 10 in Chapter 2. Then let the children use their shapes to make 'pictures' such as the two shown on the next page.

This is a very good activity as the children are not only handling the various shapes but are also picking out shapes which are identical (i.e. congruent). They are also building up their knowledge of the number of edges of a square, a triangle, etc. and learning about the properties of each shape (e.g. the opposite edges of a rectangle are the same length).

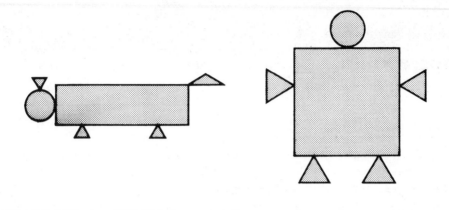

Summary

When a child has completed the many activities in this chapter he or she
should:

understand	what is meant by a *face*, an *edge*, a *vertex*
be able to	pick out and name a *cube*, a *cuboid*, a *cylinder*, a *sphere*, a *cone* distinguish between *straight* and *curved* lines pick out and name a *square*, a *rectangle*, a *triangle*, a *circle* spell the names given above
have	built up a knowledge of some of the simple properties of the above 3-D and 2-D shapes enjoyed working with shapes

Thinking about
operations

Operations

Most of us associate the word 'operation' with something that is done to our bodies in hospitals. The word, however, is also used in mathematics to describe certain activities. For example:

1 We can put a heap of beans with another heap to form one heap. This is a *combining operation*.

2 We can separate a heap of beans into two or more heaps. This is a *partitioning operation*.

3 We can find the answer to 6 + 5. This is an *addition operation*.

4 We can find the answer to 6 − 5. This is a *subtraction operation*.

5 We face North and then turn to face East. This is a *turning operation*.

Operations form a large part of mathematics and children in primary schools spend many hours dealing with simple operations. We need to understand the ideas underlying them. It is important to realize that all the simple operations with numbers are based on operations with objects. The following examples should illustrate this point.

1 The addition operation

The diagram above shows a set of boys and a set of girls. The set formed when we combine these two sets is shown on the right. This combining operation does not require the use of numbers.

We can now attach numbers to the first two sets, as below.

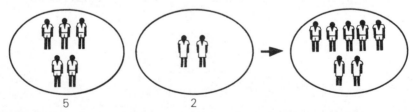

We can find the number of the combined set by counting. The finding of this number is called the **addition operation**. We record this operation by using a special symbol (+) and write: 5 + 2 = 7

2 The subtraction operation

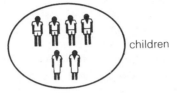
children

A set of children is shown above. The girls are removed. A set of boys is left.

boys

Using the numbers of the sets we see that we started with 6 children. Two girls were removed. The number of boys left is 4. We record this activity by using another symbol (−) and write: 6 − 2 = 4

The finding of the number of the set which is left is called the **subtraction operation**.

Another aspect of the subtraction operation arises when we need to compare the numbers of two sets and ask questions such as 'What is the difference?', 'How many more?', 'How many fewer?'. Look at the two sets shown below.

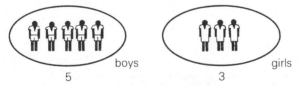
boys 5   girls 3

We can answer questions such as, 'What is the difference between the numbers of the two sets?', 'How many more boys are there than girls?', 'How many fewer girls are there than boys?', by matching the girls with the boys as below:

boys
girls

We see that:

a) the difference between the numbers is two;

b) there are two more boys than girls;

c) there are two fewer girls than boys.

We also see that we can find these answers by removing from the boys, the same number as there are girls (3). That is, we can find the answers by subtracting 3 from 5. Thus $5 - 3 = 2$.

3 The multiplication operation

The multiplication operation is based on the repeated addition of the same number. For example:

$$
\begin{aligned}
3 + 3 &= 6 \\
3 + 3 + 3 &= 9 \\
3 + 3 + 3 + 3 &= 12 \\
3 + 3 + 3 + 3 + 3 &= 15
\end{aligned}
$$

The answers to each of the repeated additions is obtained by adding 3 to the total in the line above. We use the addition operation. In time, however, we memorize the results of the additions and are able to write down the answers without using addition. When we do this we are using the **multiplication operation**. We introduce a symbol for the operation and write, for example, the last line of the repeated additions above, as: $3 \times 5 = 15$

When larger numbers are involved, such as 273×59, we cannot give the answer straightaway. We develop a technique for finding the answer in steps, *making use of the multiplications which we know*. For all multiplications we can, of course, go back to repeated addition in order to find the answer.

Note: Some teachers might think that this multiplication should be recorded as $5 \times 3 = 15$. The reason for using $3 \times 5 = 15$ is given below. Look at the set of statements:

$$
\begin{aligned}
8 + 2 &= 10 &\quad &(8 \ add \ 2) \\
8 - 2 &= 6 &\quad &(8 \ subtract \ 2) \\
8 \times 2 &= 16 &\quad &(??) \\
8 \div 2 &= 4 &\quad &(8 \ divided \ by \ 2)
\end{aligned}
$$

To follow the same pattern for multiplication as for the other three operations we need to use the phrase 8 *multiplied by* 2. The number which is repeated is written first, and the number of repetitions second. So $3 + 3 + 3 + 3 + 3 = 15$ recorded as a multiplication is written $3 \times 5 = 15$.

4 The division operation

Multiplication is based on repeated addition. We now go on to look at an operation based on repeated subtraction.

$$15 - 3 = 12$$
$$12 - 3 = \ 9$$
$$9 - 3 = \ 6$$
$$6 - 3 = \ 3$$
$$3 - 3 = \ 0$$

We see that when we start with 15 we can subtract 3 five times. We use a special symbol ($\div$) to record this activity and write: $15 \div 3 = 5$

This operation is called **division**.

The statement, $15 \div 3 = 5$, answers the question, 'How many threes make 15?'. It is, of course, closely linked with the multiplication, $3 \times 5 = 15$. If we know this multiplication statement then we can say straightaway that 5 threes make 15.

Another aspect of the division operation arises when, for example, we share 15 1-penny coins equally among 3 boys and want to know how many each boy has. We can do this by first giving each boy 1 penny (this uses 3 pennies). We then give each boy another penny and so on until we have used up all the 15 pennies. Each boy then has 5 pence. The repeated sub-traction can also be recorded as $15 \div 3 = 5$. Of course, if the multiplication statement $5 \times 3 = 15$ is known the answer to the question can be given straightaway. This emphasizes the fact that our ability to find quickly the answer to any division depends upon our knowledge of multiplication. For divisions with larger numbers, such as $644 \div 23$, we develop and use techniques for finding the answer in steps, using the simple multiplications we have memorized.

'Remainders' in division From the start it is essential that, in dealing with division, we should clarify our thinking about what are usually called 'remainders'. It is important that we should realize that some divisions can have remainders, while other types can never have 'remainders'.

1 How many teams of three can I form from twenty children? The answer is six. Two children will be left over. Here there is a 'remainder'.

2 A strip of paper, of length 9 cm, is cut into two equal parts. How long is each part? Here there can be no remainder. All the strip is used. The answer is, 'The length of each part is $4\frac{1}{2}$ cm (or 4.5 cm).'

These two examples are sufficient to indicate that we can decide whether a division can have a remainder only by considering the situation for which the division is being done. This, in effect, means that all divisions attempted by children should be based on practical problems. If children are asked, for example, to find the answer to $13 \div 2$ they do not know whether to give the answer as '6, remainder 1' or as '$6\frac{1}{2}$'. They need to know what type of situation the division comes from. They can then give the answer in the proper form.

Properties of operations

As we use operations with whole numbers various properties emerge.

1 The commutative property

Look at these statements.

$$8 + 2 = 10 \qquad 8 - 2 = 6 \qquad 8 \times 2 = 16 \qquad 8 \div 2 = 4$$
$$2 + 8 = 10 \qquad 2 - 8 = ? \qquad 2 \times 8 = 16 \qquad 2 \div 8 = ?$$

At this stage we do not know the answers to $2 - 8$ and $2 \div 8$ but we do know that $2 - 8 \neq 6$ and $2 \div 8 \neq 4$ (the sign $\neq$ stands for *is not equal to*). So we can say that a change in the order of the two numbers in a subtraction or a division results in a change in the answer. A change in the order of the two numbers in an addition or in a multiplication, however, does *not* change the answer. This is true for all additions and all multiplications. We say that the whole numbers have the **commutative property** for the operations addition and multiplication (but *not* for subtraction and division).

2 The associative property

Look at these statements.

$$\boxed{12 + 6 + 2}$$
$$(12 + 6) + 2 = 18 + 2$$
$$= 20$$
$$12 + (6 + 2) = 12 + 8$$
$$= 20$$

$$\boxed{12 - 6 - 2}$$
$$(12 - 6) - 2 = 6 - 2$$
$$= 4$$
$$12 - (6 - 2) = 12 - 4$$
$$= 8$$

$$\boxed{12 \times 6 \times 2}$$
$$(12 \times 6) \times 2 = 72 \times 2$$
$$= 144$$
$$12 \times (6 \times 2) = 12 \times 12$$
$$= 144$$

$$\boxed{12 \div 6 \div 2}$$
$$(12 \div 6) \div 2 = 2 \div 2$$
$$= 1$$
$$12 \div (6 \div 2) = 12 \div 3$$
$$= 4$$

Two ways are shown for dealing with $12 + 6 + 2$. We can only combine two numbers at one time, so we can find the answer to $12 + 6 + 2$ by using either $(12 + 6) + 2$ or $12 + (6 + 2)$. The brackets are put in to indicate which addition is to be done first. Similarly two ways are shown for dealing with the operations involving subtraction, multiplication, and division.

We notice that each of the two ways gives the same answer for the additions and also for the multiplications. But for the subtractions and the divisions a change in the way we choose our first pair results in a change in the answer.

We say that the whole numbers have the **associative property** for addition and multiplication (but *not* for subtraction and division).

3 Identity elements

Look at the pair of additions and the pair of multiplications.

$$7 + 0 = 7 \qquad 7 \times 1 = 7$$
$$0 + 7 = 7 \qquad 1 \times 7 = 7$$

These are examples of what we already know. That is:

a) if a number is combined with 0 (in either order) by addition then the result is the same number;

b) if a number is combined with 1 (in either order) by multiplication then the result is the same number.

These numbers are the only numbers which have this special property, 0 for addition and 1 for multiplication. No number has this kind of property for subtraction or division.

The number, 0, is called the **identity element** for addition.

The number, 1, is called the **identity element** for multiplication.

There is not an identity element for subtraction, nor for division. For although $7 - 0 = 7$, it is *not* true that $0 - 7 = 7$. Again $8 \div 1 = 8$ but $1 \div 8$ is *not* equal to 8.

Some of us may wonder why we need to give a special name to these two numbers (0 and 1). The reason is that as we go further in mathematics we meet and use many other operations, and for each of them it is important and helpful to find whether there is an identity element. So the idea and the name are introduced and discussed by us, as teachers, at this stage when we meet our first example of them.

Note: It is not suggested that the names of the various properties of operations discussed above should be introduced to young children. The teacher, however, should make sure that exercises are provided which will lead the children to build up their own first ideas of the properties.

Using a number line

If equally spaced points are marked on a straight line and labelled 0, 1, 2, 3, 4, etc., then we obtain what is called a **number line**, as shown below.

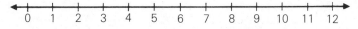

The marking and labelling of points can go on and on to the right of the mark, and later we shall find that it can also go on and on to the left (the arrow heads are used to show this). For the time being, however, we are only concerned with the part to the right. To show this we often omit the part to the left of 0, as below:

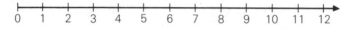

If we are dealing with numbers from 0 to 6 then we can use a line segment, as below:

A number line is very helpful in dealing with operations especially when, later, we meet negative numbers for the first time.

Here are some examples of its use.

1 For addition

$$4 + 3 = 7$$

We add four and three.

2 For subtraction

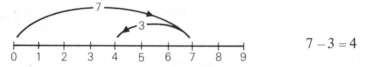

$$7 - 3 = 4$$

We subtract 3 from 7, or find the difference between 3 and 7.

3 For multiplication (repeated addition)

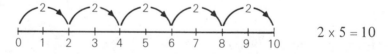

$$2 \times 5 = 10$$

4 For division (repeated subtraction)

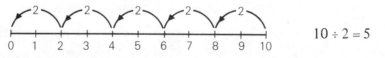

$$10 \div 2 = 5$$

Chapter 6
Addition and subtraction: first ideas

The ideas of addition and subtraction (up to 5 and then up to $9 + 9 = 18$ and $18 - 9 = 9$). The links between addition and subtraction. The words and phrases used in addition and subtraction. Memorizing the addition and subtraction facts.

Planning the work

Before we discuss the ways in which we can introduce addition and subtraction to children it might be very helpful to look back to the section 'Thinking about operations' to remind ourselves of the basic ideas underlying these two operations. We can then start to plan suitable activities to help children to understand and use the two operations.

These activities should be arranged in two stages:

a) with totals up to 10 (with subtractions from 10 or less);

b) with totals up to 18 (with subtractions from 18 or less).

Additions and subtractions which bring in numbers from 11 to 18 may involve the idea of place-value, but no techniques such as 'carrying' or the use of 'decomposition' or 'equal addition' are necessary. These become necessary only when operations involving numbers from 20 onwards are introduced. The activities should be planned so that the children can progress step by step from the practical work to written recording.

Apparatus

1 Dominoes

Dominoes can be made from card or used cartons. Using numerals to show the number of dots, a complete set contains:

```
0 – 0
0 – 1   1 – 1
0 – 2   1 – 2   2 – 2
0 – 3   1 – 3   2 – 3   3 – 3
0 – 4   1 – 4   2 – 4   3 – 4   4 – 4
0 – 5   1 – 5   2 – 5   3 – 5   4 – 5   5 – 5
0 – 6   1 – 6   2 – 6   3 – 6   4 – 6   5 – 6   6 – 6
```

2 Dice

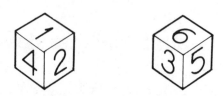

Dice can be made from cubes of wood. For young children they should not be small (an edge length of 3 cm or 4 cm is suitable). The size may depend, of course, upon the size of timber available.

The faces of each of the dice should be marked with the numerals from 1 to 6. It is usual to arrange the numerals so that those on each pair of opposite faces have a total of seven (i.e. 1 and 6, 2 and 5, 3 and 4).

3 A number sentence board

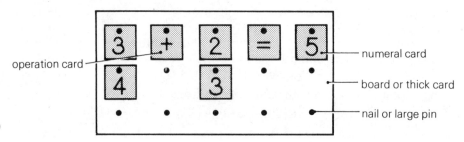

A large rectangular piece of thin wood or thick cardboard has rows of fine nails or large pins inserted as shown above. This is hung in a position where all the children can see it. Large numeral cards, operation cards, and '=' cards (each with a hole in it) are hung on the nails to make addition and subtraction sentences.

Addition (totals 10 or less)

Activities

1   The children have two sets of objects, each of a number less than 5. They count each set and write down the two numbers. They then put the two sets together to form one set. This set is then counted and the number written down. The children then say, in their own words, what they have done. No attempt is made at this stage to use the addition sign. This activity is repeated many times for pairs of sets of various numbers.

2   Activity 1 is repeated but now the teacher introduces the use of the symbols for addition and equality. He can do this by writing on the blackboard or by using a number sentence board (as described above). It is helpful, too, if the teacher links the numbers with drawings.

The two sets are first shown with their numbers.

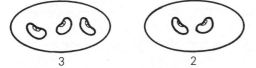

The combined set is then shown on the right of the two sets.

The addition statement is completed by putting in the '+' and the '=' signs.

The children read the completed sentence as 'Three add two is equal to five'.

Note: The writing of the completed addition in a vertical form, as shown on the right, should *not* be introduced at this stage. The vertical form becomes helpful only when place-value is first introduced.

The teacher builds up addition sentences for other pairs of sets. Then the children start to write their own addition sentences for various pairs of sets. The teacher should make sure that every child covers, through his own activities, each of the additions listed below.

$1 + 1 = 2$	$2 + 1 = 3$	$3 + 1 = 4$	$4 + 1 = 5$
$1 + 2 = 3$	$2 + 2 = 4$	$3 + 2 = 5$	$4 + 2 = 6$
$1 + 3 = 4$	$2 + 3 = 5$	$3 + 3 = 6$	$4 + 3 = 7$
$1 + 4 = 5$	$2 + 4 = 6$	$3 + 4 = 7$	$4 + 4 = 8$
$1 + 5 = 6$	$2 + 5 = 7$	$3 + 5 = 8$	$4 + 5 = 9$

$5 + 1 = 6$
$5 + 2 = 7$
$5 + 3 = 8$
$5 + 4 = 9$
$5 + 5 = 10$

It should be noted that, e.g., both $2 + 3 = 5$ and $3 + 2 = 5$ are included in the above list. This is necessary as it takes time for children to realize that $2 + 3$ and $3 + 2$ both give the same result. Eventually, of course, they must understand and use this property (the commutative property for addition).

3 A number line is drawn on the floor and marked as shown below.

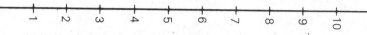

A child stands at the left end of the line. He then takes three steps along the line (to stand on the 3) and then another two steps (to stand on the 5). He then tells the class what he has done (e.g. 'I took three steps and then two more steps. I am now standing on the five.'). The activity is then recorded as the addition: $3 + 2 = 5$

This activity is repeated for many other pairs of numbers, making sure that as many children as possible have a turn. In this activity the fact that, for example, $3 + 2$ and $2 + 3$ both give the same result can be brought out.

4 The coloured number strips, as described on page 25, are used. A child picks up, for example, a 2-strip and a 3-strip. He puts the strips end-to-end and then finds another strip which is as long as the two strips together. He has to use a 5-strip.

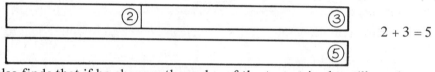

$2 + 3 = 5$

He also finds that if he changes the order of the two strips he still needs a 5-strip.

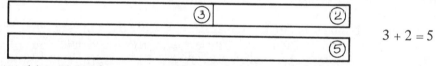

$3 + 2 = 5$

Repeat this activity for many pairs of strips.

5 Activity 3 can be repeated, using a number ladder (up to 10) as described on page 24, instead of a number line drawn on the floor. For example, using his finger, a child goes four steps up the ladder and then another one step. He finds that he is on step 5. He records the activity as $4 + 1 = 5$.

6 A child threads three beads onto a piece of string and puts a '3' numeral card after them. He then puts two more beads onto the string and a '2' numeral card. He counts the number of beads altogether and records the result as $3 + 2 = 5$.

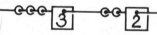

This activity should be repeated for other pairs of numbers.

7 From a set of dominoes remove the 5 – 6 and the 6 – 6. The children then find the total of the numbers of dots on each of the other dominoes. For each domino they write an addition. Some of these will include 0 as one of the two numbers (e.g. $0 + 4 = 4$, $5 + 0 = 5$).

8   Five skittles (as described on page 25) are set up close to each other. A child throws the ball at them and counts the number he knocks down. He shows the number by using a numeral card or by writing it on a piece of paper. The five skittles are set up again and the child has a second throw. He records the number he knocks down and then finds how many he has knocked down altogether in his two throws. This activity is a little more difficult than those listed earlier as the child cannot see the first set of skittles he has knocked down. For this reason some children may find it helpful to make a rough drawing of the two sets of skittles before finding the total.

This activity will almost certainly bring in the number zero and provides a good opportunity for a group of children to write down all the additions which they have which include zero. For example, $2 + 0 = 2$, $0 + 2 = 2$, $0 + 4 = 4$, $4 + 0 = 4$, $3 + 0 = 3$, etc. At this stage some children will not see the link between $0 + 2 = 2$ and $2 + 0 = 2$. It might be helpful to discuss it with them.

9   The children play the game of bean bags in a ring, as described on page 28. Each child has two turns, throwing five bags for each turn. The comments made about skittles above also apply to this activity.

10   In the activities listed so far, the children have been combining two sets of objects and finding the number of the resulting set. They are now given an addition such as $2 + 3$ and are asked to find the answer. Some children will know the result, $2 + 3 = 5$, from their previous activities. Other children may have to use counters (beans, bottle-tops, etc.) for the 2 and the 3 and find the answer by counting the combined set. Do not hurry them. It is important that they should find the answer in their own way and *very* important that they should not lose their confidence at this stage. The teacher should make sure that each child covers all the additions from $1 + 1$, $1 + 2$, etc., to $5 + 5$. When these have been dealt with additions involving zero should be given (e.g. $0 + 2$, $3 + 0$, $5 + 0$, $0 + 0$). The children can be given more practice in these additions by completing arrow graphs, such as those shown below.

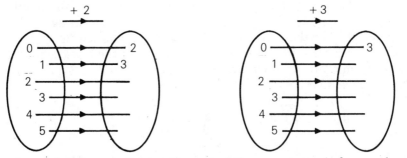

For each graph it is essential to show what the arrow stands for, as above.

11   When the children have covered the above activities successfully they should be introduced to the idea of number 'stories'. For example they put 4 beans on a table or desk and separate them into two piles in various ways. For each of these they write down an addition (e.g. $1 + 3 = 4$, $2 + 2 = 4$, $3 + 1 = 4$). Some children may suggest that they can also use $4 + 0 = 4$ and $0 + 4 = 4$. The results can be shown as:

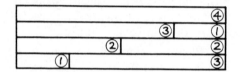

The story of 4

The additions $0 + 4 = 4$ and $4 + 0 = 4$ can also be included if the teacher thinks the children are ready for them. In the same way number 'stories' for 2, 3, and 5 can also be shown.

The coloured cardboard number strips can also be used very effectively for this activity, as illustrated below for 4.

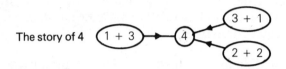

Used in this way the strips emphasize again that $1 + 3$ and $3 + 1$ both have the same answer (the commutative property).

Subtraction (from 10 or less)

Activities

a)   Taking away

1   Five children (3 girls and 2 boys) stand in front of the class. The other children count them (five). The boys return to their seats. The class count how many children are left (three). The teacher now uses the number sentence board. The two boys come to the front of the class again. The children check that there are again five children. The teacher puts a 5 numeral card on the sentence board (or writes it on the blackboard). The two boys again return to their seats and the teacher puts a 2 numeral card on the sentence board.

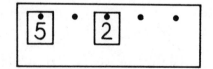

They count the number of marked parts. The teacher then tells a child to cut off two parts from his strip and to count the number of parts left. The activity is recorded as $5 - 2 = 3$. Strips divided into other numbers of parts should also be used and the number of parts cut off should be varied.

7   The children complete arrow graphs such as:

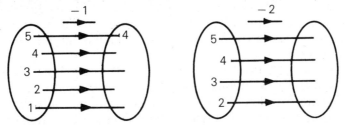

Later they can go on to arrow graphs such as:

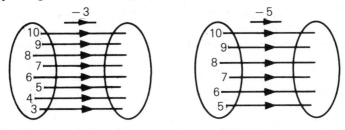

b) Comparing

In the comparing aspect of subtraction we are dealing with two sets, for example, a set of five boys and a set of two girls. And we are answering questions such as, 'How many more boys are there than girls?'. We know that we can find the answer by subtracting two from five. But to young children this is not so obvious, since no taking away seems to be involved. The use of matching, however, can help to make the subtraction clear to children. The two sets are arranged as below:

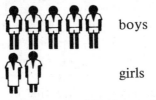

boys

girls

The two girls are matched with two of the boys. This uses two of the boys. So the number of extra boys can be obtained by taking away the two boys from the five boys (i.e. $5 - 2$).

This kind of approach can also be used to answer questions such as, 'How many fewer girls are there than boys?', 'What is the difference between the number of boys and the number of girls?'.

Comparison is an important aspect of subtraction but each activity in the early stages needs to be carefully discussed so that the children are helped to understand why subtraction can be used to find the answer. Here are some helpful activities.

1   The activity described above is repeated several times, with various numbers of boys and girls brought to the front of the class. For each the teacher discusses how the answer to the question 'How many more boys (or girls) are there than girls (or boys)?' can be found and how it is linked with a subtraction.

2   Each child puts a set of beans (e.g. five) and a set of bottle-tops (e.g. three) on his or her desk. By matching each bottle-top with a bean he finds the answer to the question, 'How many more beans are there than bottle-tops?'. He records his answer in words and also as a subtraction ($5 - 3 = 2$).

This activity should be repeated for many different pairs of sets.

3   Each child has two bead bars with a different number of beads on each. He is asked to find how many more beads there are on one bar than the other. The teacher again discusses how the answer can be thought of as a subtraction.

4

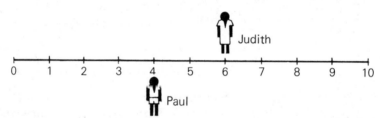

A number line (0 to 10) is drawn on the floor. Two children, Judith and Paul, stand, one on each side of the line, at the 0 mark. Judith then takes six steps along the line (to the 6 mark). Paul then takes four steps (to the 4 mark). The teacher then asks, 'How many more steps did Judith take than Paul?'. The children can quickly see that Judith took two more steps. The teacher then discusses how the answer could also be found by using $6 - 4$. Repeat with other pairs of children taking various numbers of steps.

5   The children play skittles (at first with five skittles and then with numbers up to ten). Two children, Kate and Jenny, each have a turn at throwing the ball (with all the skittles standing for each). They record the number of skittles knocked down and then find how many more one child knocked down than the other. They know, for example, that Kate knocked down five and Jenny knocked down one. They have to find the difference between five and one. Some children will be able to give the answer straight-away. Other children will need to use counters (or make a simple drawing) and use matching to find the answer.

This activity should be repeated for many pairs of children.

6 The children use a set of dominoes. For each domino they write down the difference between the numbers of the two sets of dots shown on it. For example, for the domino shown on the right they find the difference between 6 and 2.

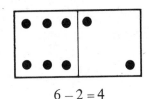

They record the difference as a subtraction.

$$6 - 2 = 4$$

The teacher may need to discuss how 'the difference between' is equivalent to 'how many more?'.

7 Each of two children throws a dice. They then find how many more one number is than the other (or the difference between them).

This activity can be repeated many times.

$$6 - 1 = 5$$

c) Linking subtraction with addition

1 Six boys and four girls stand in front of the class with each girl in front of a boy.

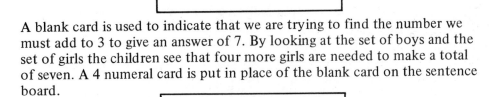

boys

girls

The teacher asks questions such as: 'Are there as many girls as boys?' 'How many more girls must we have so that there are as many girls as boys?'. The children will quickly say that two more girls are needed.

Now two other sets of boys and girls (e.g. 7 boys and 3 girls) are used. The teacher asks questions as before. At the same time he shows the numbers on a number sentence board, as below.

A blank card is used to indicate that we are trying to find the number we must add to 3 to give an answer of 7. By looking at the set of boys and the set of girls the children see that four more girls are needed to make a total of seven. A 4 numeral card is put in place of the blank card on the sentence board.

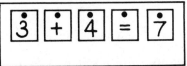

The activity is repeated for many other sets of boys and girls.

2 The children use their coloured number strips. They put, for example, a 6-strip and a 2-strip side by side on their desks.

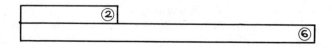

The teacher tells the children to find a strip which can be put with the 2-strip so that the two together are as long as the 6-strip. The children find that they need a 4-strip. They record the activity as $2 + 4 = 6$.

3 The children use their set of dominoes. For each domino they find how many dots must be added to the smaller number so that there are as many as the larger number. They record the answer for each domino as below.

$$1 + \boxed{4} = 5$$

For some of the dominoes a zero will appear in the answer. For example:

$$2 + \boxed{0} = 2$$

$$4 + \boxed{0} = 4$$

4 The teacher writes on the blackboard

$$3 + \square = 5$$

and discusses with the children what they think they have to do. From the earlier work with the number sentence board the children should understand that they have to find the number which when added to 3 gives an answer of 5. The teacher puts a 2 on the blank card, as below:

$$3 + \boxed{2} = 5$$

The children then try some examples on their own. For instance:

$5 + \square = 7$	$5 + \boxed{2} = 7$
$3 + \square = 6$	$3 + \boxed{3} = 6$
$1 + \square = 5$	$1 + \boxed{4} = 5$
$3 + \square = 8$	$3 + \boxed{5} = 8$

Some children may not find this an easy activity. They may need to use two sets of counters to help them find the answers.

5 Write on the blackboard: $2 + 3 = 5$
and then discuss with the children other relationships that can be written using 2, 3, and 5. If the children suggest

$$3 + 2 = 5$$
$$5 - 2 = 3$$
$$5 - 3 = 2$$

then they have a good understanding of the links between addition and subtraction. Repeat for many other examples, such as: $4 + 2 = 6$, $4 + 5 = 9$, $6 + 4 = 10$, etc.

6 To conclude this section the teacher should use two sets and ask questions, involving addition and subtraction, in as many ways as possible. For example, again using the boys and girls of Activity 1, questions should be asked such as:

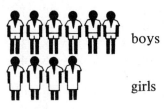

boys

girls

i) How many more boys are there than girls?

ii) How many more girls must we have so that there are as many girls as boys?

iii) $6 - 4 = \square$

iv) $4 + \square = 6$

v) What is the difference between the numbers of boys and of girls?

vi) How many fewer girls are there than boys?

vii) $2 + \square = 6$

The whole set of questions is aimed at making the children familiar with the many relationships between 2, 4, and 6. Repeat for many other pairs of numbers.

Extending addition (to 9 + 9) and subtraction (to 18 – 9)

Activities

1 When the children are confident in addition and subtraction with the smaller numbers, the activities described earlier in this chapter can be extended to larger numbers. This extension should involve additions up to 9 + 9 and subtractions up to 18 – 9. These larger numbers will need a longer number line, more skittles, and all the coloured number strips.

2   The children should also begin to make use of pattern in arranging sets of additions and subtractions. For example:

1 + 1 = 2	2 + 1 = 3	3 + 1 = 4	
1 + 2 = 3	2 + 2 = 4	3 + 2 = 5	
1 + 3 = 4	2 + 3 = 5	3 + 3 = 6	
1 + 4 = 5	2 + 4 = 6	3 + 4 = 7	
1 + 5 = 6	2 + 5 = 7	3 + 5 = 8	etc.
1 + 6 = 7	2 + 6 = 8	3 + 6 = 9	
1 + 7 = 8	2 + 7 = 9	3 + 7 = 10	
1 + 8 = 9	2 + 8 = 10	3 + 8 = 11	
1 + 9 = 10	2 + 9 = 11	3 + 9 = 12	

10 – 1 = 9	9 – 1 = 8	8 – 1 = 7	
10 – 2 = 8	9 – 2 = 7	8 – 2 = 6	
10 – 3 = 7	9 – 3 = 6	8 – 3 = 5	
10 – 4 = 6	9 – 4 = 5	8 – 4 = 4	
10 – 5 = 5	9 – 5 = 4	8 – 5 = 3	etc.
10 – 6 = 4	9 – 6 = 3	8 – 6 = 2	
10 – 7 = 3	9 – 7 = 2	8 – 7 = 1	
10 – 8 = 2	9 – 8 = 1	8 – 8 = 0	
10 – 9 = 1	9 – 9 = 0		
10 – 10 = 0			

3   The children should also have plenty of practice in making up number 'stories' such as:

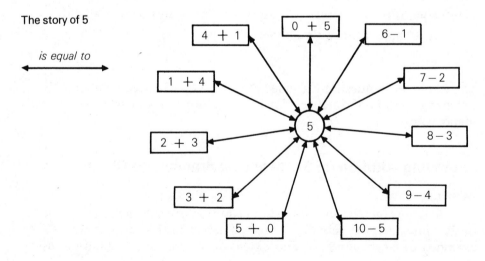

The story of 5

is equal to

4 + 1   0 + 5   6 – 1   1 + 4   7 – 2   2 + 3   5   8 – 3   3 + 2   9 – 4   5 + 0   10 – 5

4 Many examples should be given which emphasize the commutative property for addition. For example:

$7 + 3 = 10$	$5 + 7 = 12$	$8 + 6 = 14$
$3 + 7 = 10$	$7 + 5 = 12$	$6 + 8 = 14$

Memorizing addition and subtraction facts

During these many activities the children should begin to devote time to memorizing the addition and subtraction facts which they have built up. Ways of doing this are described in Chapter 16.

Summary

When a child has completed the many activities in this chapter he or she should:

understand   the idea of addition and the various aspects of subtraction

be familiar   with the relationships between various pairs of numbers

have begun   to memorize the addition and subtraction facts up to $9 + 9 - 18$ and $18 - 9 - 9$

be able to   use the many words and phrases which bring in the ideas of addition and subtraction

Chapter 7
Multiplication and division: first ideas

Repeated addition and multiplication. Repeated subtraction and division. The link between multiplication and division. Memorizing multiplication and division facts.

On pages 60 and 61 in the section 'Thinking about operations' we saw that:

a) multiplication is based on the repeated addition of the same number. For example,

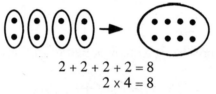

$$2 + 2 + 2 + 2 = 8$$
$$2 \times 4 = 8$$

b) division is based on the repeated subtraction of the same number. For example,

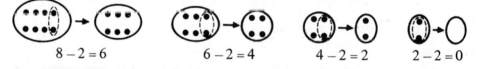

$$8 - 2 = 6 \qquad 6 - 2 = 4 \qquad 4 - 2 = 2 \qquad 2 - 2 = 0$$

To show that the repeated subtraction of 2 can be done four times we write: $8 \div 2 = 4$

Using the idea of repeated subtraction we can answer two types of questions. These are illustrated in the examples below.

i) Eight children are arranged in pairs. How many pairs are there?
The repeated subtraction of two enables us to say that there are four pairs. In a diagram we can show the activity as:

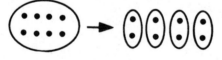

We write, $8 \div 2 = 4$.

ii) Eight children are arranged in two teams of the same number. How many are there in each team?
We can again use repeated subtraction.
For the first two children we allocate one to each team.

For the second two children we allocate one to each team.
We can repeat this allocation four times in all.
So there are four children in each team.
We write, $8 \div 2 = 4$.
In a diagram we can show the activity as:

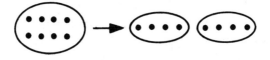

Multiplication

Activities

The first eight activities give practice in repeated addition.
The multiplication symbol is introduced in Activity 9.

1   Two children come to the front of the
class. The teacher draws a chalked loop on the
floor and the children stand in it. The teacher
writes 2 on the blackboard.

Another two children come to
the front and stand in another chalked
loop. The teacher writes on the
blackboard:

Two more children come to the front
and stand in another chalked loop.
The teacher writes on the
blackboard:

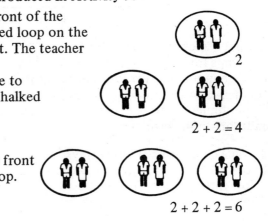

$2 + 2 = 4$

$2 + 2 + 2 = 6$

This activity continues until 5 sets of
two children have come to the front
of the class and the teacher writes on
the blackboard:

$2 + 2 + 2 + 2 + 2 = 10$

This activity should be repeated for sets of three children, four children etc.

2   Four children come to the front
of the class and stand in a line. The
first child raises his two arms.

The children are asked, 'How many
arms are raised?' and the teacher
writes:

2

The second child raises two arms and the teacher asks 'How many arms are raised now?'.
He writes on the blackboard:

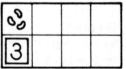

$$2 + 2 = 4$$

The third child raises two arms and the teacher writes:

$$2 + 2 + 2 = 6$$

The fourth child raises his two arms and the teacher writes:

$$2 + 2 + 2 + 2 = 8$$

This activity should be repeated for other numbers of children. It can be varied by asking the children in turn to show the fingers on one hand.

3   A chalked number line is drawn on the floor.

```
├──┼──┼──┼──┼──┼──┼──┼──┼──┼──┤
0   1   2   3   4   5   6   7   8   9  10
```

A child stands on the zero mark.
He jumps forward two steps (to 2):   2
He then jumps another two steps (to 4): $2 + 2 = 4$
He then jumps another two steps (to 6): $2 + 2 + 2 = 6$
He continues in this way and each time the teacher writes the corresponding addition on the blackboard.

4   The children use sorting trays.
In one section they put three objects and below it they put a 3 numeral card, as shown.

They then put another three objects in the next section and another numeral card, as shown. They count the number of objects and write:

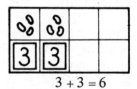

$$3 + 3 = 6$$

They then put another three objects in the third section of the tray together with a 3 numeral card. They count how many objects there are altogether and write:

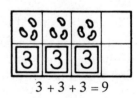

$$3 + 3 + 3 = 9$$

They continue in this way.

This activity should be repeated with two objects in each section, four objects in each section, etc.

5   The children use bead bars.

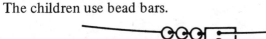

They put three beads on the bar and then a 3 numeral card, as shown. They then put three more beads on the bar and another numeral card. They go on in this way until they have four sets of three beads on the bar. They count how many beads there are altogether and record the activity as

$$3 + 3 + 3 + 3 = 12$$

This activity should be repeated for other numbers.

6   The children use sets of objects (pebbles, bottle-tops, etc.). Each child chooses four of the objects and puts them on his desk together with a 4 numeral card. He then puts down a second set of four and then a third set. He counts how many objects there are altogether and records the result as

$$4 + 4 + 4 = 12$$

This activity should be repeated for sets of various numbers.

7   The children use real or imitation coins.
They also need a sorting tray or a set of chalked loops on their desk or a set of pencilled loops drawn on paper. In the first section of the tray, or the first loop, a child puts two 1p coins. Beneath this he puts a 2p money card, as shown. In the next section of the tray he puts another two 1p coins together with another 2p money card.
He counts how many coins he has altogether and records the result as $2 + 2 = 4$

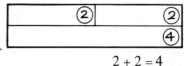

He continues in this way and then repeats for other sets of coins (three 1p coins, four 1p coins, etc.).

8   The children use their coloured number strips.
They put down two 2-strips end-to-end as shown. They then find a strip which is the length of the two 2-strips together (a 4-strip). They write

$$2 + 2 = 4$$

They go on to use three 2-strips and a 6-strip. They write

$$2 + 2 + 2 = 6$$

They continue in this way.
This activity should be repeated for sets of 3-strips, 4-strips, etc.

9

As in Activity 1 pairs of children stand in front of the class. Each pair holds up a large 2 numeral card. The teacher then asks, 'How many children are there in each set?'. He draws a large 2 numeral card on the blackboard and asks, 'How many sets of two are there?'. He shows the 4 on the blackboard, as:

$\boxed{2}$ 4

The teacher then goes on to explain that, to show that we have four twos we use a special symbol. This is called the *multiplication symbol*. He draws this between the 2 and the 4 and completes the statement:

$\boxed{2}$ x   4   =   8

This is read as: Two multiplied by four equals eight.

This activity should be repeated for other numbers of children.

The children practise drawing the multiplication symbol:

a) in the air with a finger;

b) on the desk with a finger;

c) on paper with a pencil.

It is important that children do not mix up the multiplication symbol with the addition symbol. Without practice some children do this in the early stages.

10 Some or all of Activities 1 to 9 are repeated but now each result is recorded as a repeated addition and then as a multiplication. For example using a sorting tray, as shown, the children record:

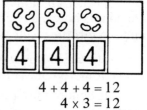

$4 + 4 + 4 = 12$
$4 \times 3 = 12$

The children should have plenty of practice in this kind of recording.

11 The children begin to make use of pattern and record sets of multiplication in order as, for example,

$2 \times 2 = 4$	$3 \times 2 = 6$	$4 \times 2 = 8$
$2 \times 3 = 6$	$3 \times 3 = 9$	$4 \times 3 = 12$
$2 \times 4 = 8$	$3 \times 4 = 12$	
$2 \times 5 = 10$		
$2 \times 6 = 12$		

Multiplication by one should not be included at first but later can be discussed and inserted at the beginning of each pattern.

The children continue to build up and understand these patterns throughout their work on multiplication. Later, as described in Chapter 16, the use of this kind of pattern helps in learning the separate multiplication facts.

12   Practice in building up patterns of multiplications can also be given by completing arrow graphs, such as those below.

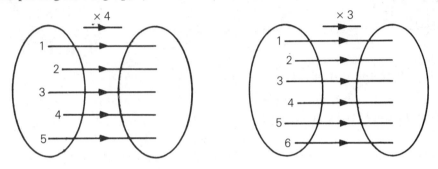

Division

Activities

Activities 1 to 6 give practice in using repeated subtraction.

1   Twelve children come to the front of the class.

The teacher draws a set of small chalked loops on the floor. He chooses two of the 12 children and they stand in one of the loops. He then chooses another two children and they stand in another small loop. He goes on in this way until all the twelve children have been used. He asks the class, 'How many twos have I?'. The children count the twos and say 'There are six'. The teacher says, 'I started with twelve children' (at the same time writing 12 on the blackboard). 'I then formed twos' (writing a 2 on the blackboard a little distance from the 12). 'I then found that I had six twos' (writing a 6 on the blackboard to the right of the 2). He then goes on to explain that to show this activity we use a special symbol. It is called the division symbol. He writes this on the blackboard between the 12 and the 2 and completes the statement: $12 \div 2 = 6$

He discusses each of the numbers in the statement. The 12 shows the number of children brought to the front. The 2 shows how they were arranged (in twos). The 6 shows the number of twos.

The teacher uses the twelve children again but now removes them three at a time.

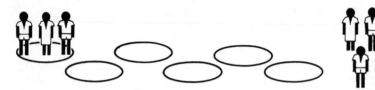

This leads to the statement: $12 \div 3 = 4$

Another twelve children can be used for removing four at a time and six at a time, leading to the statements: $12 \div 4 = 3$

$12 \div 6 = 2$

2   The children use sorting trays. They choose ten objects and put two at a time into different sections of the tray. They count the number of twos and record the activity as: $10 \div 2 = 5$

3   The children use real or imitation 1p coins and try to find the answers to questions such as, 'I have 15p, how many oranges each costing 3p can I buy?'. The children arrange the fifteen coins in threes and then count how many threes there are. They find that they can buy five oranges. The result can be recorded by a statement such as, 'I can buy five oranges' and by the division, $15 \div 3 = 5$.

4   A chalked number line on the floor is used. A child stands on the eight mark. He jumps two steps backwards to 6, then another two steps backwards to 4, then another two to 2, and then another two to zero. The class count the number of jumps (4). The teacher discusses the recording of the activity as: $8 \div 2 = 4$

Here the 8 shows the starting-point on the number line, the 2 shows the number of spaces that the child jumps each time, and the 4 shows the number of jumps. This activity should be repeated for other starting-points. (At this stage they should all be even numbers.)

A good jumper in the class may attempt jumping three steps starting at the 9 mark (or another multiple of 3).

5   Sets of prepared strips of paper with dots on them are needed for this activity. An example is shown below.

The children count the number of dots on the strip and then draw a loop round each set of 3. For the strip shown they find that they can form four sets of 3 dots.

The activity is recorded as: $12 \div 3 = 4$

This activity should be repeated for twos, fours, and sixes, and with other strips with various numbers of dots on them.

6   For this activity strips of paper marked off in squares are required.

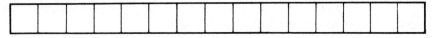

The children first count the number of squares on the strip (15). They then cut off a block of 3 squares and then another block of 3. They continue in this way until all the strip is used. They count the number of blocks of 3. The teacher discusses the recording of the activity as: $15 \div 3 = 5$

This activity should be repeated for other blocks and with different strips.

Activities 7 to 14 use repeated subtraction to find answers to questions such as, 'If ten children are arranged in two teams (of the same number) how many are there in each team?'. Initially these activities seem to be very different from Activities 1–7 but, through discussion, the children are helped to see the link between the two types of activities.

7   Eight children stand in front of the class. The teacher tells the class that the eight children are to be arranged in two teams with the same number in each. The children have to find how many there are in each team. The answer can be found by drawing two large loops on the floor and putting the children one at a time into each loop. They will find that there are four children in each loop. The children record the activity by a simple sentence: 'There are four children in each team.'

8   For this activity sorting trays are needed. The children use twelve objects. They are told to put the same number of objects into each of four sections of a tray. They probably do this by putting one object in each section in turn until they have used all the twelve objects. They record the result by a sentence such as, 'There are three beans in each section.'
    This activity should be repeated many times using various numbers of sections of the tray.

9   The children are asked to share 10p equally between two girls. They find how much each girl has by giving each girl in turn 1p until all the money is used. They record the result by a sentence such as, 'Each girl has 5p.'

This activity should be repeated many times using various amounts of money and different numbers of girls.

10 A strip of squares as used in Activity 6 is needed. The strip must be divided into an even number of squares. Each child folds his strip in half, then cuts it along the folded line. He then counts the number of squares in each part. He records the activity by a sentence such as, 'There are six squares in each part.'

In Activities 7, 8, and 9 the objects were dealt with one at a time. Now the idea of dealing with them two at a time (three at a time, etc., according to the question) is introduced. This leads to the recording of the activity as a division. This transition is not easy for some children so the teacher should go slowly and discuss each step very carefully.

11 Ten children stand in front of the class. The teacher explains that they are to be arranged in two teams and the children have to find how many there are in each team.

The teacher draws two large loops on the floor and suggests that as there are two teams, two children can be dealt with at a time. For the first two children one child is allocated to each team.

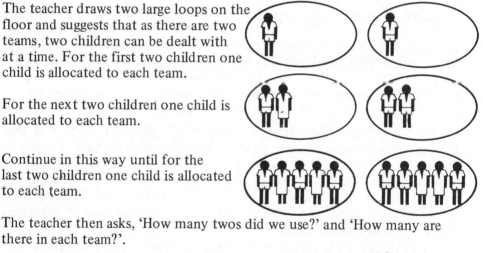

For the next two children one child is allocated to each team.

Continue in this way until for the last two children one child is allocated to each team.

The teacher then asks, 'How many twos did we use?' and 'How many are there in each team?'.

The teacher then arranges the two teams side by side as shown, and again asks, 'How many twos did we use?' He then asks, 'How can you show the number of twos?' and leads to the idea of using the statement:

$$10 \div 2 = 5$$

He discusses each of the three numbers in this statement. The ten shows the number of children, the two shows how many we use each time, and the five shows the number of twos.

He then makes the important point that the five also shows the number in each team. In this way a link is established between the number of twos which can be removed from ten and the number in each of two teams which can be formed from ten. This kind of activity should be repeated many times.

12　The children use a sorting tray. They are asked to put, for example, fifteen objects in three of the sections so that there are the same number in each. Instead of allocating the objects one at a time they now pick them up three at a time and put one in each of the three sections. They count the number of times they have to do this until they have used all of the objects.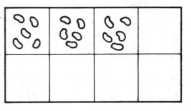

They find that they have to do it five times and that there are then five objects in each section. The result can be recorded as:　$15 \div 3 = 5$

13　The children use real or imitation 1k coins. When a child has twelve coins and is asked to share them equally among three other children, he does this by picking up three coins at a time and giving one of them to each of the three children. He finds that he can do this four times so that each child has 4k. The result can be recorded as a sentence: 'Each child has 4k' and as a division:　$12 : 3 = 4$.

14　Practice in building up division facts can be given by completing arrow graphs, such as those below.

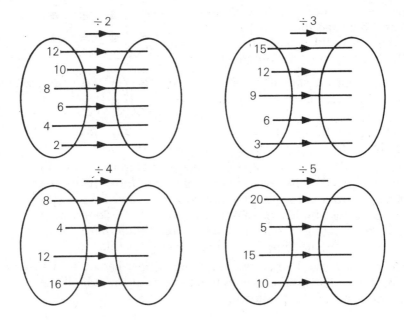

Linking multiplication and division

When the children have worked through the many activities listed above they must have some awareness of the links between multiplication and division. To make sure that this is so, here are some more activities which specifically aim at establishing these links.

Activities

1   The teacher draws a set of twelve objects on the blackboard, as shown. The children count them.

The teacher then draws loops as shown. He asks questions such as:

'How many sets have I formed?'
'What is the number of each set?'
'What multiplication can I write down from the drawing?' $(4 \times 3 = 12)$
'What division can I write down from the drawing?' $(12 \div 4 = 3)$

The teacher makes another drawing of the twelve objects, but now draws the loops as shown. He repeats the questions listed above. Now the children give $3 \times 4 = 12$ and $12 \div 3 = 4$ as the answers.

The teacher then draws the twelve objects, arranged as shown on the right. By drawing loops as shown and repeating the previous questions, the multiplication $6 \times 2 = 12$ and the division $12 \div 6 = 2$ are obtained.

By drawing loops as shown, the statements $2 \times 6 = 12$ and $12 \div 2 = 6$ are obtained.

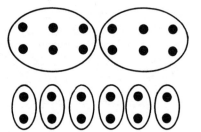

This activity should be repeated for many other numbers (e.g. 6, 8, 9, 10, 14, 15, 18, 20).

The whole of this activity is very important. It emphasizes the link between multiplication and division and helps children to move freely from a multiplication fact to a corresponding division fact. (e.g. $5 \times 2 = 10$ leads to $10 \div 5 = 2$). It also builds up an understanding of the commutative property of multiplication (e.g. $3 \times 4 = 4 \times 3$). Children should have constant practice in this kind of activity throughout the primary school.

2   The children use their coloured number strips. They take a 10-strip and find how many 2-strips must be put end-to-end at the side of the 10-strip to obtain the same length, as shown.

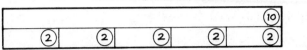

$10 = 2 \times 5$
$10 \div 2 = 5$

They record the activity as $10 \div 2 = 5$ or as $2 \times 5 = 10$. They then go on to find how many 5-strips are needed to make the same length as the 10-strip.

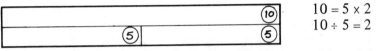

$10 = 5 \times 2$
$10 \div 5 = 2$

They record the result as $10 \div 5 = 2$ or $5 \times 2 = 10$. They repeat this activity for many other strips.

3   After these many activities involving multiplication and division the children should be ready to deal with questions such as, 'What number must I write in the ☐ to make a true statement for: $4 \times$ ☐ $= 12$?'

Here they have to understand that they are trying to find how many fours they need to make twelve. They write 3 in the box. They should then go on to deal with statements such as: $16 \div$ ☐ $= 8$.

This activity should be repeated for many statements as it demands a full understanding of the ideas of multiplication and division.

Memorizing the facts

During these many activities the children begin to devote time to memorizing the multiplication and division facts which they have built up. Ways of doing this are described in Chapter 16.

Summary

When a child has completed the many activities in this chapter he or she should

understand   the idea of multiplication and the various aspects of
                  division

be familiar with the multiplication and division relationships between
                  pairs of numbers

have begun to   memorize the multiplication and division facts for the
                  numbers up to 20

Thinking about
common fractions

Up to a few years ago children in primary and secondary schools spent many hours each year on work involving common fractions. They learned how to add and subtract two fractions, to multiply one fraction by another, and to divide one fraction by another. They were introduced to quick methods and to phrases such as 'turn upside down and multiply'. Yet, at the end of all of these many hours, very few of the children were really confident in their computation with fractions. Students on teaching practice were often asked to repeat work which the children had done before, but did not appear to understand.

With the introduction of more enlightened teaching methods and, especially, with the introduction of decimal money systems and metric measures, teachers began to ask why all this time was being given to common fractions. They tried to find out when, in mathematics or in everyday life, we need to add, subtract, multiply, or divide with fractions. To the surprise of many teachers they found it very difficult to find examples of the use of these operations with fractions in everyday life.

It was found, however, that we all need to understand the idea of a fraction and the notation used to represent it. We also need to understand and be able to use the idea of the equivalence of fractions (e.g. $\frac{1}{2} = \frac{2}{4} = \frac{5}{10} = 0.5 = 50\%$). If these ideas are fully understood then we can deal with most of the situations in which fractions occur in everyday life. It was the lack of understanding of these ideas which was the main cause of the troubles in the past.

For children who go on to secondary schools or other forms of further education, however, there is a need to be able to use operations $(+, -, \times, \div)$ with common fractions. This is particularly true in mathematics and science, especially when letters are used for numbers. For example, in solving equations and in changing formulae, algebraic fractions often occur and an understanding of the methods used for addition, subtraction, multiplication, and division is essential. It must be emphasized, however, that at the primary level this understanding should come from simple straightforward examples. The introduction of complicated calculations, involving big numbers with fractions, does not help. It is more likely to confuse.

Chapter 8
Common fractions: first ideas

The important ideas in working with fractions. The use of the notation for a fraction. Helpful activities. A fraction of a set of objects. First ideas of equivalence.

In the section 'Thinking about fractions' it was emphasized that the two most important ideas which children need are:

a) the idea of a fraction and the notation used;

b) the idea of equivalence.

These ideas are, of course, best built up through suitable activities and also by making use of the occasions when fractions occur in an incidental way.

The use of correct and appropriate words and phrases in describing fractions can be of great help in building up the right ideas. For example, the fraction $\frac{2}{7}$ should be described in words as *two*-sevenths, with the emphasis on the two. (A phrase such as *two over seven* should be avoided.) The introduction of the words *numerator* and *denominator* is not necessary in the early stages and may confuse the children. The words *top* and *bottom* are more descriptive and within the range of a child's experience.

The meaning of $2\frac{1}{4}$ is well understood by us as teachers. But it is surprising how many children, even at the secondary level, do not understand that it represents $2 + \frac{1}{4}$ (even though they can use a 'rule' to change it to $\frac{9}{4}$). We need to remember this and make sure that they have plenty of experience of changing $2 + \frac{1}{4}$ to $2\frac{1}{4}$. In the early stages it is essential that children should always associate a fraction with a specific object (e.g. a quarter of a paper square; a quarter of a piece of string). If they use the symbol alone they may think that all quarters are equal to each other. This is particularly important when children have to find, for example, a quarter of a set of objects (e.g. a quarter of a set of eight sticks of chalk). Now, the *whole* is the set and no breaking of a stick of chalk is necessarily involved. If the idea of a fraction is clearly understood this should cause no difficulties but discussion is usually needed to make sure the children do not become confused.

Some activities which may help children to build up their ideas about fractions are listed on the following pages.

The idea and notation of a fraction

Folding and cutting activities

1   Apparatus: strips of paper; pieces of string; paper rectangles, squares, and circles.

A child folds a strip of paper into two parts of the same length. He cuts along the fold line. He then holds up one of the two parts and says, 'This is one-half of the strip.' He holds up the other part and again says, 'This is one-half of the strip.' He holds up both parts and says, 'Two halves make a whole.'

The notation for one-half is introduced and the child writes $\frac{1}{2}$ on each of the two strips.

This activity is repeated with other materials and objects, as listed above. It is not possible, of course, to write $\frac{1}{2}$ on a piece of string. In this case, a child can put one of the two parts of the string on a piece of paper and write $\frac{1}{2}$ on the paper, near the string.

2   Activity 1 above can be extended to quarters by folding twice. The children should count the equal parts to make sure that there are four.

A child holds up one of the four equal parts and says, 'This is one-quarter of the strip.' He repeats this for each of the other three parts. He holds up all the four parts and says 'Four quarters make a whole.' He writes $\frac{1}{4}$ on each of the four parts.

The child then holds up two of the four parts and says, 'I am holding up *two* quarters of the strip.' He should emphasize the *two*. The notation ($\frac{2}{4}$) for two quarters is then introduced and discussed.

Three quarters are then held up, discussed, and the notation, $\frac{3}{4}$, is introduced.

Four quarters should again be held up to emphasize the fact that four quarters make a whole.

If long strips of paper are available the folding may be extended to eighths with the able children.

Thirds are not easily obtained by folding so other ways of introducing them should be used (see below).

3   Strips of paper (all the same length) and marked by the teacher as shown are needed. The unmarked strip is kept as a whole strip. The children then use each strip in turn. For example, using the strip divided into three parts, they first count the number of parts (three). They then cut along the marked lines and, by placing the three strips on top of each other,

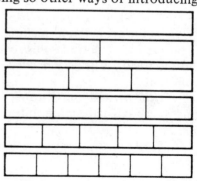

check that they are all the same length. The notation for one-third is then introduced and the children write $\frac{1}{3}$ on each of the three parts. They then hold up strips to show *one*-third, *two*-thirds, *three*-thirds.

When the children have used each of the strips in this way they can arrange their labelled strips as shown on the right. This is not easily organized as some children tend to get the small strips mixed. It is worth trying, however, as it brings in some of the ideas of equivalence.

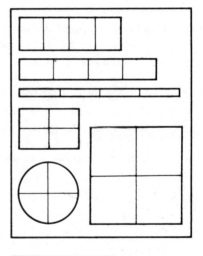

Drawing and colouring activities

4   Each child is provided with a sheet of paper on which a set of shapes (each divided into four equal parts) are drawn. The children count the number of parts in each shape. One child can use an extra copy of the shapes to check, by cutting out, that the four parts of each shape are the same size. The children then colour, or shade, one of the four equal parts and write $\frac{1}{4}$ on it, as shown.

This activity is repeated for each of the other shapes.

5   Activity 4 is repeated on another sheet but now the children colour or shade three-quarters of each shape. At the side of the coloured shape they write $\frac{3}{4}$, as shown.

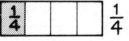

6   On other copies of the sheet the children show two-quarters ($\frac{2}{4}$) and then four-quarters ($\frac{4}{4}$).

For the two-quarters many children will say that it is the same as one-half (one of the first ideas of equivalence).

Activities such as 4, 5, and 6 are repeated for sets of shapes divided into thirds, fifths, sixths, etc.

Activities leading to the idea of a fraction of a set

7   Each child has, for example, a set of eight identical objects (e.g. beads, matchboxes, wooden cubes, coins). He counts them and is then told to divide the set into two parts with the same number in each. The idea that each part is a half of the original set is then discussed. The children write, 'One-half of 8 is 4.' This activity is repeated for many other numbers (these should all be even numbers in the early stages).

For each set the children can make a simple drawing, as below.

8   Activity 7 is repeated for other fractions of suitably chosen numbers. For example, one-third of six, one-fifth of ten, one-sixth of twelve. For each a statement should be written and a simple drawing made.

9   The children repeat Activities 7 and 8 but now they find, for example, three-quarters of eight, four-fifths of ten, etc. For each of these, two drawings can be made, as shown in the example below.

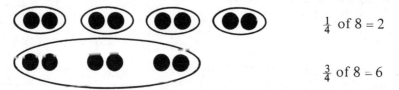

$\frac{1}{4}$ of 8 = 2

$\frac{3}{4}$ of 8 = 6

It is particularly essential in an example of this kind that the children think of $\frac{3}{4}$ as *three*-quarters and emphasize the three in saying the fraction. In these activities, ideas of equivalence will occur and should be discussed. For example, children will quickly see that there are as many objects in two-quarters of 8 as in one-half of 8.

10   Each child is provided with a sheet of shapes.

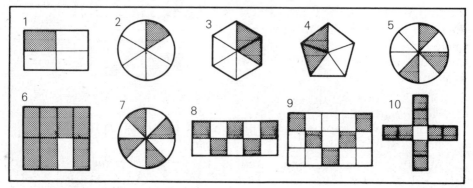

A fraction of each shape is shaded, as shown. The children have to write down the fraction at the side of the shape.

Activities leading to the idea of equivalence

In most of the activities listed above the idea of equivalence occurs and every opportunity should be taken of discussing it with the children. The idea should grow out of the children's experience rather than being taught as a separate topic. However, it is helpful at times to draw together the various ideas which the children have acquired.

11 With the children the teacher makes a simple fraction board. Long strips of thick paper or thin card can be used for this. One strip is first pinned to the blackboard and a 1 written on it. Then an identical strip is divided into two equal parts and $\frac{1}{2}$ written on each. These are pinned underneath the 1-strip. Quarters and eighths are then made and pinned up as shown. The teacher and the children then discuss the fraction board. From this discussion the children see that, for example, $\frac{1}{2} = \frac{2}{4} = \frac{4}{8}$; $\frac{3}{4} = \frac{6}{8}$; $\frac{2}{2} = \frac{4}{4} = \frac{8}{8} = 1$.

12 Another simple board can be made for thirds and sixths. From this the children should see that
$\frac{1}{3} = \frac{2}{6}$; $\frac{2}{3} = \frac{4}{6}$; $\frac{3}{3} = \frac{6}{6} = 1$.

13 For the able children it may be appropriate to use the two sets from Activities 11 and 12 together, as shown. From this combined board the children will be able to find more sets of equivalent fractions, e.g. $\frac{1}{2} = \frac{2}{4} = \frac{3}{6} = \frac{4}{8}$ and $\frac{2}{2} = \frac{3}{3} = \frac{4}{4} = \frac{6}{6} = \frac{8}{8} = 1$.

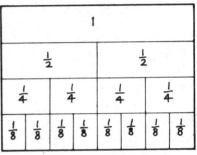

This fraction board is also helpful for comparing fractions. If the first part of each set is coloured or shaded, as shown, then the children can quickly see that, for example: $\frac{1}{2} > \frac{1}{3}$; $\frac{1}{3} > \frac{1}{4}$; $\frac{1}{6} > \frac{1}{8}$, etc. This can lead to much useful discussion. For example, the children can be asked to explain why one-third is greater than one-quarter.

14 For this activity the children need two identical glass bottles or other suitable containers. They fill one of them with water (or sand) and are then asked to find one-half of the amount of water. They do this by pouring some of the water from the full bottle into the empty bottle. They then stand the two bottles side by side to see whether the water level is the same for each. If not they pour water from the larger part into the other bottle. They continue in this way until the two levels are the same.

Using more bottles the children can go on to find one-quarter of the water. Some of the more able children can try to find one-third of the water, using the same kind of method.

15 For this activity the children need a lump of soft clay and a simple balance. They find one-half of the clay by using the 'trial and error' method of Activity 14. They can then go on to divide the clay into quarters.

Summary

When a child has completed the many activities described in this chapter he or she should:

understand	the idea of a fraction of a whole
	the notation used for showing a fraction
	the idea of equivalence of fractions
	the idea of a fraction of a set
be able to	change a fraction to a simple equivalent fraction
	use the notation for describing a fraction

Thinking about
place-value

Nowadays we accept that from an early age we all learn to count. But it was not always so. For example, a shepherd boy long ago could not count. But he needed to make sure that he did not lose any of his sheep. He could not count them so he made use of some form of one-to-one matching. Perhaps he used a pebble to represent each sheep, or cut a notch in a stick or tied a knot in a strip of leather. In this way he was able to check that, at the end of the day, there was a sheep for each pebble, notch, or knot.

Gradually, however, people did begin to learn to count. At first they did not find it easy to count beyond three. In their own language they could use *one*, *two*, *three* but for greater numbers they used the one word *many*.

Simple forms of counting were adequate while people lived in small communities but when they began to farm, build, and trade, it became essential to extend their counting. In many cases this was done by making use of fingers and toes, and using five, ten, or twenty as the base of their numbers.

It also became necessary to record numbers in a more convenient form than the use of stones, notches, knots, etc. This led to the making of marks on stone and thus the introduction of symbols for numbers. About a thousand years ago, a method of writing numbers was introduced which made it much easier to do written calculations. This method originated in India and was developed and extensively used by the Arabs. For this reason it is called the Hindu–Arabic system. It is the system we all now use. Like many of the earlier systems the Hindu–Arabic system is based on *ten*.

Its most important difference from other systems is that a symbol is introduced for zero. With this symbol and the symbols 1, 2, 3, 4, 5, 6, 7, 8, 9 it is possible to show any number by using the idea of place-value. For example,

	H 100	T 10	U 1
3 *hundreds*, 4 *tens*, and 6 *ones* is shown as 346	3	4	6
4 *hundreds*, 3 *tens*, and 6 *ones* is shown as 436	4	3	6
6 *hundreds* and 5 *ones* is shown as 605	6	0	5

The use of the 0 in 605 enables us to show that there are no *tens*. If we did not have a symbol for zero we might show 6 *hundreds* and 5 *ones* as 65. This would then be confused with sixty-five.

During recent years the development and use of computers has led to an increasing interest in bases other than ten. The underlying need was to use fewer symbols than those used for base ten (i.e. 0 to 9). A way in which this can be done, requiring only the ability to count to three and the use of the symbols 0, 1, and 2, is illustrated below.

Look at the set of objects represented by dots below.

Using our ability to count up to three, we first arrange the set in *threes* (with one left over).

As we can only count up to three we cannot say how many *threes* we have. So we combine three of the *threes* to form *three-threes*, as below.

We can now say that we have:
1 *three-threes*, 2 *threes*, and 1 *one*.
Using column headings and numerals the number of the set at the top of the page can be shown as:

three-threes	threes	ones
1	2	1

If there were one more object in the set the number would be shown as:

three-threes	threes	ones
1	2	2

The next number in order would be shown as:

three-threes	threes	ones
2	0	0

Going on in this way, using only the numerals 0, 1, and 2, but increasing the number of columns as necessary, we can show the number of any set.

Without column headings, the numbers above could be shown as 121, 122, and 200. But now we have to understand that the value shown by a numeral depends upon its place. For example, the right-hand 2 in 122 represents 2 *ones*, but the 2 in the middle represents 2 *threes*. This is the underlying idea of what is called **place-value**.

When we work in threes, as we did above, we say that we are using *base three*. From early times, man made use of his fingers in counting and so he naturally worked in *base five, base ten*, or *base twenty*. Some people, however, used other bases, such as seven. Nowadays *base ten* is generally used, but during recent years another base has become important. This is *base two*. In this base only two numerals are used — 0 and 1. This is very helpful in designing and using computers so with the very rapid expansion of this kind of aid in industry and commerce during recent years the importance of *base two* has increased.

Some examples of numbers shown in *base two* are given below, using column headings.

	eights	fours	twos	ones
fingers on one hand		1	0	1
days in a week		1	1	1
fingers on two hands	1	0	1	0

The importance of place-value for children is not, however, that they should understand the modern computer. Rather, it is that a real understanding of place-value is an essential requirement in using numbers and in computation. A lack of this understanding is a major stumbling block for many children in primary schools.

Chapter 9
Place-value: first ideas

The importance of place-value. Why many children fail to understand place-value. Some activities for introducing place-value.

A clear and full understanding of place-value is essential if a child is to progress in addition, subtraction, multiplication, and division. But many children quickly become confused when they try to use these ideas. Why?

Is it because children are not given sufficient practical activities in their early years at school to help them to build up ideas about place-value? Is it because they go on to written computation too quickly? Is it because the words and phrases which are imposed on children when they start to use place-value in calculations confuse them rather than help them? What real meaning can words and phrases such as *borrow, pay back, goes into, bring down the seven, add a zero, move the decimal point*, have for children? They are not linked with any of the practical activities which they may have done. In fact, they do not correctly describe what is being done. To *borrow* from one number and to *pay back* to another number is nonsense. The difficulty here is that, as teachers, we tend to use the words and phrases which we ourselves used at school. We accept them without thinking about them. And this is something a teacher must always be on guard against. It is a good thing to develop the habit of looking at all the words and phrases we use and asking ourselves what they really mean — both to ourselves and to children.

So, before we start to blame children because they do not understand place-value we ought to make sure that:

a) we provide them with plenty of practical activities which help in building up the right ideas;

b) we do not introduce complicated written calculations before the children are ready for them (if we do, the children can cope only by doing them parrot-like, without any real understanding);

c) we look very carefully at the words and phrases we use when place-value comes into calculations.

With these thoughts and warnings in our minds we can begin to think about how best to introduce and develop the idea and use of place-value.

In doing this we quickly find that we have to make a decision. We have to decide whether we are going to use only *base ten* or whether we are going to give children a broader background by using a variety of other bases before concentrating on *base ten*. One of the disadvantages of using only *base ten* is that it is not always easy for the teacher to decide whether a child really understands the underlying place-value ideas. It is easy for a child to deal with numbers up to 99 without understanding place-value. If simple, straightforward activities are provided in other bases, however, a child has to use more than two columns very quickly. For example in *base three* a third column has to be used as soon as there are more than eight (*base ten*) objects.

Another advantage of using bases other than ten is that a child's attention is focused all the time on the column headings and on the relationships between them. In *base four*, for example, he must understand that he can never have a 4 in any column. As soon as he gets one more than three (i.e. four) in any column, he must change it to a 1 in the column to the left. There is a constant use of four-ness.

A variety of activities in other bases should help children in their understanding of place-value in *base ten*. There is, however, no real need to use the language of bases in these activities. This is well illustrated in the activities which are discussed below.

Activities

For each activity the children should work individually, in pairs, or in small groups, depending upon the amount of apparatus and material available. (For convenience, the activities are described for individual working.)

1   For this activity each child needs:

a)   a set of empty matchboxes;

b)   some elastic bands or pieces of string;

c)   a set of beans or other objects which are approximately the same size. They should be small enough that several beans will go into a matchbox. The child starts with a heap of beans (about twenty to thirty). He puts the same number (e.g. four) into matchboxes until he has used as many fours as possible. Any beans left over he leaves on his desk. He does not put them into a matchbox.

The child then goes on to arrange his filled matchboxes in bundles of four. He puts an elastic band around each bundle. An example of what the child may now have on his desk is shown below.

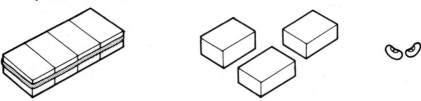

He says, 'I have one bundle, three boxes, and two beans'. Then he records the activity. This recording is an essential and very important part of the activity. Without it, the activity loses much of its value.

The recording should be done in two ways:

a) by a simple drawing, as on page 103, with the number of bundles, boxes, and single beans shown;

b) by using columns, as shown below.

bundles	boxes	ones
1	3	2

The results should be fully discussed. For example, questions such as the following should be asked:

a) How many beans are there in a box?

b) How many boxes make a bundle?

c) How many beans are there altogether in a bundle?

d) How many beans are there in two boxes?

e) How many beans are there altogether if I have two boxes and three single beans?

f) If I have the beans shown above and then have one more bean, how would I show, using columns, the number of beans altogether?

g) If I have the beans shown above and then have two more beans, how would I show, using columns, the number of beans altogether?

The activity should be repeated, starting with the same number of beans, but putting a different number in a box (and this new number of boxes in a bundle). Care must be taken, however, to make sure that the number of bundles does not lead to the need for another column. (For example if three beans are put in a box and this leads to four bundles, then three of these bundles should be combined to form a still larger set. This is best avoided in the early stages but can be introduced later.) Twenty-two is a convenient number of beans, as shown in the table below.

Number in a box	bundles	boxes	ones
3	2	1	1
4	1	1	2
5		4	2
6		3	4

At this stage it is best to avoid having only two beans in a box, as four columns are needed for only eight beans.

Twenty beans is a suitable number to use to bring in zeros in some of the columns, as shown below.

Number in a box	bundles	boxes	ones
3	2	0	2
4	1	1	0

It is important that the children should include the empty column when they give the result in words. For example, when twenty beans are arranged in threes the children should say, 'I have two bundles, no boxes, and two beans.' It is the use of the zero which makes it possible to record numbers, using place-value, when we do not put in the column headings (i.e. nine hundreds and five ones has to be shown as 905, *not* 95).

2   For this activity the following materials are required.

a)   A good supply of beads.

b)   A lump of clay (or plasticine) into which pieces of wire (or other suitable material) are stuck. Each piece of wire should be long enough to take three beads, but not four.

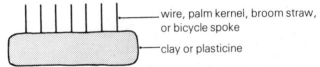

wire, palm kernel, broom straw, or bicycle spoke

clay or plasticine

c)   Another lump of clay with wires, as for (b), but with each piece of wire long enough to take nine beads (but not ten).

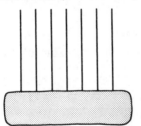

A child first uses the 3-bead wires. He fills as many as possible with his beads. (Make sure that each wire used is completely filled. Any surplus beads should be left on the desk, not put on a wire.)

The child then uses the beads on the 3-bead wires to fill as many as possible of the 9-bead wires. Again make sure that all the 9-bead wires used are completely filled.

If, for example, the child starts with 23 beads he should finish with:

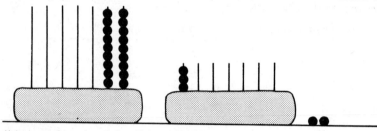

The child says, for example, 'I have filled two long wires, one short wire, and have two beads on the table.' He might also say, 'I have two nines, one three, and two ones.'

Note: Not more than 26 beads should be used with this apparatus.

The child then goes on to record the activity by:

a) a simple drawing as above;

b) using columns, as below.

nines	threes	ones
2	1	2

A result such as that shown above provides a good opportunity to discuss what each of the twos represents. If a child understands that the first 2 represents two nines and the second 2 represents two ones, he is beginning to understand place-value.

3   Each child collects a set of small flowers. He then arranges the flowers on his desk. First he arranges them in, for example, fours.

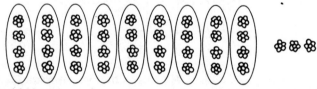

He is then told that four rows of four make a 'field'. So he separates the rows into fields (either by drawing a chalk loop around each field or by using a piece of string).

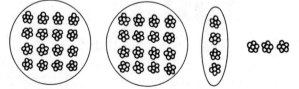

He says, 'I have two fields, one row, and three flowers'.

He records the activity by:

a) a simple drawing;

b) using column headings.

fields	*rows*	*flowers*
2	1	3

The activity should be repeated for different numbers in a row and for different numbers of flowers. For each, the recording in columns needs to be checked carefully.

4 In the activities described above the children have been able to see all the objects as they have been rearranged. They have not replaced a number of them by a new object, as is often done in using an abacus. For example, the number 13 is represented on an abacus by one bead on the 'tens' wire and three beads on the 'ones' wire, as shown below.

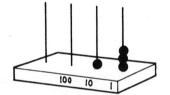

This, of course, is a true representation but it is a big step forward for the children, especially as the one bead on the 'tens' wire is often identical to the beads on the 'ones' wire. Children can quickly become confused. To avoid this a bridge needs to be formed between the earlier activities and the use of the abacus.

One way of doing this is to use the coloured number strips described on page 25. The children work in pairs, so that they have twenty 1-strips between them. (Later some more 1-strips may have to be provided.) One child is provided with a set of 1-strips (e.g. 13). The other child has a set of 5-strips. They cover a 5-strip with 1-strips to make sure that they both understand that a 5-strip is equivalent to five 1-strips. The child with the 1-strips is then told to change as many as possible of his 1-strips for 5-strips. He counts five of his 1-strips and gives them to his partner in exchange for one 5-strip. He then counts another five 1-strips and again exchanges them for a 5-strip. He still has three 1-strips but his partner will not give him a 5-strip in exchange for them. The first child then says, 'I have two 5-strips and three 1-strips' and records the number using column headings as:

5-strips	*1-strips*
2	3

This activity has the advantage that the 5-strip is actually the same size as five 1-strips together. So a child finds the changing and the recording straightforward.

The activity should be repeated many times, using various numbers of 1-strips (but not more than 24). The strips into which they are changed can also be varied (taking care that a second changing is never necessary).

When the children understand the idea and use of column headings the idea of working in tens should be introduced. Several helpful activities are given below.

5   The use of coloured numbered strips as described in Activity 4 is extended to include the 10-strip. The number of 1-strips should at first be not greater than nineteen. Then numbers from twenty to thirty can be used. For each set of 1-strips the children use column headings to record the changing of each set of ten 1-strips to one 10-strip. For example:

10-strips	1-strips
1	5
2	3

The number names for each set of 1-strips are now linked with the above recordings. The names for the numbers eleven to nineteen need careful explanation and discussion. The number names from twenty onwards follow a regular pattern. The spelling of the number names should be practised as soon as they are introduced.

6   Each child has a set of small drinking straws (or other suitable objects) and two tins. One tin should be labelled *tens* and the other *ones*.

A child counts ten of his straws and fastens them together, using an elastic band (or a piece of string, cotton, or other suitable material). He puts this bundle into the *tens* tin. For numbers up to nineteen he finds that he cannot make up another ten so he puts the single straws into the *ones* tin. He records the activity, for example, as shown below.

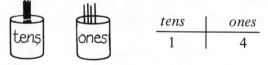

tens	ones
1	4

He repeats this activity with all the numbers from eleven to nineteen.

The child then starts again with one set of straws in the *tens* tin.

He puts one straw in the *ones* tin and records the number in three ways, as below,

tens	*ones*
1	1

11   eleven

He then puts one more straw in the *ones* tin and records:

tens	*ones*
1	2

12   twelve

In this way he goes on to build up and record the numbers up to nineteen.

When one more straw is added to the nineteen the idea of putting the ten straws together to form a second *ten* should be discussed. The child then does this and moves the *ten* to the *tens* tin. The need to put a zero in the *ones* column when recording should be emphasized.

tens	*ones*
2	0

20   twenty

The child continues in this way up to twenty-nine and then goes on to 30, 40, etc.

7   Each child has a duplicated sheet of squares (with 10 squares in each column). On this he colours a set of squares to show a number, as below.

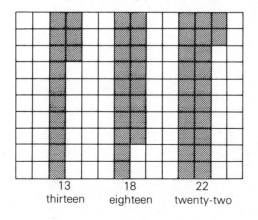

13	18	22
thirteen	eighteen	twenty-two

This is a straightforward activity but it does give variety and may help some children to move from half understanding to full understanding. Some teachers may, of course, prefer to use 10 by 10 square grids. These are used later in several activities and it may be appropriate to introduce them at this stage.

8   There is some excellent commercially produced apparatus available which reduces the teacher's preparation and which gives good results if used sensibly. Its cost, however, may be beyond the resources of some schools. But all teachers should be aware of it and should try to obtain some of this kind of apparatus to try out in their own school. They will then be able to assess its possible value and decide whether it is worth making a special effort to obtain more.

Summary

When a child has completed the many activities in this chapter, he or she should:

understand	the idea of place-value
be able to	record numbers using column headings
	use a zero for an empty column
	record numbers without column headings

Chapter 10
Addition: using place-value

Planning the work in suitable steps. Useful apparatus. Addition of 2-digit numbers with no 'carrying'. Addition of 2-digit numbers with 'carrying' to the *Tens*. Addition of three 2-digit numbers with and without 'carrying'.

Planning the work

Here is one way of arranging the work in suitable steps.

1 Give plenty of practice in learning the addition facts, up to $9 + 9 = 18$ (see Chapter 16). The learning of the addition facts requires as much time and effort as the learning of the multiplication facts. To introduce the use of place-value before the children are confident in their knowledge of the addition facts will only confuse them and result in a lack of success.

2 Introduce the use of the vertical form in dealing with additions such as $24 + 13$, where the total of the units *is less than 10*. Give plenty of practice in this way of recording.

3 Extend (2) to examples where the total of the units is 10. This introduces the idea of changing 10 units to 1 ten and recording in the vertical form.

4 Extend (3) to examples where the total of the units is greater than 10. Gradually introduce the shortened form of recording the addition.

5 Introduce the addition of three or more numbers (with total not greater than 99). Some of these should involve the changing of the units to one or more tens.

6 Gradually dispense with the use of the column headings. Careful watch must be kept of the way in which the children set down their additions. Errors often arise because of careless setting down, resulting in tens becoming mixed up with the units. Children need to keep their tens and units columns well apart.

7 At the appropriate time additions can be introduced with a total greater than 99. If the children understand the basic ideas this should be accepted as a straightforward extension of the work already done. (This extension is discussed in detail in Chapter 19.)

Apparatus

1   Short straws, sticks, etc. which can be made into bundles of ten by tying with elastic bands, string, cotton, etc. It is a good idea for each child to have two tins, labelled *tens* and *ones*, as shown on the right. He can then put single sticks and bundles of ten in these to represent a number. The number can be shown by putting numeral cards in front of the tins.

2   A set of coloured number strips, as described on page 25.

Activities

1   The children work in pairs. The first child shows a number (e.g. 15) by putting one bundle of ten in his *tens* tin and five single sticks in his *ones* tin. The second child shows a number (e.g. 23) in the same way. The children then find how many sticks there are altogether. They do this by putting all the bundles of tens in one of the *tens* tins and all the single sticks in one of the *ones* tins. They count the number of bundles in the *tens* tin, then put a 3 numeral card in front of the tin. They then count the single sticks and put an 8 numeral card in front of the *ones* tin. They say that they have thirty-eight sticks altogether.

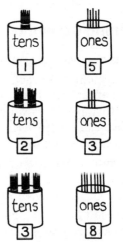

The recording of the addition in a vertical form is now introduced. This is an important step and needs to be discussed fully. It follows, of course, the use of columns and column headings introduced in Chapter 9. Now the column headings are *tens* and *ones*. Using these the children record the addition, as shown on the right. This kind of recording follows naturally from the activity and should be straightforward for the children to follow.

	tens	*ones*
	1	5
+	2	3
	3	8

2   Repeat Activity 1 for many other pairs of numbers (remembering that the total for each column should not be greater than nine).

3   Repeat Activity 1 using number strips. The children first use the strips to show each of the two numbers, as below.

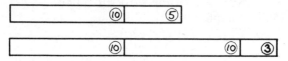

They then put the strips together, arranged as below.

Finally they replace the 5-strip and the 3-strip by an 8-strip.

In this way they show that when the strips for the two numbers (15 and 23) are put together they show the number 38. They record the addition in a vertical form, again using *tens* and *ones* for the column headings.

4 Repeat Activity 3 for many other pairs of strips (again remembering that the total for either column should not be greater than nine).

5 Repeat Activity 1 but now choose two numbers so that the total of the *ones* is ten (e.g. 16 and 14). When the children put the sticks together they find that they have ten sticks in the *ones* tin. Discuss the changing of these to one bundle of *tens*. The children should tie them together and then move the bundle ('carry' it) to the *tens* tin. They now find that there are 3 bundles in the *tens* tin. There are no sticks in the *ones* tin. Make sure that the children understand that altogether there are 30 sticks.

Now repeat this activity but at each step record on the blackboard what is done. First show the addition to be, done.

tens	ones
1	6
+ 1	4

The children deal with the single sticks. They put these together to get ten sticks. Use coloured chalk or dotted numerals to show this, as on the right.

tens	ones
1	6
+ 1	4
	10

The children then tie the ten sticks together to get one bundle of ten and no single sticks. To show this first rub out the coloured (or dotted) 10. Then write an 0 in the units column of the answer. Go on to explain that we show the one *ten* by writing a '1' in the *tens* column, under the answer line, as on the right.

tens	ones
1	6
+ 1	4
	0
1	

The children then deal with the bundles of ten. There is one bundle of ten for the 16, one for the 14, and one which was formed from the single sticks. They add these to get three *tens*. These are shown by writing a '3' in the *tens* column of the answer, as on the right.

tens	ones
1	6
+ 1	4
3	0
1	

6 Repeat Activity 5 for many other pairs of numbers for which the total of the *ones* is ten (remembering that the answer should not be greater than 90).

7 Repeat Activities 5 and 6 using the number strips. For 16 + 14, the 6-strip and the 4-strip together are changed to a 10-strip. This illustrates the changing very well.

8 Repeat Activity 1 but now choose the two numbers so that the total of the *ones* is greater than ten (e.g. 17 and 25). The recording can now be shown as on the right. Check that the children understand and can explain this way of recording.

tens	ones
1	7
+ 2	5
4	2
1	

At this stage discuss the use of abbreviations for *tens* and *ones*. Explain that T and O could be used but that O might be confused with the symbol for zero. To avoid this another word for *one* is used. This is the word *unit*. For this, the abbreviation U can be used and the column headings can be abbreviated to T and U. This is another example of taking care to explain to children why particular words are used in mathematics.

9 Repeat Activity 8 for many other pairs of numbers for which the total of the *ones* is greater than ten (but with answers not greater than 99).

10 Repeat Activities 8 and 9 using number strips.

11 Use the same kind of apparatus to introduce and give practice in the addition of three numbers (total not greater than 99). In recording these additions teachers are sometimes not sure where to put the '+' sign. Some teachers use two of them. The simplest way is to write 'add' at the top of the three numbers and omit the + sign, as shown on the right. At times in these additions 2 *tens* have to be 'carried' from the *units* to the *tens*. This step needs careful demonstration and discussion.

Add	
T	U
1	5
1	8
2	3
5	6
1	

12   If the teacher thinks the children are ready for it, the addition of two 2-digit numbers which have a total of more than 100 can be introduced at this stage (e.g. 62 + 46, 75 + 58).

For these the children find that there are ten or more bundles in the *tens* tin. So they use ten of these to form a big bundle of 10 *tens* (i.e. one hundred). They put this big bundle in a tin labelled *hundreds* and the use of the HTU heading is introduced in the recording.

If the children have understood the work with TU headings they should find this extension straightforward to understand.

Note: Addition of larger numbers is discussed in detail in Chapter 19.

Summary

When a child has completed the many activities in this chapter, he or she should:

understand	the use of place-value in addition
	the idea of writing additions in a vertical form
	the idea of 'carrying'
be able to	add two or more 2-digit numbers

Chapter 11

Subtraction: using place-value

Methods used in subtraction. The use of 'Decomposition'. Planning the work in suitable steps. Useful apparatus. Subtraction of a 1-digit number from 20, 30, 40, . . ., 90. Subtraction of a 2-digit number from 20, 30, 40, . . ., 90. Subtraction of a 2-digit number from another 2-digit number.

Deciding on the method to use

Before we start to discuss ways of introducing the use of place-value in subtraction to children, it is essential that we clarify our own thinking about the various methods that can be used for a subtraction such as $45 - 27$. These are listed below.

a) Counting on

Add 3 to 27 — to make 30.
Add 10 to the 30 — to make 40.
Add 5 to the 40 — to make 45.
$3 + 10 + 5 = 18$. So 18 was added to 27 to make 45.
The difference between 45 and 27 is 18.
$45 - 27 = 18$.
     This method is often used in shops and markets in giving change.

b) Decomposition

Dealing first with the *units*, we cannot subtract 7 from 5. So we use one of the 4 *tens* and change it to 10 *units*. We show this as on the right. The real thinking is now completed.

$$\begin{array}{r} TU \\ 4\ 5 \\ -2\ 7 \\ \hline \end{array} \qquad \begin{array}{r} TU \\ {}^{3}\!4\,{}^{10}\!5 \\ -2\ 7 \\ \hline \end{array}$$

    We can now deal with the *units* in two ways:

i) by subtracting 7 from 15 ($15 - 7 = 8$);

ii) by subtracting 7 from 10 and adding 5 to the result ($10 - 7 = 3$; $3 + 5 = 8$).

$$\begin{array}{r} TU \\ {}^{3}\!4\,{}^{10}\!5 \\ -2\ 7 \\ \hline 8 \end{array}$$

It should be noted that if (i) is used all the subtraction facts up to $18 - 9$ *must* be known. For (ii), only the subtraction facts from 10 *must* be known.

We now complete the subtraction by dealing with the *tens* ($3 - 2 = 1$). The language associated with this method involves only: 'use one of the four *tens* and change it to ten *units*'. This describes simply and exactly what is done.

```
    T U
   3 10
    4 5
 - 2 7
 ─────
    1 8
```

c) Equal additions

Dealing first with the *units*, we cannot subtract 7 from 5.

```
   T U
   4 5
 - 2 7
 ─────
```

So we add 10 *units* to the 45 and *at the same time* we add 1 *ten* to the 27. We record these two additions as shown.

```
      T U
       10
      4 5
     3
 -   2 7
 ─────
```

We now deal with the subtraction of the *units* in one of the two ways described for *decomposition*.

```
      T U
       10
      4 5
     3
 -   2 7
 ─────
        8
```

We complete the subtraction by dealing with the *tens*: ($4 - 3 = 1$).

```
      T U
       10
      4 5
     3
 -   2 7
 ─────
      1 8
```

The language associated with this method involves the use of a phrase such as: 'add ten *units* to the five *units* (in the 45) and *at the same time* add one *ten* to the two *tens* (in the 27)'.

This method makes use of the fact that the difference between two numbers remains unchanged if we add the same number to each. For example, $8 - 5 = 18 - 15 = 28 - 25 = 108 - 105$.

In the example shown, $45 - 27$, we add 10 *units* to the 5 *units* (in the 45) in order to get more *units* and at the same time add 1 *ten* to the 2 *tens* (in the 27).

This is not difficult for us to understand but it is complicated for young children. It is made somewhat more complicated by the fact that, although the children are 'taking away', the method used is based on 'what is the difference?'.

Decomposition is much easier to explain and understand and is preferred to *equal additions*. The children should be familiar with the idea of *counting on* but it takes up too much time when used with larger numbers (e.g. 3654 − 1367). For these reasons *decomposition* will be the method used throughout this book.

Planning the work

Here is one way of arranging the work in suitable steps.

1 Make sure that each child knows all the subtractions from 10 (e.g. $10 - 4 = 6$, $10 - 8 = 2$, etc.). Without this basic knowledge a child will be wasting his or her time in going on to more complicated subtractions.
Give more practice in learning all the subtraction facts up to $18 - 9 = 9$.

2 Introduce ways of subtracting a 1-digit number from 20 (e.g. $20 - 4$). Then go on to the subtraction of a 1-digit number from 30, 40, . . ., 90 (e.g. $30 - 4$, $50 - 9$, $80 - 6$, etc.).

3 Introduce ways of subtracting a 2-digit number from 20, 30, . . ., 90 (e.g. $30 - 17$, $50 - 24$, $90 - 63$, etc.).

4 Introduce ways of subtracting a 1-digit number from any 2-digit number (e.g. $47 - 5$, $33 - 9$, $51 - 4$, etc.).

5 Introduce ways of subtracting any 2-digit number from another 2-digit number (e.g. $56 - 24$, $82 - 19$, $78 - 59$, etc.).

6 Extend the methods used in (2) to (5) above to larger numbers. (This extension is discussed in detail in Chapter 19.)

There are, of course, other possible orders in which the various steps can be arranged. The one described above concentrates on the changing of 1 *ten* to 10 *units* followed by subtraction from ten.

Apparatus

1 *Tens* and *ones* tins with single sticks or straws and bundles of *tens*, as used for addition.

2 Coloured number strips, as used for addition.

Activities

1 Plenty of practice in learning the subtraction facts from 10 should be provided (for ways of doing this see Chapter 16). A knowledge of these

facts is essential. At the same time the children should have more experience leading to the learning of all the subtraction facts (up to $18 - 9 = 9$).

2   The children use their *tens* and *ones* tins. In the *tens* tin they have two bundles of ten straws. The *ones* tin is empty.

The children are told to remove four of the straws and find how many are left. After discussion, they use one of the bundles of ten. They untie it and put the ten separate straws in the *ones* tin. Now they remove four of the straws from the *ones* tin and count how many are left in the tin. They then say how many are left altogether (1 *ten* and 6 *ones*). The activity is recorded as on the right.

```
 TU
 2 0
-  4
 ───
 1 6
```

The teacher then goes on to explain how the children can show, in their recording, what they did. This needs to be done very neatly so as to set a good standard for the children. This activity should be repeated for all the possible subtractions of a one-digit number from 20

```
  TU
 1 10
 2 0
-  4
 ───

```

$(20 - 7, 20 - 2, \text{etc.})$. The activity should then be extended to subtractions of a one-digit number from 30, 40, 50, ..., 90.

3   The children use their coloured number strips.

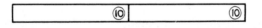

They place two 10-strips end-to-end to make a 20-strip.
The children are asked, 'What strip remains if I remove a 4-strip from the 20-strip?' One way of finding the answer is to replace one of the 10-strips by ten 1-strips.

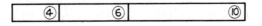

The removal of four 1-strips from the 20-strip leaves one 10-strip and six 1-strips: $20 - 4 = 10 + 6$
$$= 16$$

This result can also be shown by replacing a 10-strip by a 4-strip and a 6-strip, as below.

4   The children repeat Activity 2 but now subtract a two-digit number from 20, 30, . . ., 90. For example, they start with two bundles of ten in the *tens* tin.

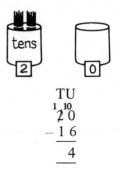

They are then told to remove sixteen straws and find how many are left. The children should realize that they have to remove 1 bundle of ten and 6 single straws. To remove the six straws they should first untie one bundle and put them in the *ones* tin. The activity is recorded as shown on the right.

$$\begin{array}{r} TU \\ \overset{1}{\cancel{2}}\overset{10}{0} \\ -\ 1\ 6 \\ \hline 4 \end{array}$$

This activity should be repeated for the other two-digit numbers between 10 and 20. Then it should be extended to subtractions from 30, 40, 50, . . ., 90. (e.g. 30 – 16, 50 – 14, 80 – 12, etc.) When the children are confident in dealing with these subtractions they can go on to deal with the subtractions of any two-digit number from 30, 40, . . ., 90 (e.g. 30 – 23, 50 – 37, 80 – 59, etc.).

5   The children now go on to the last step in the introduction of subtraction. That is, to discuss an example such as 45 – 17.

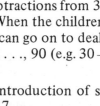

They again use their *tens* and *ones* tins. Four bundles of ten and five single sticks are put in the tins, as shown. The children have to remove 17 of them and find how many are left.

To do this they remove one of the bundles from the *tens* tin and untie it to get ten single sticks. They can now go on in one of two ways:

a)   remove 7 sticks from the 10 single sticks and place the remaining 3 sticks in the *ones* tin (so that they now have 8 single sticks); or

b)   put the 10 single sticks in the *ones* tin so that they now have 15 single sticks together. They then remove 7 of these (leaving 8 single sticks).

The children have now removed 7 sticks. They then remove one bundle of ten from the *tens* tin leaving 2 bundles of ten. Altogether 28 sticks are left (45 – 17 = 28).

The subtraction is recorded as on the right.

$$\begin{array}{r} TU \\ \overset{3}{\cancel{4}}\overset{10}{5} \\ -\ 1\ 7 \\ \hline 2\ 8 \end{array}$$

The way in which the subtraction in the *units* column is done when a 10 has been added needs to be fully discussed with the children. If they know all the subtraction facts (up to 18 – 9) then they can deal with 15 – 7 in one step. Otherwise in the early stages, it may be best for them to use two steps. That is, 10 – 7 = 3, then 3 + 5 = 8. Many children will, of course, use one step for the facts they know and two steps for those for which they are not confident. The children should be encouraged, however, to learn all the subtraction facts and use only one step. Otherwise, they might go on using two steps for the rest of their lives. This is an unnecessary waste of time.

6 The children repeat Activity 5 for many other subtractions which involve changing 1 ten to 10 units. Insist that the 'changing' is shown neatly. Otherwise errors will occur.

Summary

When a child has completed the many activities in this chapter he or she should:

understand	the idea and use of 'decomposition' in subtraction
be able to	use the subtraction facts to subtract any 2-digit number from another 2-digit number

---

Chapter 12
Multiplication: using place-value

Repeated addition and multiplication. The need to know the multiplication facts. Apparatus needed. Planning the work. Multiplying a 2-digit number by a 1-digit number. Multiplying by ten.

Repeated addition and multiplication

The need for the use of place-value arises when multiplications outside the known facts have to be done (e.g. 14 x 6, 27 x 3, etc.). The methods used for these demand that all the multiplication facts (up to 9 x 9 = 81) are known. So every effort should be made to help children to memorize these facts. Ways of doing this are discussed in Chapter 16.

It is important that, throughout the work on multiplication, children are constantly reminded of the link between repeated addition and multiplication. From the start they should understand that, for example, 6 x 4 is another way of thinking of 6 + 6 + 6 + 6. They should also understand that any multiplication can be done by repeated addition. For example, the answer to 65 x 7 can be found by the addition of seven sixty-fives. When the multiplication facts are known and the use of place-value is understood, however, the answer is found much more quickly by multiplication.

In the early stages it is helpful to set down a multiplication, such as 23 x 4, both as an addition and as a multiplication, as shown below.

Add	Multiply
TU	TU
2 3	2 3
2 3	x 4
2 3	1 2 (3 x 4)
2 3	8 0 (20 x 4)
1 2 · (3 + 3 + 3 + 3)	9 2 (23 x 4)
8 0 (20 + 20 + 20 + 20)	
9 2 (23 + 23 + 23 + 23)	

This kind of double recording not only emphasizes the link between addition and multiplication but also helps the children to understand the various steps in the multiplication.

Some of the less able children will benefit by recording multiplications in the way shown above for a long time. When, however, the more able children understand and are able to use this method of recording they can be introduced to the shorter way of setting down the working. Again it should be linked with repeated addition, as shown below.

Add	Multiply
TU	TU
2 3	2 3
2 3	× 4
2 3	9 2
2 3	1
9 2	
1	

The linking of multiplication with addition at this stage in recording can be of great help to all children. It emphasizes that the short form of multiplication is based on the method which they have been using for addition. It is not a new idea. In fact, the more experience we have in teaching multiplication the more we realize the importance of linking it with addition. If place-value and addition are well understood, then multiplication needs only a sound knowledge of the multiplication facts.

Apparatus

1 *Ones*, *tens*, and *hundreds* tins with single sticks and bundles of tens.

2 Coloured number strips.

Planning the work

The following steps are suggested.

1 Provide plenty of practice in the learning of the multiplication facts.

2 Introduce the use of place-value in dealing with multiplication outside the known facts, through examples such as 14 × 3. Record, in full, as an addition and as a multiplication. The examples should be chosen so that the answer is not greater than 99.

3 Introduce the shorter form of recording a multiplication. Bring in examples where no carrying is necessary. Also make sure that for some examples a zero appears in the units column of the answer (errors sometimes occur because children do not put in the zero).

4 Extend 2 and 3 to multiplications in which hundreds appear in the answer, as in the example, shown in two ways, on the next page.

```
    TU                              TU
    2 7                             2 7
  × 6                             × 6
  ─────                           ─────
    4 2   ( 7 × 6)                 1 6 2
  1 2 0   (20 × 6)                ─────
  ─────                               4
  1 6 2   (27 × 6)
  ─────
```

5 Introduce multiplication by 10. This is a very important step.

Activities

1   The children need a supply of objects arranged in tens and ones. As an example, straws in *tens* tins and *ones* tins can be used. Working in pairs or in small groups (depending upon the amount of apparatus available), the children put 13 straws (as 1 *ten* and 3 *ones*) in each of four pairs of tins.

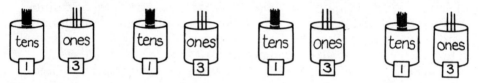

The children record the number in each tin. They are then told to put all the straws together in another pair of tins. This they do. They are then asked to find how many there are altogether. Most children will quickly say that there are 4 *tens* and 12 *ones*. They should also understand that the 12 straws can be made into a bundle of ten together with two single straws. This ten they put in the *tens* tin. So, altogether, there are 5 *tens* and 2 *ones*. That is, there are 52 straws.

   The recording of this activity is then discussed. First, as an addition, it is shown in two ways below. Then it is shown as a multiplication.

```
  Add           Add
  TU            TU              TU
  1 3           1 3             1 3
  1 3           1 3           × 4
  1 3           1 3           ─────
  1 3           1 3             1 2   ( 3 × 4)
  ───           ───             4 0   (10 × 4)
  1 2           5 2           ─────
  4 0           ─             5 2   (13 × 4)
  ───           1             ─────
  5 2
  ───
```

The link between these two way of recording should be repeated many times for other numbers in the tins and for other numbers of pairs of tins.

2 Activity 1 can be usefully repeated using coloured number strips.

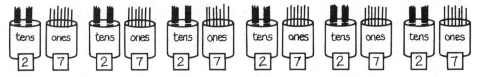

3 Activity 1 is extended to multiplication where hundreds appear in the answer. Using 27 × 6 as an example, the children put 2 *tens* and 7 *ones* in six pairs of *tens* and *ones* tins.

They then put all the straws in another pair of *tens* and *ones* tins.
The children change the 42 straws to 4 bundles of ten and 2 single straws.
The 4 *tens* are then moved to the *tens* tin. There are now 16 *tens*. Ten of these *tens* are now made into a bundle of one hundred and put into a *hundreds* tin, so that the straws are now arranged as below.

The activity is recorded in several ways, as below.

Add	Add	Multiply	Multiply
HTU	HTU	HTU	HTU
27	27	27	27
27	27	× 6	× 6
27	27	42 (7 × 6)	162
27	27	120 (20 × 6)	4
27	27	162 (27 × 6)	
27	27		
42	162		
120	4		
162			

It is important that the second way of recording as a multiplication is used only when the children understand the first way.

Multiplication by 10

During these many activities the idea of multiplying a one-digit number by 10 will arise. This is a very important idea and should be discussed in detail whenever the opportunity occurs. The ability to deal with this multiplication is essential when the children come to a division (by a one-digit number) which is outside the known facts (e.g. $42 \div 3$).

The children should have no difficulty with multiplications such as 10×2, 10×3, 10×4, etc. For, if they understand the symbols used, they can think of these as $10 + 10$, $10 + 10 + 10$, $10 + 10 + 10 + 10$, etc. They should then be able to write these as 20, 30, 40, etc. The values of multiplication such as 2×10, 3×10, 4×10, etc. may, however, need to be discussed. The answers can be obtained either by repeated addition

$$2 + 2 + 2 + 2 + 2 + 2 + 2 + 2 + 2 + 2$$
$$3 + 3 + 3 + 3 + 3 + 3 + 3 + 3 + 3 + 3$$
$$4 + 4 + 4 + 4 + 4 + 4 + 4 + 4 + 4 + 4 \text{ etc.}$$

or by using the commutative property for multiplication. That is, by recognizing that 2×10 is equal to 10×2, etc.

A rule for multiplying by 10 should *not* be introduced at this stage. It is important that not only should the children be able to multiply any one-digit number by 10, but also that they should be able to explain how the answer is obtained.

Summary

When a child has completed the many activities in this chapter he or she should:

understand	the link between repeated addition and multiplication
	the use of place-value in multiplication
	the multiplication facts (up to $9 \times 9 = 81$)
be able to	multiply a 2-digit number by a 1-digit number
	multiply a 1-digit number by 10

Chapter 13
Division: using place-value

Why many children find division difficult. Ways of finding the answer to a division. Recording a division. Dividing any 2-digit number by a 1-digit number. Remainders in division.

Why many children find division difficult

Almost all teachers say that children find division the most difficult of the four basic operations with numbers. Some of the reasons for this are clear to see.

a)   A sound knowledge of the multiplication facts (to $9 \times 9 = 81$) is essential for division. Too many children do not know these facts.

b)   The traditional formal way of setting down a division is often imposed too early.

c)   The language used often has no meaning for the children. For example, 'goes into' has no link with what children have done in their practical activities.

We need to remember these causes of difficulties when we introduce divisions which are outside the known facts (e.g. $42 \div 3$).

A method for division outside the known facts

In the early stages each division should arise from a practical situation. For example, the division $42 \div 3$ can arise from 'There are 42 children. They are arranged in threes. How many threes are there?' (We need to make sure, of course, that all the children do understand that $42 \div 3$ can be used to represent 'How many threes make forty-two?')

Discuss with the children ways of finding the answer. Here are some suggestions they might make.

a)   Use 42 objects (beans, pebbles, bottle-tops, etc.) and arrange them in threes. Count the number of threes. (This should be done in the early stages. It helps children to understand what they are doing.)

b)   Use 42 objects and use repeated subtraction to find how many threes can be made up and removed.

c) Without using objects.
     i) Use repeated subtraction of 3. That is, $42 - 3 = 39$; $39 - 3 = 36$, etc. This is a long and tedious method and mistakes can arise in the subtractions. It is, however, worth doing.
     ii) Build up in threes (i.e. repeated addition) until the total is 42. Again, this takes a long time but should be done.

All of this discussion takes time. But it is better to use time now rather than to hurry over this introduction and then have to spend time on explanation again and again in the future.

In these early discussions some children may suggest using multiples of three within the known facts. For example, the children know that $3 \times \boxed{9} = 27$. But this is only part way to 42. By subtraction, however, the children can find the difference between 27 and 42 ($42 - 27 = 15$). So if they now find how many threes make 15 they can find how many threes altogether make 42. They know that $3 \times \boxed{5} = 15$. So, they can think of 42 as being made up of 9 threes (27) and 5 threes (15). That is, 42 is made up of $9 + 5 = 14$ threes. So, $42 \div 3 = 14$.

This method is well illustrated on a number line, as below.

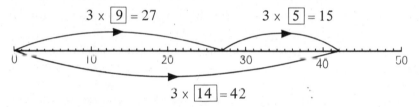

The children then suggest other ways in which 42 can be made up using threes. Some examples are shown on number lines below.

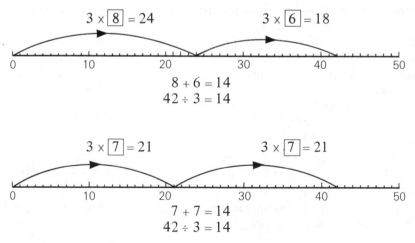

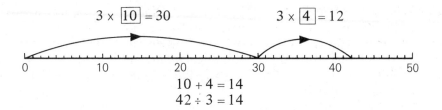

$$3 \times \boxed{10} = 30 \qquad\qquad 3 \times \boxed{4} = 12$$

$$10 + 4 = 14$$
$$42 \div 3 = 14$$

If a small number of threes is first chosen then the division may have to be done in more than two steps, as the difference is still outside the known facts for three. An example is given below.

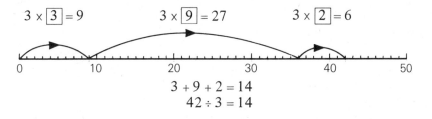

$$3 \times \boxed{3} = 9 \qquad 3 \times \boxed{9} = 27 \qquad 3 \times \boxed{2} = 6$$

$$3 + 9 + 2 = 14$$
$$42 \div 3 = 14$$

The children go on to discuss, in the same way, divisions such as $56 \div 4$, $34 \div 2$, $60 \div 5$, $96 \div 8$, $98 \div 7$, $84 \div 6$. Each of these should start as a simple everyday problem. For example, 'How many oranges at 4k each can I buy with 56k?'

From these many examples the children will begin to see that it is helpful to make the first step as large as possible. For example, the best first step for $96 \div 8$ is $8 \times \boxed{10} = 80$. This deals with as many of the 96 as possible within the known facts. This use of 10 as the first multiplier always provides the best first step. It also has the advantage that multiplication by 10 is very easy when place-value is understood.

Recording a division

The children can now go on to setting down the working of a division in a vertical form. An example is shown on the right. This method of setting down has the advantages:

a) it records, step by step, what the children do;

b) it does not introduce the use of strange phrases such as 'goes into';

c) it shows the link between multiplication and division.

$$
\begin{array}{r}
\text{TU} \\
4\ 2 \\
-3\ 0 \quad (3 \times \mathbf{10}) \\
\hline
1\ 2 \\
-1\ 2 \quad (3 \times \mathbf{4}) \\
\hline
 \\
42 \div 3 = 14
\end{array}
$$

It must be very strongly stressed that any method of setting down this division has meaning only if the children fully understand the meaning of 42 ÷ 3 (so often this is not the case). So it is essential, in the early stages, that the teacher insists on the children explaining, in their own words, what each division means. For example, 'Forty-two divided by three tells me to find how many threes make forty-two'.

Here are two other divisions set down in the same way as the example above.

64 ÷ 4	75 ÷ 5
TU	TU
6 4	7 5
−4 0 (4 × 10)	−5 0 (5 × 10)
2 4	2 5
−2 4 (4 × 6)	−2 5 (5 × 5)
— —	— —
64 ÷ 4 = 16	75 ÷ 5 = 15

If the children understand the commutative property for multiplication (e.g. 3 × 5 = 15 and 5 × 3 = 15) they will understand that if 3 × 14 = 42 then 14 × 3 = 42. This enables them to say that if 42 children are arranged in three teams of the same number then there will be 14 in each team. This can, of course, be checked by multiplication (14 × 3 = 42).

For a division such as 78 ÷ 3, the working has to be done in three steps, as shown on the right.

TU
7 8
−3 0 (3 × 10)
4 8
−3 0 (3 × 10)
1 8
−1 8 (3 × 6)
— —
78 ÷ 3 = 26

This, again, can be well illustrated on a number line, as shown below.

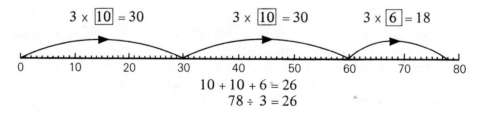

3 × ⬚10⬚ = 30   3 × ⬚10⬚ = 30   3 × ⬚6⬚ = 18

0   10   20   30   40   50   60   70   80

10 + 10 + 6 = 26
78 ÷ 3 = 26

Some children, who understand multiplication by 20, 30, 40, . . ., 80, 90, will see that the working of the above division can be shortened by multiplying by 20, as shown on the right. This, however, is a very big step for many children. It is discussed further in Chapter 19.

$$
\begin{array}{r}
\text{TU} \\
7\ 8 \\
-6\ 0 \quad (3 \times \textbf{20}) \\
\hline
1\ 8 \\
-1\ 8 \quad (3 \times \textbf{6}) \\
\hline
\end{array}
$$

$$78 \div 3 = 26$$

Some teachers may feel that they would like the children to move on to recording a division in the traditional way, as shown on the right.

$$
\begin{array}{r}
1\ 4 \\
3\overline{)4\ 2} \\
-3\ 0 \\
\hline
1\ 2 \\
-1\ 2 \\
\hline
\end{array}
$$

$$42 \div 3 = 14$$

This should create no problems provided that the new layout is explained and discussed with the children. As a first step it may be helpful to show the 10 and the 4 of the answer separately as on the right. This provides a more direct link with the method used in the early stages.

$$
\begin{array}{r}
4 \\
1\ 0 \\
3\overline{)4\ 2} \\
-3\ 0 \\
\hline
1\ 2 \\
-1\ 2 \\
\hline
\end{array}
$$

$$42 \div 3 = 14$$

The traditional method of recording has no special advantages over the method introduced here. It happens to be the method used by many teachers themselves when they were at school. If the 'short' method of recording a division is introduced, this should be done only when the step-by-step method is fully understood.

$$
\begin{array}{r}
1\ 4 \\
3\overline{)4\ 2}
\end{array}
$$

It is 'short' because much of the working is not recorded. The subtractions, for example, are done in the head. They are not written down. Some children are able to do this easily but for other children it will cause many difficulties. (They will still need to write down the subtractions but will now do them on scraps of paper.) So great care needs to be taken in introducing this method of recording. The children should then be given the choice of using either the short or the step-by-step method.

Remainders in division

A remainder occurs in the division which arises from, for example, 'An orange costs 4p. How many can I buy with 70p?'
The working is shown on the right.
17 oranges can be bought.
All the money is not used.
2p remains.

```
TU
 70
-40   (4 × 10)
 ───
 30
-28   (4 × 7)
 ───
   2
```

Many examples like this should be discussed with the children. For example:

a)   A strip of ribbon is 85 cm long. How many 6 cm strips can I cut from it? How much is not used?

b)   How many 3p stamps can I buy with 50p? How much change do I have?

It is important that each is based on a practical situation. This helps children to understand what they are doing.

Note: Division with larger numbers is discussed in Chapter 19.

Summary

When a child has completed the many activities in this chapter he or she should:

understand	how repeated subtraction and repeated addition can be used for division
	how the use of multiples of a number saves time
	how the use of multiples of ten simplifies a division
	how remainders occur in division
be able to	divide any 2-digit number by a 1-digit number

Thinking about
decimal fractions

Everyday usage of decimal fractions does not necessarily bring in, to the full, the ideas of place-value. For example, a length of timber such as 7.645 m is more likely to be thought of as 7 metres and 645 millimetres than 7 metres, 6-tenths of a metre (6 decimetres), 4-hundredths of a metre (4 centimetres), and 5-thousandths of a metre (5 millimetres). This arises from the fact that in using a decimal system of measures it is usually less complicated to use only two units. For example:

money	pounds and pence
timber lengths	metres and millimetres
capacity	litres and millilitres
mass	kilograms and grams

So we must not assume that because children can use the decimal notation for money they understand the ideas of decimal fractions.

Our objective, then, in introducing decimal fractions to children is to help them to understand that the notation used is an extension of place-value, as used for units, tens, hundreds, etc. The decimal point is used to make clear where the whole numbers end and the fractions begin.

To use decimal fractions effectively it is necessary to:
a) understand the notation. That is, to realize that it is an extension of the notation used for whole numbers (based on ten and the use of place-value);
b) understand the equivalence of decimal fractions and other forms of fractions (e.g. common fractions and percentages).

In operations with decimal fractions the use of 'rules' needs to be approached with caution. In particular, multiplication of decimal fractions by ten needs to be linked with the multiplication of whole numbers by ten. If the latter has been based on place-value, then the same phrases can be used with decimal fractions: *when a number is multiplied by 10 the same digits appear in the answer but each is one place to the left*. If 'add a zero' has been used for whole numbers and then 'move the decimal point' is used for decimals, children are likely to become confused and to add a zero when multiplying a decimal by 10.

As a footnote it is worth mentioning that, at all levels, many children find difficulty with equivalences such as $0.37 = \frac{37}{100} = 37\%$.

Chapter 14
Decimal fractions: first ideas

The decimal notation for tenths and for hundredths. The link between the decimal notation and place-value. Showing a fraction in various forms.

Nowadays the decimal notation is used for money but it is doubtful whether children think of it as such. It is more likely that they think of, for example, ₦5.24 as 5 naira and 24 kobo. It is unlikely that they think of the '2' as representing 2-tenths of a naira and the '4' as representing 4-hundredths of a naira. They do not link the notation with the ideas of place-value. Nevertheless the use of a decimal point as a means of separating two kinds of units is not strange to them. We can make use of this in our early work with decimal fractions.

Introducing the decimal notation for tenths

Note: The children need to be able to measure in centimetres and millimetres before they start these activities. Make sure they can do this.

Activities

1 Measuring lines A duplicated set of straight lines is very helpful for this activity. The children measure the length of the first line.

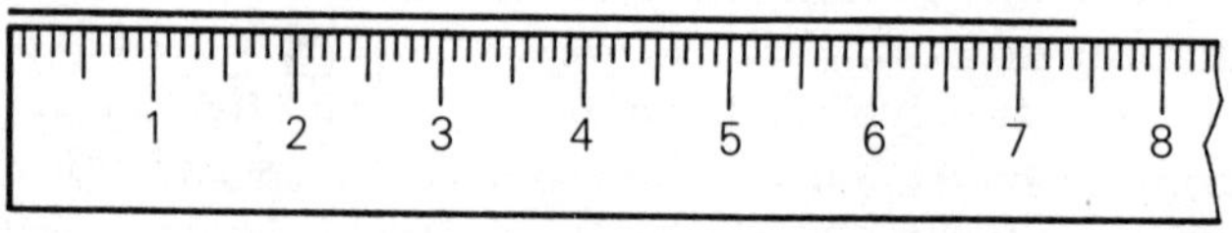

They find that it is 7 cm and 4 mm. The 4 mm is $\frac{4}{10}$ of a centimetre, so the length can be written as 7 cm + $\frac{4}{10}$ cm or as $7\frac{4}{10}$ cm.

The idea of writing this length as 7.4 cm is then introduced. At this stage this is thought of as a shorter way of showing the tenths.

The children record the length in three ways:

    7 cm 4 mm $7\frac{4}{10}$ cm   7.4 cm

The children measure many other lines in this way and record each measurement in the three ways shown above.

Some of the lines should be less than 1 cm so that the use of a zero in the units place can be introduced (e.g. 0 cm 8 mm is shown as 0.8 cm).

2 Using a number line The marked edge of the ruler is, of course, a kind of number line so the children can move easily from measuring with a ruler to marking points on a number line. For these activities sets of duplicated number lines are very helpful.

On one of these lines a point is marked, as shown below.

$2\frac{7}{10}$

```
0        1         2    2.7  3         4         5
```

The children show the position of the point on the line in two ways: as $2\frac{7}{10}$ and as 2.7.

They give the positions of many other points in this way. Some of these should be between the 0 and 1 markings on the line so that results such as $\frac{8}{10}$ and 0.8 are recorded.

Throughout these activities the children should be encouraged to look at the common fractions they record and, if possible, write them in other ways. For example:

$4\frac{5}{10}$	$4\frac{1}{2}$	4.5
$4\frac{8}{10}$	$4\frac{4}{5}$	4.8
$\frac{6}{10}$	$\frac{3}{5}$	0.6

This kind of recording emphasizes the various equivalent forms in which a fraction can be written.

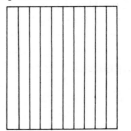

3 The children are provided with a duplicated sheet of squares, each divided into tenths, as shown. They count the number of parts into which the square is divided (ten) and discuss the fact that each is $\frac{1}{10}$ of the square.

The children colour or shade one of the parts and, below it, write $\frac{1}{10}$ and also 0.1. They then colour several parts of a square, as shown in the example on the right below, and write the fraction in two ways.

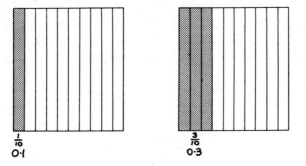

$\frac{1}{10}$
0·1

$\frac{3}{10}$
0·3

Using a new square for each, the children then colour, in turn, all of the other possible fractions.

Note: This is an important activity, as it leads into one of the activities for introducing the decimal form for hundredths.

4 Relating the decimal notation (for tenths) to place-value In the two activities above the decimal form of a fraction is thought of as another way of showing tenths. The place-value aspect can now be usefully discussed.

For whole numbers the children know that the column headings are as shown on the right. Reading the numbers, 100, 10, 1, from left to right, each is one-tenth of the number before it. (This needs to be carefully discussed.)

H	T	U
100	10	1

So, moving on to the right, the next column heading is one-tenth of 1. That is, $\frac{1}{10}$. With this extra column the headings are as shown on the right ('t' is used for tenths).

H	T	U	t
100	10	1	$\frac{1}{10}$

The children should be given plenty of practice in reading numbers under these column headings. In the example shown the children should read the first number as two hundreds, five tens, eight units, and three tenths.

H	T	U	t
100	10	1	$\frac{1}{10}$
2	5	8	3
7	9	4	5
	2	3	9
	4	0	6

At this stage the reason for using a decimal point can be discussed more fully. With column headings there is no need for a point. Without headings, some way of separating the whole numbers from the fractions must be used. It would be wrong to write the first number as 2583. The use of a point is a very simple way of showing the end of the whole numbers and the beginning of the fractions.

The children should now read each of the numbers shown above, using decimal language. For example: two hundred and fifty eight point three.

Introducing the decimal notation for hundredths

Activities

1 Using a 100-square   Square grids, such as shown on the right, are needed for this activity. (A duplicated sheet of several squares is most useful.)

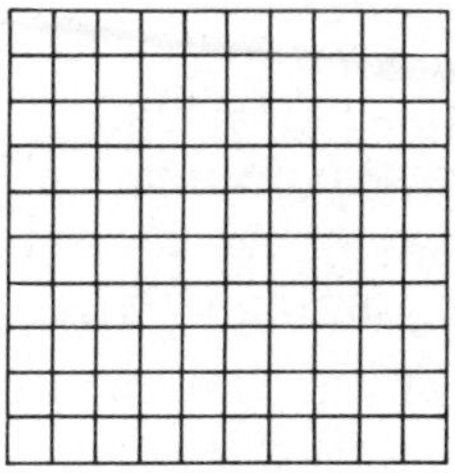

a)   The children first find the number of squares in the grid (100). They then colour or shade one of the squares. They write down the fraction of the grid which is coloured ($\frac{1}{100}$).

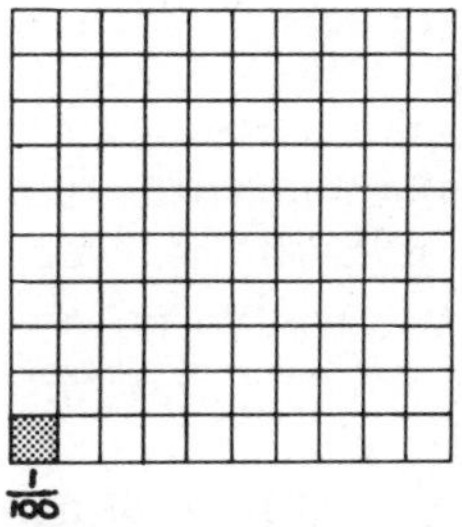

$\frac{1}{100}$

The children then colour or shade one column of squares. The number of coloured squares is counted (10). The children write down the fraction of the grid which is now coloured. The various ways in which this can be done are discussed. For example,

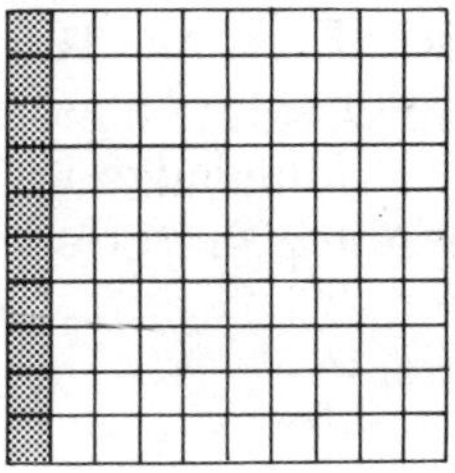

   i) Thinking of the 10 small squares (each of which is $\frac{1}{100}$ of the grid), the fraction is $\frac{10}{100}$.
   ii) By counting, the children find that there are 10 columns altogether. So each column is $\frac{1}{10}$ of the grid.
   iii) As a decimal $\frac{1}{10}$ is written as 0.1. So 0.1 of the grid is coloured.

From this activity the children should understand that each square is $\frac{1}{100}$ of the grid and that each column is $\frac{1}{10}$ (or 0.1) of the grid.

b) The children now colour 17 squares, as shown, and are asked to write down, in various ways, the fraction of the grid which is coloured. They should be able to show this fraction as $\frac{17}{100}$ and also as $\frac{1}{10} + \frac{7}{100}$. Some children might also write the second form as $\frac{10}{100} + \frac{7}{100}$. Each of these three ways should be discussed to make sure that all the children understand them. Then many other examples of this kind should be done by the children (e.g. colour 39 small squares, leading to $\frac{39}{100}$; $\frac{3}{10} + \frac{9}{100}$; $\frac{30}{100} + \frac{9}{100}$).

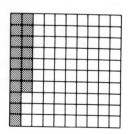

2 Relating hundredths to place-value

The use of place-value to show each of the fractions recorded in Activity 1 should now be discussed. In example b) the children showed the amount coloured in three ways.

$$\frac{17}{100} \qquad\qquad \frac{10}{100} + \frac{7}{100} \qquad\qquad \frac{1}{10} + \frac{7}{100}$$

They can show the $\frac{1}{10}$ as a decimal, but they have no column in which to show the $\frac{7}{100}$. The introduction of another new column for hundredths needs to be discussed. From the 100-grid the children see that $\frac{1}{100}$ is 1-tenth of $\frac{1}{10}$, so the pattern of column headings previously used can be extended as shown on the right. The $\frac{1}{10} + \frac{7}{100}$ can then be recorded as shown.

H	T	U	t	h
100	10	1	$\frac{1}{10}$	$\frac{1}{100}$
			1	7

The children should record this fraction as 0.17 and read it as zero point one seven.

Note: For later work it is important that the children should have practice in writing this fraction in its several forms:

$$0.17 \qquad \frac{1}{10} + \frac{7}{100} \qquad \frac{10}{100} + \frac{7}{100} \qquad \frac{17}{100}$$

The link between 0.17 and $\frac{17}{100}$ is often ignored. This can cause difficulties in later work (particularly when changing decimal fractions to percentages).

The children should go on to write each of the other fractions in Activity 1 in its decimal form, in words, and in its various forms using tenths and hundredths.

3 Using tenths and hundredths with whole numbers The children should have practice in reading and writing numbers such as those shown on the right, in their many ways. The first, for example, could be shown in the following ways:

H	T	U	t	h
100	10	1	$\frac{1}{10}$	$\frac{1}{100}$
	2	7	4	9
1	5	4	3	7
	2	0	6	3
	5	2	0	4
	8	0	0	9
		8	8	8
	2	3	2	3

2 tens   7 units   4 tenths   9 hundredths

20 + 7 + $\frac{4}{10}$ + $\frac{9}{100}$

27 + $\frac{4}{10}$ + $\frac{9}{100}$

27 + $\frac{49}{100}$

27 + 0.4 0.09

27.49

It should be read and written as twenty seven point four nine.

The link with notation used for money can usefully be discussed at this stage. For example, £27.49 can be thought of as:

27 1-pound banknotes and 49 1-penny coins;

27 1-pound banknotes, 4 10-pence coins, and 9 1-penny coins;

2 10-pound banknotes, 7 1-pound banknotes, 4 10-pence coins, and 9 1-penny coins.

Note: When the use of the decimal notation for tenths and hundredths is fully understood, the extension to thousandths and beyond is usually straightforward.

Summary

When a child has completed the many activities in this chapter he or she should:

understand	the decimal notation for tenths and hundredths
	the relationship between the decimal notation and place-value
be able to	write tenths and hundredths as decimals
	change decimal fractions to tenths and hundredths

Thinking about
standard measures

There are several principles which we should remember when we are preparing measuring activities for children. These are listed below.

a) In order to build up a good understanding of any measure, children must use the measure in practical activities.

b) Before making any measurement children should make an estimate of the probable result. They should then compare their estimate with the actual measurement. In this way children gradually build up a better idea of the actual size of the measure being used and become more proficient in their estimating.

c) Children should be encouraged to think about the most appropriate measure to use when making a measurement. For example, in measuring the length of a room, they should think about using metres and centimetres, rather than centimetres and millimetres.

d) Children should realize from the start that most measurements are accurate only within the limits of the measures used. This aspect of measuring was discussed fully on page 37.

e) In order to deal quickly and easily with calculations involving measures children should be confident in writing measurements in a decimal form (e.g. 2 m 35 cm is 2.35 m). With this understanding of the decimal form of measures, established methods can be used for all the necessary calculations.

f) In industry and technology never more than two units are used in any measurement e.g. in measuring timber, lengths are given in metres and millimetres. So a length could be 7m 285 mm. This avoids the use of 7 m 28 cm 5mm. It could of course be written as 7.285 m.

This kind of limitation needs to be remembered in our teaching. We need to avoid making up examples, for practice in computation, which bring in more than two different units.

g) The introduction of a smaller unit of measure serves two purposes.

i) It enables more accurate measurements to be made (e.g. instead of giving a length as '7 cm to the nearest cm' we can say that it is 7 cm 4 mm, to the nearest mm).

ii) It enables small amounts to be measured (e.g. a length less than 1 cm can be measured).

We need to keep these principles in mind.

Chapter 15
Measuring and measures: using standard units

Using standard measures for length (m and cm) and mass (kg and $\frac{1}{2}$ kg). Telling the time in quarter-hours and minutes. The equivalence of coins. Buying and getting change.

In Chapter 4, 'Measuring and measures: first ideas', ways of introducing the ideas of measuring were discussed. Except for time and money, non-standard measures were used (pieces of cane, tins, lumps of clay, etc.). For the reasons given in the section 'Thinking about measuring and measures', a start must be made in the early years on using standard measures. The most appropriate of these at this stage are the measures for length and mass, together with an extension of the work on time and money.

Length

A decision has to be made as to which unit of length should be introduced first — the metre, the decimetre, or the centimetre. The metre is a large unit and not very helpful for measuring small lengths (e.g. the edge of a book); the decimetre is a convenient size for children but is rarely used in practice; the centimetre is useful for measuring small lengths but not for longer distances (e.g. the length of the classroom). What must be avoided in the early stages, of course, is introducing the use of two units at the same time. One unit must be introduced and through their activities the children themselves should see the need for a larger or smaller unit. It should be remembered that, for example, if a metre is used first, then a smaller unit is required for two reasons: a) to measure lengths more accurately; b) to measure lengths smaller than a metre.

It is probably best to start with an unmarked metre stick or cane. Later, this can be divided into a hundred centimetres. This enables the name *centimetres* to be explained. Then rulers, *marked in centimetres only*, can be used for smaller lengths.

It is important that the symbols for metre and centimetre should be used correctly. The symbol for metre is **m** (without a full stop) and the symbol for centimetre is **cm** (again without a full stop). It is important that the teacher understands that these are symbols. They are *not* abbreviations. No 's' is required for the plural. For example:

$$1 \text{ metre} = 1 \text{ m} \quad ; \quad 7 \text{ metres} = 7 \text{ m}$$
$$1 \text{ centimetre} = 1 \text{ cm} \quad ; \quad 13 \text{ centimetres} = 13 \text{ cm}$$

Activities

1   The children are provided with *unmarked* metre sticks or canes. With these they measure suitable lengths such as: the length and width of the classroom; the height of the door; the length of a table; the distance between two marks on the floor; various lengths outside the classroom.

For each of these lengths it is unlikely that the measurement will be a whole number of metres. It is sufficient at this stage, however, for the children to give each answer to the nearest metre. They should use the ideas of, for example: 'a little more than four metres', 'nearly seven metres', 'about six and a half metres'.

The children quickly realize that they cannot measure very accurately with an unmarked metre stick. Neither can they measure lengths smaller than a metre. Ways of overcoming these two difficulties should be discussed and the idea of dividing a metre into smaller parts introduced. The children should themselves suggest the number of parts into which a metre could be divided. This should lead to the idea of using tens and hundreds to link with our number system. The idea of a decimetre can be mentioned and discussed briefly but, in order to keep the measuring as simple as possible, it is probably best to go straight to the centimetre as the smaller unit.

2   After a discussion about dividing a metre into smaller parts the children are provided with metre sticks marked in centimetres.

(The use of commercially produced metre rulers, marked in centimetes and millimetres, should be avoided at this stage. The millimetre markings may confuse some of the children.) The children first use these marked sticks to measure lengths less than a metre. It is unlikely that the lengths will be an exact number of centimetres, so the idea of measuring to the nearest centimetre will have to be used. Phrases like those used in measuring in metres will again have to be used in stating the results.

3   The measuring, in centimetres, of lengths associated with the body appeals to most children. For example, each child, with the help of a friend, can measure:

his height (this can sometimes best be done by the child lying on the floor);

the length of an arm;

the length of a foot;

the length between his finger tips when he stands with both arms outstretched to the side;

the length of a stride;

the length of a jump, etc.

4   The children now go on to use rulers (20 cm, 25 cm, or 30 cm) marked in centimetres only, to measure lengths of various objects in the classroom (e.g. the length and width of a book; the length of a pencil; the edges of a card, paper rectangle, triangle, etc.).

5   To check easily the children's ability to measure accurately in centimetres it is useful to use duplicated sheets on which a number of straight lines and shapes are drawn, as in the example below. (*Note:* Each line should be an exact number of centimetres.)

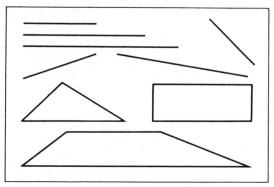

The children write the measurement for each line near to it. The children's work can then be checked easily and quickly.

6   When the children are confident in measuring in centimetres they can go on to measure longer lengths using metres and centimetres. They may be helped in building up the right ideas if, for example, in measuring the length of the classroom, they first place as many as possible unmarked metre sticks end-to-end along the floor. A metre stick, marked in centimetres, is then used to measure the gap between the end of the last stick and the wall.

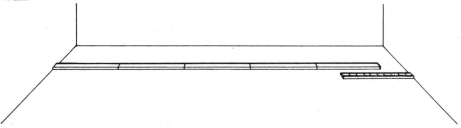

The children record each measurement as, for example, 'The length of the room is 9 m 56 cm'.

7   The children work in groups. Each group has a set of about 40 drinking straws of various lengths. The children measure the length of each straw, to the nearest centimetre. They then show their results in table form and also by a graph, as in the examples on the next page.

Length (to nearest cm)	10	11	12	13	14	15	16	17	18	19	20
Number of straws	2	3	5	6	4	0	7	4	8	2	7

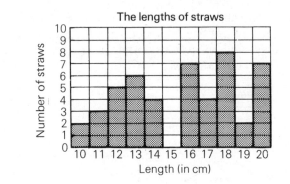

The lengths of straws

8   When the children are confident in measuring to the nearest centimetre the use of millimetres (mm) can be introduced. This enables the children to measure more accurately. To make the checking and marking easier it is helpful to provide each child with a duplicated set of lines to measure, as in Activity 5. Each measurement is recorded as, for example, 'The length of the line is 7 cm 4 mm'. (Until the use of decimal fractions has been introduced the writing of the length as 7.4 cm cannot be used.)

Small variations in the children's answers should be expected.

The children then go on to measure, in cm and mm, suitable lengths in the classroom.

Mass

In Chapter 4, ways in which children can be introduced to the idea of balancing and to the use of a set of identical objects (coins, bottle-tops, etc.) as 'weights' in measuring the mass of an object are described.

When the children are confident in this kind of activity they can be introduced to the standard measure for mass, that is, the kilogram. If standard metal kilogram 'weights' are not available, then adequate alternatives can be made by using the fact that the mass of 1 cubic centimetre of water is approximately 1 gram. So 1000 cm³ of water will have a mass of approximately 1000 grams, that is, one kilogram.

Make a cardboard open cube, with edges of 10 cm. Make it watertight by sealing the edges with gummed paper or several coats of paint. (*Note:*   1000cm³ = 1 litre.)

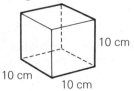

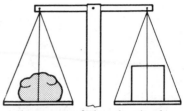

Put the cube on one of the pans of a balance.
Fill it with water. On the other pan of the
balance place a lump of soft clay and add
more clay or remove some until it balances
the water.

The mass of the water is approximately 1 kg so the mass of the clay is also
approximately 1 kg.

Several clay 'weights' can be made in this way. By dividing 1 kg of clay
into two parts which balance each other, $\frac{1}{2}$ kg 'weights' can then be made
and, if necessary, $\frac{1}{4}$ kg 'weights'. Sand or other suitable material can be used
instead of clay. This has to be put into bags of cotton or other material
which keeps the sand intact. Each bag should be labelled appropriately,
e.g. '1 kg'.

Activities

1   The children handle the 1 kg masses to get the feel of them. They then
try to decide whether a particular object (e.g. a large book, a stone, a boot)
weighs more than or less than 1 kg. They do this by holding the 1 kg mass
in one hand and the object in the other. The feel of their muscles helps
them to decide which is the heavier. A balance is then used to check the
answer.

This activity should be repeated for many objects. Some of these
should be made of metal while others should be made from lighter materials,
such as a feather pillow. In this way the children should begin to see that
the mass of an object does not depend only on its size.

2   Activity 1 is extended to include objects which weigh two or more
kilograms. A balance with larger pans may be needed to hold some of the
objects.

It is unlikely that any of the objects will weigh a whole number of
kilograms so the idea of 'more than 2 kg but less than 3 kg', 'nearly 2 kg',
etc. will have to be used. To get some idea of, for example, how much
less than 2 kg an object weighs, sand can be put into the pan containing the
object until the two pans balance.

3   The children themselves may try to divide a kilogram of clay or sand
into two parts so that they balance each other. They can then use their 1 kg
and $\frac{1}{2}$ kg 'weights' to measure masses to the nearest $\frac{1}{2}$ kg. The results can
also be recorded as, for example, 'The stone weighs more than 1 kg but less
than $1\frac{1}{2}$ kg'.

4   The children use their 1 kg and $\frac{1}{2}$ kg 'weights' to obtain, for example,
1 kg of beans, $\frac{1}{2}$ kg of flour, $1\frac{1}{2}$ kg of potatoes. Local materials and produce
should be used, as far as possible, for this activity.

Time

Activities

1 Using quarter-hours When children are confident in telling the time in hours and half-hours they can be introduced to the use of quarter-hours. This brings in the new ideas of 'past' and 'to' (a quarter *past* three, a quarter *to* four). To help children to understand this idea a clock with its face divided into two parts, as below, can be used.

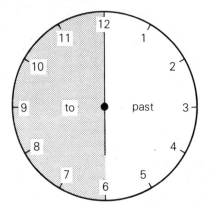

One half of the face should be coloured (or shaded), and the words 'to' and 'past' written on the face, as shown. The children then practise turning the minute hand through a whole turn as the time changes from, for example, 2 o'clock to 3 o'clock. They then turn the hand half way round and say that the clock shows 'half past two'. The idea of moving the hand a quarter of a turn is discussed, making sure that the children understand that after a quarter-turn the hand points to the 3. The children say, 'The clock shows a quarter past two'. The hand is now given another quarter-turn and the children say the time as 'two-quarters past two' or 'half past two'. This gives more practice on the equivalence of one half and two-quarters.

Another quarter-turn brings the minute hand to the 9 and the children say the clock shows 'three-quarters past two'. The idea that at 'three-quarters past two' the time will soon be 3 o'clock is discussed. Help the children to see that in another quarter of an hour it will be 3 o'clock. When this is understood the use of 'a quarter to three' can be introduced and discussed. Some children will need much practice in the use of 'past' and 'to' and the activity should be repeated many times, using all the hours round the clock.

Note: During each of these activities it is a good idea to move the hour hand as well as the minute hand. This will help the children to understand that in half an hour the hour hand moves half-way from, for example, the 2 to the 3. In a quarter of an hour it moves a quarter of the way from the 2 to the 3.

2 Using minutes Another important aspect of telling the time which children need to understand is the use of minutes and the way in which these are read from the clock-face. A child can quickly become confused when he hears someone say that the time is 'ten minutes past eight' but on the clock-face the minute-hand points to the 2.

The dividing of an hour into sixty small parts (minutes) to help in telling the time more accurately needs to be explained to the children. A large clock-face showing the minute marks should be available for all the children to see. In turn each minute mark should be pointed to and counted from one to sixty.

Practice in counting in fives up to sixty should then be given. Ample time should be given to this and various ways of showing the repeated additions should be used. For example:

a) a number line for 0 to 60 can be used.

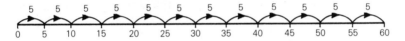

b) the fives can be shown as multiplications.

5 x **1** = 5
5 x **2** = 10
5 x **3** = 15
5 x **4** = 20
5 x **5** = 25
5 x **6** = 30
5 x **7** = 35
5 x **8** = 40
5 x **9** = 45
5 x **10** = 50
5 x **11** = 55
5 x **12** = 60

It is helpful to show the 1, 2, 3, 4, . . ., 12 in colour. This provides a link with the numerals on the clock-face.

c) the idea of fives can be shown more clearly on a clock-face drawn on the blackboard, as shown.

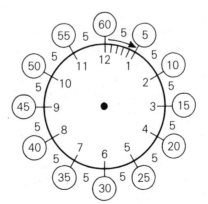

The use of minutes in telling the time, together with the use of *past* and *to*, can then be introduced and practised. A large clock-face, which all the children can see and read, as shown below, is very helpful.

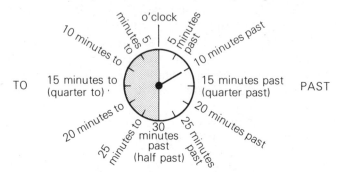

When these ideas have been introduced regular daily practice should be provided until all the children can tell the time confidently and accurately.

Money

In the money activities described in Chapter 4, 'Measuring and measures: first ideas', the children used 1p coins to buy one article and then two articles with a total cost of not more than 10p. Now several other aspects of the use of money need to be introduced. These are:

a) the equivalence of coins;

b) buying one or more articles and paying for them with mixed coins;

c) buying and getting 'change'.

Some suitable activities for introducing these aspects are listed below.

a) The equivalence of coins

In dealing with equivalence it is important to remember that some children may not fully understand why, for example, a 5p coin is not five times the size of a 1p coin. It needs to be explained that the value of a coin depends not on its size but on what can be bought for it. If one article can be bought with a 1p coin, then five can be bought with a 5p coin. That is, a 5p coin is equivalent *in value* to five 1p coins. The children need many activities to help them to understand clearly this idea of equivalence.

Activities

1   A child places a real or imitation 5p coin on his desk and at the side of it places 1p coins which together have the same value. He shows the result by a simple drawing.

(the arrow is used to show *has the same value as*)

This activity is repeated for a 2p coin and a 10p coin.

2   The children show the equivalence of a 10p coin to 2p coins and 5p coins:

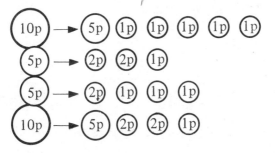

(In Activities 1 and 2 each coin is shown as a number of coins of the same value. A mixture of coins is not used at this stage.)

3   The children now take an important step forward and try to find different sets of coins equivalent to a particular coin. For example:

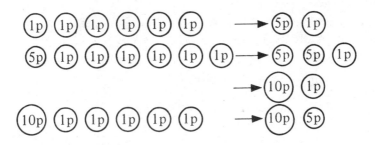

The children use coins to show each of these equivalences (working in groups may be necessary if sufficient coins are not available). They then show each result by a simple drawing.

    This is a very helpful activity and children should have plenty of practice in showing this kind of equivalence.

4   The children reverse Activity 1. That is, each child has a set of coins and has to change them to coins of higher value. For example:

149

There are many possible examples which can be provided and children should be given as much regular practice as possible in this kind of changing of coins.

b) Buying with a mixture of coins

Activities

1   Buying an article at the classroom 'shop' and paying for it with a mixture of coins provides further practice in the use of the equivalence of coins. For example, a child buys a small pencil which costs 7p. He decides how he can pay for it from the coins which he has. He records the various ways by drawings, such as:

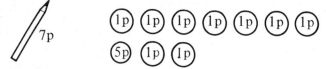

This activity should be repeated for many articles.

2   The children buy two articles and have to work out and record the total cost. They can also record the coins they used to pay for the articles. For example:

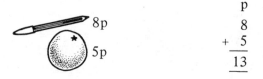

$$\begin{array}{r} p \\ 8 \\ +\ \ 5 \\ \hline 13 \end{array}$$

The pen and the orange cost 13p.

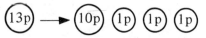

This activity should be repeated many times for various pairs of objects.

Some children may then go on to buying three articles, again recording the activity as above.

c) Getting change

It should be remembered that in giving change in a shop the method of 'counting on' is usually used. For example, if an article is bought for 76p and paid for with a £1 bank note, then the change is worked out as:

four 1p coins	(to make 80p)
one 10p coin	(to make 90p)
another 10p coin	(to make £1).

At this level, it is not usual to calculate the change by subtracting 76 from 100.

Children should use and understand both the 'counting on' method and the subtraction method. It should be noted that the aspect of subtraction used is that of *finding the difference*. The two ways need to be discussed fully in order to help the children as much as possible to understand what they are doing.

Activities

1   A child buys one article, costing less than 10p, from the shop and gives the child in charge of the shop a 10p coin. The two children then have to agree on how much change should be given. For example, if a pen costing 8p is bought, the two children should agree that the change is 2p. The child records the activity as below.

8p ✏	I bought a pen for 8p	p
(10p)	I gave 10p	10 − 8
(1p) (1p)	My change was 2p	2

This activity should be repeated many times, for various articles, and getting change from a 5p coin and a 10p coin.

2   The children go on to buy one or more articles and get change from 20p, 30p, 40p, 50p. Later this can be extended to getting change from amounts up to £1.

Summary

When a child has completed the many activities described in this chapter he or she should:

understand   the idea of a standard measure

be able to   measure lengths, using metres and/or centimetres
measure mass, using kilograms and simple fractions of
    kilograms
tell the time, using minutes and *past* and *to*
change coins for other denominations
find the cost of two articles
calculate the *change* in buying and selling

Thinking about
learning number facts

Each of the statements $3 + 4 = 7$, $8 - 5 = 3$, $7 \times 4 = 28$, $18 \div 9 = 2$ is a number fact. Each states the result of using one operation on a pair of numbers.

To be able to calculate quickly and accurately we need to memorize some of these number facts. Fortunately we do not have to memorize too many of them. In addition, for example, because we use *base ten*, we have to memorize only the facts from $0 + 0 = 0$ to $9 + 9 = 18$. If we know these facts and understand place-value, then we can quickly and accurately deal with an addition such as $27 + 54$. There is no need to learn the fact $27 + 54 = 81$. For the same kinds of reasons we have to memorize multiplication facts only from $0 \times 0 = 0$ to $9 \times 9 = 81$.

Addition facts

The necessary addition facts can be conveniently shown in table form, as below.

Second number

+	0	1	2	3	4	5	6	7	8	9
0	0	1	2	3	4	5	6	7	8	9
1	1	2	3	4	5	6	7	8	9	10
2	2	3	4	5	6	7	8	9	10	11
3	3	4	5	6	7	8	9	10	11	12
4	4	5	6	7	8	9	10	11	12	13
5	5	6	7	8	9	10	11	12	13	14
6	6	7	8	9	10	11	12	13	14	15
7	7	8	9	10	11	12	13	14	15	16
8	8	9	10	11	12	13	14	15	16	17
9	9	10	11	12	13	14	15	16	17	18

First number

When we look at this table we notice that:

a)   there is a kind of symmetry about the diagonal line from 0 to 18. This arises from the commutative property of addition. That is, for $4 + 5 = 9$ on one side of the line there is a corresponding addition, $5 + 4 = 9$, on the other side of the line.

   This means that, if we understand this property, we can reduce the amount of effort needed to memorize all the facts. For example, at the same time as we memorize $3 + 7 = 10$ we should also be memorizing $7 + 3 = 10$.

b)   the addition of zero to any number leaves the number unchanged. If we understand this idea there is no real need to memorize any fact in which zero is one of the two numbers.

c)   there are several additions, which have, for example, a result of 7. These are: $0 + 7$, $1 + 6$, $2 + 5$, $3 + 4$, $4 + 3$, $5 + 2$, $6 + 1$, $7 + 0$. If we ignore the $0 + 7$ and $7 + 0$, and also make use of the commutative property, then the pairs of numbers which, for addition, give a result of 7 are: 1 and 6, 2 and 5, 3 and 4. So instead of trying to memorize eight different facts we need to concentrate our attention on three only.

   If a), b), and c) are taken into account then the pairs of numbers for which we have to memorize addition facts are as shown below.

Other number of pair

+	1	2	3	4	5	6	7	8	9
1	2								
2	3	4							
3	4	5	6						
4	5	6	7	8					
5	6	7	8	9	10				
6	7	8	9	10	11	12			
7	8	9	10	11	12	13	14		
8	9	10	11	12	13	14	15	16	
9	10	11	12	13	14	15	16	17	18

One number of pair

That is, there are 45 different pairs of numbers for which we have to learn addition facts. Of these, nine involve the addition of one only. ($1 + 1$, $2 + 1$, $3 + 1$, ..., $9 + 1$). These are very easy to memorize — so, in fact, there are only 36 pairs of numbers which we need to consider seriously when memorizing addition number facts.

Subtraction facts

In the section 'Thinking about operations' the link between addition and subtraction was discussed. This link is an essential basis for dealing with subtraction facts. For example, if we know the addition fact $7 + 9 = 16$ and think of it as,

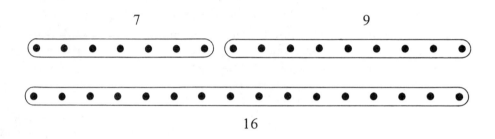

then even without any memorizing, we see that $16 - 7 = 9$ and $16 - 9 = 7$.

For quickness in calculation, however, we do not want to have to go through these steps from the addition. We need to memorize the subtraction facts. The use of the link with addition facts, however, should make the memorizing easier. It also indicates that instead of learning the addition and subtraction facts separately we ought to be looking at all the relationships between, for example, 7, 9, and 16. That is, once $7 + 9 = 16$ has been established we ought to link it with $16 - 7 = 9$ and $16 - 9 = 7$. The subtraction facts which need to be known are shown in the table opposite.

When we look at the table opposite we see that:

a) there is no line of symmetry, as in the addition table. This is because subtraction does not have the commutative property. That is, for example, $7 - 2 \neq 2 - 7$.

b) there are 100 subtraction facts altogether (the same as the number of addition facts shown on the table on page 152). Practice in memorizing all of these facts, however, is not necessary, as:

 i)   the answer to facts involving the subtraction of zero can be given straightaway (e.g. $7 - 0 = 7$).

 ii)   the facts which involve the subtraction of one, demand only the ability to count in order (e.g. $7 - 1 = 6$).

 iii)   the facts which involve the subtraction of a number from itself depend only on an understanding of subtraction (e.g. $7 - 7 = 0$).

If we delete the facts covered by i), ii), and iii) from the 100 subtraction facts, those which have to be memorized are shown in the table on page 156.

Note: In $13 - 8$, for example, 13 is the 'First number' and 8 is the 'Second number'.

Second number

−	0	1	2	3	4	5	6	7	8	9
0	0									
1	1	0								
2	2	1	0							
3	3	2	1	0						
4	4	3	2	1	0					
5	5	4	3	2	1	0				
6	6	5	4	3	2	1	0			
7	7	6	5	4	3	2	1	0		
8	8	7	6	5	4	3	2	1	0	
9	9	8	7	6	5	4	3	2	1	0
10		9	8	7	6	5	4	3	2	1
11			9	8	7	6	5	4	3	2
12				9	8	7	6	5	4	3
13					9	8	7	6	5	4
14						9	8	7	6	5
15							9	8	7	6
16								9	8	7
17									9	8
18										9

First number

Note: i) The upper right hand part of the table is empty as negative numbers are needed to fill the spaces.

ii) The lower left hand part of the table is empty as the results of the subtraction can be found by using place-value.

Second number

−	0	1	2	3	4	5	6	7	8	9
0										
1										
2										
3										
4			2							
5			3	②						
6			4	3	②					
7			5	4	③	②				
8			6	5	4	③	②			
9			7	6	5	④	③	②		
10			8	7	6	5	④	③	②	
11			9	8	7	6	⑤	④	③	②
12				9	8	7	6	⑤	④	③
13					9	8	7	⑥	⑤	④
14						9	8	7	⑥	⑤
15							9	8	⑦	⑥
16								9	8	⑦
17									9	⑧
18										9

First number

Some of the facts shown above have a circle round the answer. Each of them is closely linked with another fact in the same row. For example, $9 - 6 = ③$ is linked with $9 - 3 = 6$. Both of them are based on $6 + 3 = 9$. This again emphasizes the need to look at these three facts together.

Multiplication facts

The multiplication facts are shown in the table below.

Second number

First number

x	0	1	2	3	4	5	6	7	8	9
0	0	0	0	0	0	0	0	0	0	0
1	0	1	2	3	4	5	6	7	8	9
2	0	2	4	6	8	10	12	14	16	18
3	0	3	6	9	12	15	18	21	24	27
4	0	4	8	12	16	20	24	28	32	36
5	0	5	10	15	20	25	30	35	40	45
6	0	6	12	18	24	30	36	42	48	54
7	0	7	14	21	28	35	42	49	56	63
8	0	8	16	24	32	40	48	56	64	72
9	0	9	18	27	36	45	54	63	72	81

Looking at this table we notice that:

a) there is a kind of symmetry about the diagonal going from 0 to 81. This, as for addition, comes from the commutative property for multiplication (e.g. $7 \times 5 = 5 \times 7 = 35$).

b) there is a row and a column of zeros. These appear because when a zero occurs in a multiplication the result is always zero.

c) there are several multiplications which give a result of, for example, 12. This is also true for several of the other numbers which appear in the matrix.

d) multiplications which involve the number 1 have as their answer the other number of the pair (e.g. $7 \times 1 = 7$, $1 \times 4 = 4$).

Making use of a), b), and d) we can reduce the number of multiplication facts on which we have to concentrate our memorizing to the 36 pairs shown in the table on the next page.

We remember that in multiplying by numbers greater than nine, the whole of our working is based on multiplication by 10, 100, 1000, etc., together with the use of known multiplication facts. So in order to multiply successfully we must know the multiplication facts, be able to multiply by 10, 100, etc., and also understand and use the ideas of place-value.

Other number of pair

x	2	3	4	5	6	7	8	9
2	4							
3	6	9						
4	8	12	16					
5	10	15	20	25				
6	12	18	24	30	36			
7	14	21	28	35	42	49		
8	16	24	32	40	48	56	64	
9	18	27	36	45	54	63	72	81

One number of pair

Division facts

When we:

a) understand multiplication,

b) know the multiplication facts,

c) understand division,

then we also know the division facts. For example if

a) we understand that 5×3 can be thought of as

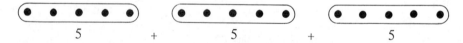

     5   +   5   +   5

b) we know that $5 \times 3 = 15$,

c) we understand that $15 \div 5$ can be thought of, in words, as 'How many fives make fifteen?',

then we can give the answer, 3, straightaway. There is no need to spend time and effort in memorizing the division fact $15 \div 5 = 3$.

    We shall be confused, however, if we attempt to deal with division facts before we know the multiplication facts. No amount of learning division facts like parrots will help us.

Chapter 16
Number facts: ways of learning

Objectives. Understanding and learning number facts. Building up the facts. Helping children to memorize number facts. Apparatus and activities. Organizing the learning. Testing.

Objectives

To be able to calculate quickly and accurately children must know the number facts. That is, they must be able to give quickly the answer to, for example, $7 + 5$, $12 - 8$, 8×6, $56 \div 7$. As teachers, our objective is to help children to build up a knowledge of the facts in an efficient and pleasurable way. The word *efficient* is used to emphasize that we must look very carefully at the methods we use. We need to make sure that our methods are simple and straightforward and do not create difficulties for the children. (We have all met children who cannot give the answer to 7×8 without saying a 'table' which they have learned. This is *not* very efficient.) The word *pleasurable* is used to indicate that as far as possible the children should enjoy the activities designed to help them in learning the number facts. If they enjoy the activities, instead of being under stress, they are more likely to learn the facts.

It must be emphasized that the learning of number facts is a continuous process. There are many occasions during mathematical work when a number fact occurs. Teachers should make use of these opportunities. The fact should be discussed and a minute or so spent on helping the children to memorize it. A fact met in this way in an activity is more likely to be remembered than if it is dealt with on its own without any background.

Understanding and learning number facts

If a child is to learn the number facts efficiently and pleasurably he must:

1 understand the operations $(+, -, \times, \div)$;
2 understand the link between:
   a) addition and subtraction,
   b) multiplication and division;
3 have experience of building up each fact;

4 understand the special properties of:
   a) 0 for addition and multiplication,
   b) 1 for multiplication;

5 understand the commutative property for addition and multiplication;

6 make use of patterns in sets of facts;

7 have plenty of suitable practice to consolidate the memorizing of the facts.

All of these aspects of learning the facts are essential. It is very wasteful of time and effort (and often very frustrating!) if attention is directed only to 7). Without the background of knowledge involved in 1) to 6) the children can only learn like parrots. The facts may have no real meaning to them.

A full understanding of some of the ideas listed above comes only slowly to many children. For example, the commutative property for addition gradually emerges from the children's experiences. They do not recognize or think about the property in their early activities. But teachers who are aware of its importance in learning number facts will discuss the idea with the children when suitable occasions arise. (There is, of course, no need to use the phrase *commutative property*. It is sufficient if the children begin to see, for example, that 2 + 3 and 3 + 2 have the same answer.) After many examples the children will, in their own ways, begin to generalize the results.

In the same way an understanding of the special properties of 0 and 1 comes only as a result of many experiences. But, again, a teacher who is aware of their importance will make sure that the children have these experiences.

In fact one of the main influences in helping children to learn number facts is the teacher's own awareness and understanding of the many aspects involved. Items 1) and 2) were discussed in detail earlier in this book, in the appropriate chapter. So we will go on and look at ways of helping children with the other aspects of learning the facts.

Building up the facts

Before children attempt to memorize any number fact they themselves must have built up the fact through their own experiences. That is, before they attempt to memorize 3 + 4 = 7 they must have taken part in activities based on the idea of combining a set of number three with a set of number four to form a set of number seven. They must also have recorded the fact each time it occurs.

Providing these activities is not a difficulty. The teacher's main problem is one of organization. He or she has to make sure that each of the many facts is dealt with in turn. One way of doing this is to deal first with the easier facts and then, later, go on to the more difficult facts. Using the addition facts as an example, the children could first have experiences of all the facts with a total of not more than five, as shown in the table below.

Second number

+	0	1	2	3	4	5
0	0	1	2	3	4	5
1	1	2	3	4	5	
2	2	3	4	5		
3	3	4	5			
4	4	5				
5	5					

First number

Note: At this stage use is not made of the commutative property as most children are not ready for it. Every opportunity should be taken, however, to discuss pairs of results such as $3 + 1 = 4$ and $1 + 3 = 4$.

At this stage the children do not use this kind of table to show their results. They record each result as, for example, $4 + 1 = 5$. They can, however, make a start on using pattern and show their results in a simple table form. One possible way of doing this is shown below.

$1 + 1 = 2$	$2 + 1 = 3$	$3 + 1 = 4$	$4 + 1 = 5$
$1 + 2 = 3$	$2 + 2 = 4$	$3 + 2 = 5$	
$1 + 3 = 4$	$2 + 3 = 5$		
$1 + 4 = 5$			

It is probably best not to include the facts in which zero appears, but to discuss these wherever they occur. In this way, even at this early stage, children begin to understand that whenever zero is one of the two numbers the result is the same as the other number.

When the children have built up this set of facts they should begin to memorize them. Some children will quickly do this through the activities themselves but many will need to have further directed practice.

When this first set of facts are understood and known by the children they can go on to build up more facts. For example, they can go on to cover all the facts with a total of ten or less. The children again take part in further activities directed at helping them to memorize all these facts (especially the set of new facts). As part of these activities the children extend the tables started for the earlier facts, to include all additions with a total of 10 or less.

During these activities the addition of zero should again be discussed and by the end of this stage the children should be familiar with the commutative property of addition (though the phrase itself should not be introduced). Finally, the remaining facts, up to $9 + 9 = 18$, are introduced. The tables are completed and children are helped, through many further activities, to memorize all the facts.

Breaking down the set of addition facts in this way helps the teacher to organize the children's work and also helps the children to progress step by step in their understanding and memorizing of the facts. There are, of course, many other ways of arranging the various steps. A teacher must decide which is the best way for himself or herself and for the children. What is most important is that each teacher should have a plan for organizing the work of the children.

At *each* stage in the introduction of addition facts the corresponding *subtraction* facts should be introduced through many and mixed activities. For example, following the introduction and learning of $2 + 3 = 5$, the children should link it with the subtractions $5 - 2 = 3$ and $5 - 3 = 2$. They should begin to think of the various relationships between 2, 3, and 5.

This is a most important step and much time should be given to it. The children should again make use of pattern by showing their results in table form. One way of doing this for the first set is shown below.

$1 - 1 = 0$	$2 - 1 = 1$	$3 - 1 = 2$	$4 - 1 = 3$	$5 - 1 = 4$
	$2 - 2 = 0$	$3 - 2 = 1$	$4 - 2 = 2$	$5 - 2 = 3$
		$3 \quad 3 = 0$	$4 - 3 = 1$	$5 - 3 = 2$
			$4 - 4 = 0$	$5 - 4 = 1$
				$5 - 5 = 0$

The children can begin to memorize these facts, but what is more important is that they should know the addition facts (the learning of these is often neglected in schools) and should clearly understand the links between addition and subtraction. If these are understood and known then the subtraction facts follow naturally from the addition facts.

The organization of the learning of the *multiplication* facts can be based on a similar pattern to that used for the addition facts. Here are suggestions for the various stages:

1) multiplications with a result not greater than 14;

2) multiplications with a result not greater than 48;

3) multiplications with a result not greater than 81.

Look at page 157 to see how to show these facts in table form.

In the activities leading to the building up of the facts, the special case of when zero is one of the two numbers should occur at each stage. Also, as for addition, the commutative property for multiplication (e.g. $4 \times 5 = 20$ and $5 \times 4 = 20$) should be discussed and used at each stage. Patterns should be used to show the result in table form at each stage. Those for the first stage are shown below.

$1 \times 1 = 1$	$2 \times 1 = 2$	$3 \times 1 = 3$	$4 \times 1 = 4$	$5 \times 1 = 5$	$6 \times 1 = 6$
$1 \times 2 = 2$	$2 \times 2 = 4$	$3 \times 2 = 6$	$4 \times 2 = 8$	$5 \times 2 = 10$	$6 \times 2 = 12$
$1 \times 3 = 3$	$2 \times 3 = 6$	$3 \times 3 = 9$	$4 \times 3 = 12$	$5 \times 3 = 15$	$6 \times 3 = 18$
$1 \times 4 = 4$	$2 \times 4 = 8$	$3 \times 4 = 12$	$4 \times 4 = 16$	$5 \times 4 = 20$	$6 \times 4 = 24$
$1 \times 5 = 5$	$2 \times 5 = 10$	$3 \times 5 = 15$	$4 \times 5 = 20$		
$1 \times 6 = 6$	$2 \times 6 = 12$	$3 \times 6 = 18$	$4 \times 6 = 24$		
$1 \times 7 = 7$	$2 \times 7 = 14$	$3 \times 7 = 21$			
$1 \times 8 = 8$	$2 \times 8 = 16$	$3 \times 8 = 24$			
$1 \times 9 = 9$	$2 \times 9 = 18$				

$7 \times 1 = 7$	$8 \times 1 = 8$	$9 \times 1 = 9$
$7 \times 2 = 14$	$8 \times 2 = 16$	$9 \times 2 = 18$
$7 \times 3 = 21$	$8 \times 3 = 24$	

It must again be emphasized that *each* of the above facts should be established through activities before any attempt is made to put them in a table form. It is each individual fact which is important to the children, not the ability to chant a set of facts in table form.

It must be remembered that children can learn all the number facts without even putting them in table form. The main advantage of a table is that it emphasizes the regular pattern of the results. This regularity may help some children to link an unknown fact with a known fact.

When the children understand and know the first set of multiplication facts the corresponding *division facts* should be introduced. For example, when $2 \times 6 = 12$ and $6 \times 2 = 12$ are understood and known, the division facts $12 \div 2 = 6$ and $12 \div 6 = 2$ should be introduced. And, as for addition, the relationships between 2, 6, and 12 should be established (i.e. $2 \times 6 = 12$, $6 \times 2 = 12$, $12 \div 2 = 6$, $12 \div 6 = 2$). These relationships are very important. They give further understanding to both the multiplication and division facts and can be of great help to children in memorizing both sets of facts. The children will quickly see that if they know the multiplication facts they also know the division facts. It is a waste of time for children to start learning division facts until they are confident in their knowledge of the corresponding multiplication facts.

Helping children to memorize number facts

When children have built up a set of facts, and have partially memorized them, they need more activities and practice to help to fix them in their minds. This further work should cover *all* the facts which the children have built up and should be as pleasurable as possible. To make sure that all the facts are covered the activities must be carefully organized, and to make the activities enjoyable use should be made of apparatus and suitable games. Each of these requirements is discussed in detail below.

1 Making sure that all the facts are covered

As an example we shall consider how the work can be organized when the children have built up all the multiplication facts where the result is 24 or less. These are shown in the table below (the zero facts are included to make sure we do not ignore them).

Second number

x	0	1	2	3	4	5	6	7	8	9
0	0	0	0	0	0	0	0	0	0	0
1	0	1	2	3	4	5	6	7	8	9
2	0	2	4	6	8	10	12	14	16	18
3	0	3	6	9	12	15	18	21	24	
4	0	4	8	12	16	20	24			
5	0	5	10	15	20					
6	0	6	12	18	24					
7	0	7	14	21						
8	0	8	16	24						
9	0	9	18							

(First number — vertical label at left)

Looking at this matrix we see that:

a) there are 67 facts altogether;

b) 19 of the facts have zero as one of the two numbers;

c) there are some facts which children memorize easily (e.g. $4 \times 1 = 4$, $3 \times 2 = 6$) and some facts which children find more difficult (e.g. $3 \times 7 = 21$, $8 \times 3 = 24$);

d) there are usually two facts for each pair of numbers (e.g. for 3 and 4 there are the two facts $3 \times 4 = 12$ and $4 \times 3 = 12$). This is always true except when the same two numbers appear in the multiplication (e.g. for 3 and 3 there is only one fact $3 \times 3 = 9$);

e)   four facts have 12 as the result (3×4, 4×3, 6×2, 2×6) and four facts have 24 as the result (6×4, 4×6, 3×8, 8×3). This occurs for other sets of four facts and later, when more facts are built up, more than four have the same result. (In this table there are 19 facts with zero as the result. The zero facts, however, are a special case.)

Taking into account the five items a) to e) listed above, one way of organizing the learning is to arrange the 67 facts in sets of ten, say, and to concentrate on each of these in turn. Each set should contain:

1)   at least one zero fact;

2)   some easy facts;

3)   some more difficult facts;

4)   the second fact which is linded to a fact because of the commutative property (e.g. if $3 \times 5 = 15$ is included then $5 \times 3 = 15$ should also be included).

      Not all the facts with 1 or 0 as one of the two numbers need to be included in the sets as the children should understand the general principles for these facts rather than the specific facts. Five possible sets are given below (to save space only the left-hand side of each fact is shown).

Set

1) 1×6 3×7 1×0 2×2 5×4 8×2 6×1 7×3 2×8 4×5

2) 9×1 2×7 2×6 3×4 3×3 7×0 4×3 6×2 7×2 1×9

3) 5×2 3×8 1×7 4×4 6×3 0×8 3×6 7×1 8×3 2×5

4) 2×9 1×4 2×4 5×3 1×1 0×3 3×5 4×2 4×1 9×2

5) 2×3 6×4 2×4 0×0 3×8 7×3 2×9 4×2 4×6 3×2

Note: In set 5) the facts 3×8, 7×3 and 2×9 are shown for the second time, to give extra practice.

Each of these five sets can, in turn, be used for further practice by the children. Each provides a limited objective for the children. They can concentrate on ten facts at a time instead of trying to memorize the whole of the 67 facts. When sets 1) and 2) have been learned the children can, of course, be *tested* on the facts in the two sets. So step by step they accumulate a knowledge of all the facts.

As each set of multiplication facts is learned, the corresponding division facts should be learned. For example, the learning of the following division facts (left-hand side only shown) should follow the learning of set 1) of the multiplication facts.

$6 \div 1$ $21 \div 3$ $0 \div 1$ $4 \div 2$ $20 \div 5$ $16 \div 8$ $6 \div 6$ $21 \div 7$ $16 \div 2$ $20 \div 4$

In this way the links between each set of multiplication facts and the corresponding set of division facts are emphasized.

When the multiplication facts with a result of 24 or less have been memorized then *all* the facts with a result of 48 or less can be dealt with in the same way. Here are some possible sets for these facts.

Set

1) 5×9 6×7 1×8 2×6 2×2 0×5 6×2 8×1 7×6 9×5

2) 2×4 4×9 5×7 6×1 3×3 7×0 1×6 7×5 9×4 4×2

3) 4×3 7×1 3×9 4×7 4×4 6×0 7×4 9×3 1×7 3×4

4) 8×2 3×7 1×9 2×9 5×5 0×2 9×2 9×1 7×3 2×8

5) 6×5 5×2 2×7 3×8 6×6 0×0 8×3 2×5 7×2 5×6

6) 5×3 6×8 8×4 3×6 2×1 9×0 6×3 4×8 8×6 3×5

7) 6×4 8×5 2×3 5×4 3×1 0×8 4×5 3×2 5×8 4×6

When these facts have been memorized then *all* the facts up to $9 \times 9 = 81$ can be arranged in suitable sets. Throughout the whole of this organization the corresponding division facts should be learned for each set of multiplication facts.

The above discussion on arranging facts in suitable sets is based on multiplication facts. A similar approach can be used for the addition facts and the corresponding subtraction facts.

2 Helpful activities and apparatus for memorizing number facts

Many activities are listed below. Some deal with a specific set of facts. Others deal with facts as they occur in day-to-day situations. By providing this variety of approaches all children should be helped and encouraged in their memorizing of the facts.

a) **Practice cards** For each set of facts $(+, -, \times, \div)$, a card is prepared on which the set is written. An example is shown on the right. Each card is given a reference letter and number (e.g. M2) to help the teacher in keeping records of each child's work.

M2 Multiplication
2 x 4 =
4 x 9 =
5 x 7 =
6 x 1 =
3 x 3 =
7 x 0 =
1 x 6 =
7 x 5 =
9 x 4 =
4 x 2 =

Each child works through a card three times:

    i)   using apparatus, if necessary, he finds the answer to each fact and writes the complete fact in his exercise book. (These are checked by the teacher.)

    ii)   he repeats i) without using apparatus.

    iii)   he writes the answers only on a slip of paper which he then passes to the teacher to be marked.

Practice cards can also be prepared to link subtraction with addition and to link division with multiplication. For example, a card can be prepared with a set of multiplication facts on the front of it and the corresponding set of division facts on the back, as shown below.

        front   back

MD 6 Multiplication	MD 6 Division
5 x 3 =	15 ÷ 5 =
6 x 8 =	48 ÷ 6 =
8 x 4 =	32 ÷ 8 =
3 x 6 =	18 ÷ 3 =
2 x 1 =	2 ÷ 2 =
9 x 0 =	0 ÷ 9 =
6 x 3 =	18 ÷ 6 =
4 x 8 =	32 ÷ 4 =
8 x 6 =	48 ÷ 8 =
3 x 5 =	15 ÷ 3 =

These cards should, of course, be used only when a child is confident in his knowledge of the set of multiplication facts.

    A child writes the completed multiplication facts in his exercise book. Then at the side of each he writes the corresponding completed division fact from the other side of the card. Another method is for a child to copy each set of facts side-by-side in his exercise book. He then, in turn, writes the answers to each multiplication fact and the corresponding division fact.

b) Flash cards

 front   back $5 + 3 = 8$

Suitable sizes.   For children: about 7 cm by 4 cm
            For teachers: about 20 cm by 10 cm

Sets of cards are prepared; many for the children and some for the teacher. A corner (in the same position for each card) is cut off, so that when a set of cards are put together the 'fronts' will all be uppermost.

On the front of each card an incomplete fact is written. On the back of the card the completed fact is shown.

The cards can be used in a variety of ways. But the basic idea is that a child shows the front of the card to another child for one or two seconds (i.e. he 'flashes' the card to the other child). The second child then says the answer. The first child checks the answer by looking at the back of the card. In this way both children are involved in thinking about the fact.

c) Daily activities

i) *Using the date*   Each day a few minutes can be used by the children to write down as many different facts as they can which have the day of the month as the answer. For example, on 12 March, they could write down some or all of the facts:

$9 + 3 = 12$, $3 + 9 = 12$, $8 + 4 = 12$, $4 + 8 = 12$,
$7 + 5 = 12$, $5 + 7 = 12$, $6 + 6 = 12$.
$3 \times 4 = 12$, $4 \times 3 = 12$, $6 \times 2 = 12$, $2 \times 6 = 12$.

ii) *Using the clock*   Each day use can be made of the clock-face. One day, for example, the teacher can put a card, with **+4** written on it, as shown, on the clock-face. Children, in turn, then add four to each of the numbers from 1 to 12.

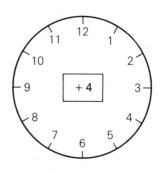

Another day the card can be **x3**. Practice of this kind adds variety to the learning. The children enjoy it.

d) Using tables

i)   Children often enjoy showing the facts they are learning in table form. Two examples are given on page 161 for additions up to a total of 5. Both these table forms are helpful in picking out the various additions which have, for example, 4 as the answer. This is a very useful activity.

ii) A number square from 1 to 100 can also be used to show patterns in sets of facts. For example, in the square on the right multiplication by 9 is shown. The children see the 9, 18, 27, . . ., 81, in a line. For each successive multiple the answer moves one place down and to the left. For multiplication by other numbers different patterns emerge. These can help individual children in memorizing the facts.

1	2	3	4	5	6	7	8	9	10
11	12	13	14	15	16	17	18	19	20
21	22	23	24	25	26	27	28	29	30
31	32	33	34	35	36	37	38	39	40
41	42	43	44	45	46	47	48	49	50
51	52	53	54	55	56	57	58	59	60
61	62	63	64	65	66	67	68	69	70
71	72	73	74	75	76	77	78	79	80
81	82	83	84	85	86	87	88	89	90
91	92	93	94	95	96	97	98	99	100

iii) The children look at multiplication by various numbers and notice:
— for *multiplication by 9* the sum of the digits is always 9.

9	9
18	$1 + 8 = 9$
27	$2 + 7 = 9$
36	$3 + 6 = 9$
45	$4 + 5 = 9$ etc.

— for *multiplication by 5* the units digit of the answer is either 0 or 5.

Summary

When a child has completed the many activities described in this chapter he or she should:

understand	the idea of a number fact
	how addition and subtraction facts are related
	how multiplication and division facts are related
	how commutativity helps in learning number facts
	the special importance of 0 and 1 in the facts
know	all the addition facts up to $9 + 9 = 18$, together with the corresponding subtraction facts
	all the multiplication facts up to $9 \times 9 = 81$, together with the corresponding division facts
have enjoyed	building up and learning the facts

---

graphs

Why we draw graphs

In everyday life and in mathematics, science, technology, commerce, etc., people do not spend time drawing a graph unless it serves some useful purpose when it is finished. We need to remember this in our teaching.

A graph can be useful in various ways. For example:

a) it can show information in a form which can be quickly and easily understood;

b) it can provide information which we previously did not have;

c) it can indicate relationships between the members of two sets.

Examples of these three uses are given below.

a) to show information

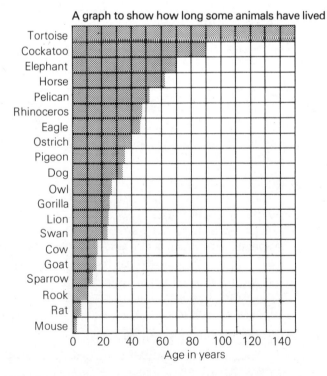

A graph to show how long some animals have lived

b) to obtain more information

Number	0	1	2	3	4	5	6	7	8	9	10
Square of number	0	1	4	9	16	25	36	49	64	81	100

Using the information in the above table we can draw the graph shown:

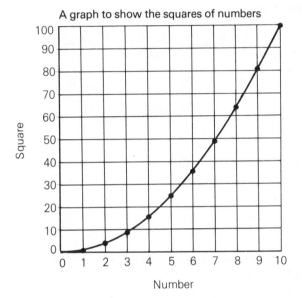

A graph to show the squares of numbers

From this graph we can:

a) find the approximate values of the squares of numbers such as 2.7, 3.2, 4.8, 8.7, etc.;

b) find the numbers whose squares are 20, 32, 67, etc. (i.e. we can find the square roots of these numbers).

c) to indicate relationships

The graph below shows the *extension* of a piece of elastic when one end is fastened to a nail in a wall and various masses are attached to the other end.

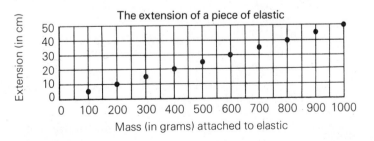

The extension of a piece of elastic

This graph indicates that, for example,

a) when the weight is doubled the extension is doubled;

b) when the weight is trebled the extension is trebled, etc.

That is, the extension varies directly as the weight attached. This is an important relationship which is clearly shown by the graph.

Types of graphs

Before we start to draw a graph we must decide on the best way to show our information. Some of the possible ways are shown, with examples, below.

1 by drawing simple pictures

The ages of our group

6	👤	👤	👤	👤				
7	👤	👤	👤	👤	👤	👤	👤	

A graph like this is called a **picto-graph** or an **iso-type**. This one shows that there are four children aged 6 and seven children aged 7 in our group.

2 by using an arrowed line

The idea underlying this type of graphical representation is that instead of writing a sentence such as

Carl is the brother of Winston

we show it as

Carl ————————→———— Winston.

The phrase *is the brother of* is replaced by the arrowed line.

This kind of representation is helpful:

a) in the early stages when children are not confident in their writing and spelling but wish to record an activity. For example, the children show the sentence

The bucket holds more than the bottle

by a drawing such as

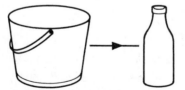

Here the arrowed line is understood to stand for *holds more than*.

172

b) when a set of statements have to be shown, as in the example below.

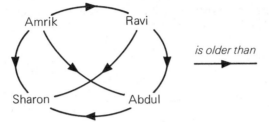

In this example *is older than* is shown near the graph to make clear what the arrowed line stands for. This is essential if the graph is to be understood and should be insisted upon in all graphs of this kind.

Graphs in which an arrowed line is used in this way are called **arrow graphs**. Arrow graphs are used in various ways. Some are described below.

i) *To show relationships between the members of a set*   A straightforward example of this use is shown in b) above. Many other examples of this type occur regularly throughout the work in mathematics and full use should be made of them.

In some examples further ideas have to be introduced. For example:

a)

Martin — Eric

Denise   Harriet

is the brother of

For the children shown in this graph:
Martin *is the brother of* Eric and Eric *is the brother of* Martin.
These two sentences are shown by putting two arrow heads on the line.

b)

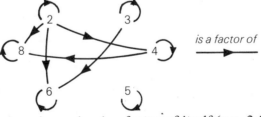

In the above graph each number is a factor of itself (e.g. 2 *is a factor of* 2). This is shown by drawing a looped arrowed line round the numeral.

The use of a loop occurs in many graphs in which the word *same* appears in the phrase. For example, *lives in the same street as, is the same age as, wears sandals of the same size as.*

ii) *To show relationships between the members of two or more sets*
Some examples of arrow graphs which show the relationships between
members of two sets are shown below.

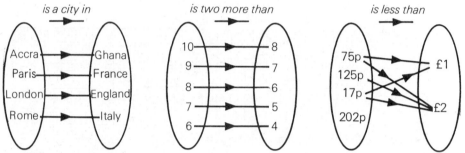

In the third graph it will be noticed that more than one arrowed line goes
from some members of the first set. For one member of the first set there is
no arrowed line.

3 by using squares on a grid

A graph like that shown is called
a **block graph**, a **column graph**, or
a **bar graph**.

A graph to show how many children in a
class had the marks 0,1 ..., 10 in a test

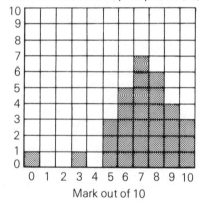

Number of children

Mark out of 10

4 by using a circle

An example is shown on the right.
A graph like this is called a **pie graph**
or a **pie chart**.

Allocation of money
for development

5 by using points on a grid

Two examples are shown below.

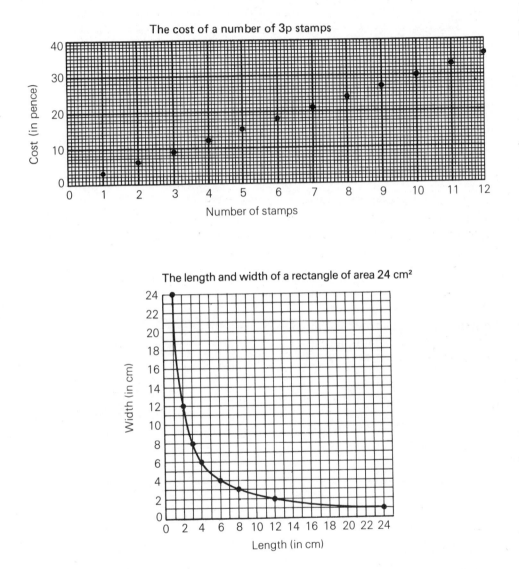

Each point on a graph of this kind represents a pair of numbers, written in a given order. For example, the point which allows the cost, 21p, of 7 stamps represents the pair of numbers 7 and 21. This pair is usually written as (7, 21). It is called an *ordered pair*.

It will be noticed that in the first graph the points are not joined by a line, but in the second graph they are joined. The reason for this is that in the first graph we can only have whole numbers of stamps, but in the second graph we can have lengths which are not whole numbers. We need to think carefully before we start drawing a line through the points on a graph of this kind. We also need to think about whether the line should be straight or curved.

One important advantage of this type of graph is that it can help us to see *relationships*. For example, from the second graph we can see very clearly that as the length increases the width decreases. In the first graph, however, the cost increases uniformly as the number of stamps increases.

Graphs like the two shown are called **Cartesian graphs** after the mathematician Descartes. The two numbers which form the pair for a point are called the **Cartesian co-ordinates** of the point.

6 by using points in the squares (or rectangles) of a grid

Two examples of this type of graph are shown below. On each, a dot represents one child.

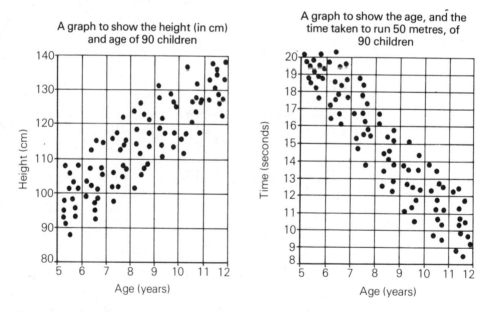

A graph to show the height (in cm) and age of 90 children

A graph to show the age, and the time taken to run 50 metres, of 90 children

A graph of this type is called a **scattergram** or **scatter graph**.

From a graph of this kind we can often see a general relationship rather than an exact relationship. For example, from the first graph we see that, in general, the older a child is the greater is his height. At the same time, however, we see that there are some children aged 8 years who are taller than some children aged 10 years. From the second graph we see that, generally, the older a child is the shorter time he takes to run 50 metres. But, again, there are exceptions.

A scatter graph sometimes shows that there is little or no relationship between two sets of measurements, as in the example below.

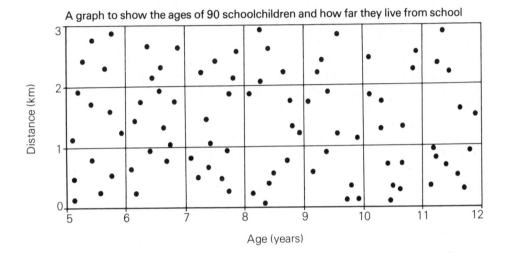

A graph to show the ages of 90 schoolchildren and how far they live from school

The various graphical forms listed above are those which are usually used. There are others. But first it is essential to understand and be able to use these. What is most important is that we should be sure in our minds about why we are drawing a graph. Then we can decide on which type of graph will best suit our purpose.

Chapter 17
Graphs

More block graphs. Ways of labelling the axes. Grouping information. Pie graphs. Showing pairs of numbers by points on a grid. Scatter graphs. Reading and using graphs.

Graphical work is not usually taught on its own as a separate topic. A graph should be drawn and used during any activity when it serves a useful purpose, as discussed in 'Thinking about graphs'. Most teachers believe that the drawing of a graph not only clarifies a child's understanding of an activity but is also a good mathematical habit to develop. Generally, children enjoy graphical work and many take pride in producing neat, tidy, and colourful work. They are particularly pleased when their drawings are displayed in the classroom. Children do not usually experience much difficulty with the early work in the use of picto-graphs, arrow graphs, and block graphs provided, of course, that each form is discussed fully and the work is not hurried. The drawing of a graph does take time and children vary very much in the rate at which they do their drawings.

As the use of graphs is extended, however, and new ideas are introduced, some children might need much help and guidance.

Extending the use of block graphs

Most children are able to draw a simple block graph. But they often need more help and guidance when they are introduced to:

1 the idea of not always starting the numbering of an axis at zero;

2 the idea of arranging information in groups;

3 ways of representing measurements by a block graph.

Activities

An activity which brings in the first two of these ideas is described below.

1 The children quietly count *one, two, three, four*, etc. and each child writes down the number reached in one minute (the teacher tells them when to start and stop). The results for a class of 39 children are given, in order, below.

      81, 83, 85, 87, 88, 92, 96, 96, 98, 99, 100, 100, 101,
    103, 104, 106, 107, 107, 109, 110, 110, 112, 112, 112, 113, 114,
    114, 115, 116, 117, 119, 119, 121, 123, 123, 126, 127, 129, 136.

The showing of these results by a block graph requires careful thought and discussion. The children will probably agree that two axes should be used and labelled as shown.

The marking of the *Number reached* axis may lead to some discussion. If it is marked like a number line then it may be difficult to decide where to draw the column for each number, e.g. 92.

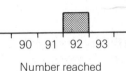

Will it be drawn to the left of 92? to the right? or with the 92 in the middle of its base? It is easier to mark the spaces rather than the lines, as shown on the right. The drawing of each column then causes no difficulties.

When the axis is marked in this way the children will quickly see that all the columns will come to the right of the 80 mark. All the space between 0 and 80 will be wasted. This provides a good opportunity for introducing the idea of *not* starting at 0 but at 80. This not only saves space but also allows a larger scale to be used.

If the same scale is used for each of the two axes the graph will consist of very small rectangles:

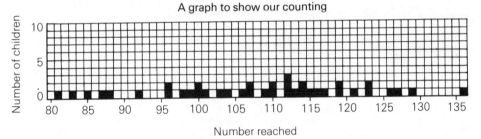

One way of making the graph easier to draw and read is to use a different scale for the *Number of children* axis. This needs to be discussed. An example is shown below.

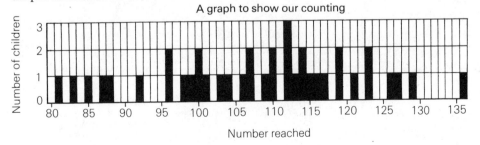

The drawing of this graph takes much time and would become very tedious if there were more children involved. Time and effort can be saved — and possibly a better picture of the results obtained — if the *Number reached* results are arranged in groups. For example, the grouping could be:

80 to 84, 85 to 89, 90 to 94, 95 to 99, 100 to 104, etc.

(*Note*: It is important that the groups should all be the same size. Otherwise the graph may be distorted and not easy to read correctly.)

In table form, the results can now be shown as below.

Group	80–84	85–89	90–94	95–99	100–104	105–109	110–114
Number of children	2	3	1	4	5	4	8

Group	115–119	120–124	125–129	130–134	135–139
Number of children	5	3	3	0	1

(*Note*: i) It is important to include zero groups, like the 130–134 group, in this table, and to show them on the graph.

ii) It is usual to arrange the size of the groups so that there are about 10 to 12 groups altogether.)

These groups can now be shown on a graph, as below.

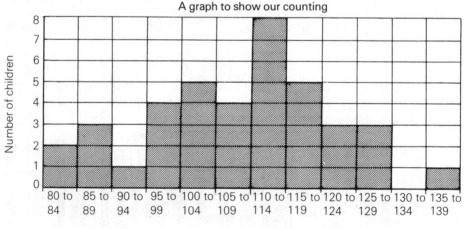

A graph to show our counting

Number of children

80 to 84, 85 to 89, 90 to 94, 95 to 99, 100 to 104, 105 to 109, 110 to 114, 115 to 119, 120 to 124, 125 to 129, 130 to 134, 135 to 139

Number reached

This kind of grouping has the advantages that the graph is easier to draw and to read. The general picture of the results is more clearly seen.

It must be understood, however, that the individual results are not now shown. For example, the graph shows that five children counted to one of the numbers from 100 to 104, but it does not show to which number each child counted. If our purpose is to obtain a general picture of the children's counting then the loss of individual results is not important. If, however, the individual results are important, then grouping the results would not serve our purpose.

2   The third extension to block graphs which sometimes causes difficulties arises when a set of measurements have to be shown. For example, let us think of an activity in which children are given a set of drinking straws of various lengths. The children have to measure the length of each straw to the nearest centimetre and show their results by a graph. A set of results, in table form, may be as below.

Length (to nearest cm)	10	11	12	13	14	15	16	17	18	19	20
Number of straws	2	3	5	6	4	0	7	4	8	2	7

Before these are shown by a graph the children have to decide how to label the bottom axis. If *spaces* on the axis are used then the labelling can be done as shown on the graph below.

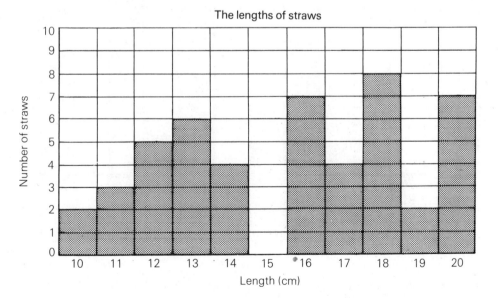

The lengths of straws

181

If, however, the bottom axis is thought of as a continuous number line, then much discussion becomes necessary.

For example, on the number line above, how is the column for the length of 13 cm to be positioned? Is it to be drawn to the right or to the left of the mark? To answer these questions we must think of what we mean when we say that a length is 13 cm, to the nearest centimetre. We do not mean that it is exactly 13 cm. It can be any length between 12.5 cm and 13.5 cm. We show this by drawing the column for 13 cm as below.

The column for the 12 cm lengths will, in the same way, be drawn between 11.5 cm and 12.5 cm. That for 14 cm will be drawn between 13.5 cm and 14.5 cm. The resulting graph will then look like the one shown below.

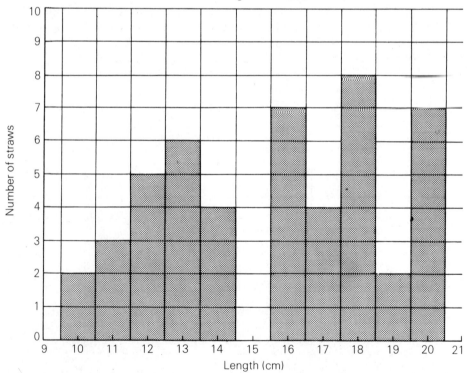

The lengths of straws

The ideas underlying the drawing of a graph in this way are very important and need to be fully discussed with the children.

Drawing pie graphs

A pie graph is often used when we want to show the proportions of various quantities, rather than the quantities themselves. For example, this pie graph shows the proportions of a class of children choosing a particular sport as their favourite.

Children should have experience in reading this kind of graph for examples appear in Geography books, Science books, newspapers, and magazines. They should be encouraged to collect them so that they can be discussed.

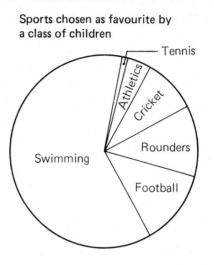

Sports chosen as favourite by a class of children

The drawing of a pie graph, however, is not as easy as reading one. This can be illustrated by looking at the steps involved in drawing a pie graph to show the following information.

The population of a village			
Men	Women	Boys	Girls
165	219	369	330

Step i) Find the total population.

$$165 + 219 + 369 + 330 = 1083$$

Step ii) Show each number as a fraction of the total.

Men $\frac{165}{1083}$ Women $\frac{219}{1083}$ Boys $\frac{369}{1083}$ Girls $\frac{330}{1083}$

Step iii) Find the fractions of 360°

Men $\frac{165}{1083}$ of 360° = 54.8° (to one place of decimals)

Women $\frac{219}{1083}$ of 360° = 72.8° (to one place of decimals)

Boys $\frac{369}{1083}$ of 360° = 122.7° (to one place of decimals)

Girls $\frac{330}{1083}$ of 360° = 109.7° (to one place of decimals)

Step iv) Check that the total of the four angles is 360°.

$$54.8° + 72.8° + 122.7° + 109.7° = 360°$$

Note: There might be a small difference from 360° owing to the approximating of each angle.

Step v) Show these angles at the centre of the circle. Label the various parts. Write the heading for the graph.

The drawing of a graph like this is not beyond the scope of an able child but it might be too demanding for a less able child. The teacher must decide to what extent the children themselves should draw graphs of this kind.

A graph to show how the population of a village is made up

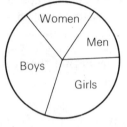

Showing ordered pairs by a graph

It is a big step from showing information by using a picto-graph, an arrow graph, a block graph, a pie graph, to using a point to show an ordered pair, especially as in some everyday activities an ordered pair is used to denote an area. For example, a map reference such as (A,7) is often used to denote a square on a map. One way of introducing the idea is described below.

A simple straightforward arrow graph is drawn, such as the one on the right. The ordered pairs shown on the graph are written down as: (1,2), (2,4), (3,6), (4,8), (5,10).

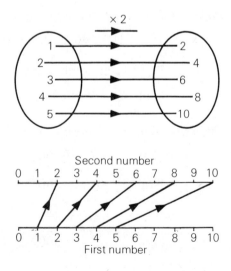

The ordered pairs are now shown by using two parallel number lines, as on the right.

The idea of arranging the two number lines at right-angles, with a common end-point, is then introduced, as shown below left.

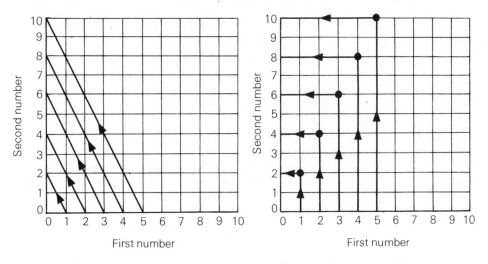

The idea of making use of the lines on a grid of squares is introduced, as shown above right, together with the idea of marking the point of intersection of the two lines.

As a last step the arrows are not shown (they have to be thought of in the mind). Only the points are shown.

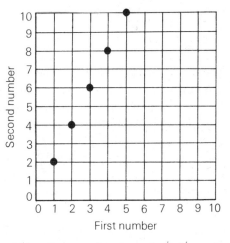

Several simple examples of this kind should be discussed and worked through with the children. They should then begin to understand the link between the ordered pairs shown by the arrow graph and those shown by the points on the grid.

It is important that this marking of points on a grid is *not* thought of as an end in itself. What is more important is that the children should look at the pattern made by the dots and link it with the relationship between the second and first members of each ordered pair. For example, for the graph above, each marked point represents an ordered pair for which *the second number* is twice *the first number*. The points lie on a straight line, and, if this line is drawn, every point on it represents an ordered pair for which *the second number* is twice *the first number*.

One of the mistakes that children often make in the early stages of using ordered pairs is that they write or say the two members in the wrong order. This is a serious mistake and needs to be watched for very carefully.

The need to write or say the two members of an ordered pair in the correct order can be reinforced through the children's playing the game of *Four in a line*. This game also has the advantage that a square grid is used on which points are marked. The game is played by two children. A third child acts as referee.

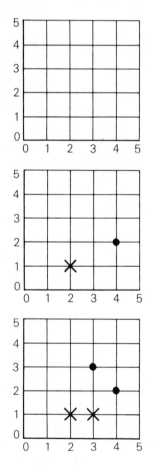

The game is played on a grid as shown on the right. This can be drawn by the children or the teacher can provide duplicated copies.

The game can best be described by showing a game between two children Paula and Chan. Paula starts. She says *four, two* (4,2) and puts a dot in the position shown. Chan then says *two, one* (2,1) and puts a cross in the position shown.

Paula is trying to get four dots in a line. Chan is trying to get four crosses in a line. Paula now says *three, three* (3,3) and puts a dot as shown. Chan says *three, one* (3,1) and puts in a cross as shown.

Paula says *two, four* (2,4).
Chan says *five, one* (5,1).
(Why did he choose this pair?)

Paula says *one, five* (1,5).
Paula has won the game.
She has four dots in a line.

Note: The referee checks that each dot or cross is put in its correct position. If a child says, for example, *two, four* but marks (4,2) he or she loses that turn.

Most children enjoy this game and they should be given plenty of opportunities for playing it. It helps in developing a good attitude towards mathematics.

Reading and using graphs

The ability to read and understand a graph is as important as being able to draw a graph. So, throughout their work in mathematics, children should have regular practice in looking at graphs and discussing what the graph tells them and what they can find out from it. The teacher should make good use of graphs which occur in subjects other than mathematics (e.g. science, geography, history). This will widen the children's experience and at the same time help them to develop the habit of looking at a graph critically. The children will also become aware that graphs can give very interesting information.

multiples, factors, and prime numbers

Children need to know about factors, multiples, and prime numbers. The idea of each of these is essential if the children are to deal successfully with operations with fractions. The ideas are also very necessary later when algebraic expressions involving fractions have to be dealt with. It is, however, the basic ideas which need to be well understood. It is not necessary for the children to become involved with large numbers or complicated examples. There is little necessity for the children to become involved in learning 'rules'. If the numbers are kept small then the children can deal with factors and multiples through their own thinking.

The definition we use for a prime number is important, for on it depends whether we regard the number *one* as being a prime number.

One definition says that a prime number has no factors other than itself and one. Using this the number *one* is a prime number (as are 2, 3, 5, 7, 11, etc.). Another definition says that a number is prime if it has two, *and only two*, different factors. Using this definition, 2, 3, 5, 7, 11, etc. are prime numbers (2 has the factors 2, 1; 3 has the factors 3, 1, etc.,) but the number *one* is not a prime number. It has only one factor (itself).

Either of these definitions is permissible, but the second is now generally used. The reason for this occurs in rather more advanced mathematics when we want to say that the square of any number is not a prime number. We can say this if *one* is not a prime number.

We do not, of course, discuss these two definitions with the children at this stage. We use the ideas of the second definition throughout our thinking and working.

Chapter 18
Numbers: multiples, factors and primes

Multiples, common multiples, least common multiple. Factors, common factors, greatest common factor. The idea of a prime number.

Multiples

Children use the idea of a multiple when they begin to think about repeated addition and multiplication. For example, each of the numbers 2, 4, 6, 8, 10, 12, is a multiple of two. Likewise each of the numbers 3, 6, 9, 12, 15, 18, is a multiple of three. In telling the time, multiples of five are used in counting the minutes corresponding to the numerals on a clock face.

Some children will also have realized that, for example, 6 is a multiple of 2 and also a multiple of 3.

We can build on these experiences. Here are some activities.

Activities
1   The examples quoted above can be used to introduce the word **multiple.** It may be helpful to write $2 \times 3 = 6$ on the blackboard with the words:

      multiply
      multiplication
      multiple.

Explain that we start with 2. The 'x 3' tells us to *multiply* the 2 by 3. We use *multiplication* to get the answer (6). Six is a *multiple* of two. Repeat this activity for other multiplications.

2   Write two sets of multiples on the blackboard, as shown in the example below.

multiples of 2   2 4 6 8 10 12 14 16 18 20

multiples of 3   3 6 9 12 15 18 21

Tell the children to look at the multiples and to say what they notice.

They quickly see that some numbers are multiples of 2 and also of 3. Draw loops around these pairs, as below.

multiples of 2   2 4 6 8 10 12 14 16 18 20

multiples of 3   3 6 9 12 15 18 21

Introduce the use of the phrase **common multiple**.
Say, '6 is a multiple of 2 and of 3'
　　　'6 is a common multiple of 2 and 3'.
The children use these statements for 12 and then for 18.

　　Some children may be able to go on to give other common multiples of 2 and 3. Ask the children which is the least of these common multiples (6). Introduce the use of the phrase **least common multiple**. (Some teachers use **lowest common multiple**.)

Note: In dealing with addition and subtraction of fractions it is not essential that the least common multiple is used. But it does simplify the working if it is used.

3　Repeat Activity 2 for many other pairs of numbers, for example: 2 and 5, 3 and 4, 3 and 5, 4 and 6.

4　Another useful and helpful way of showing common multiples is described below. On the blackboard show a rectangle, or other shape, and in it write all the whole numbers from 1 to 20.

Whole numbers from 1 to 20

1	2	3	4	5	6
7	8	9	10	11	
12	13	14	15	16	
17	18	19	20		

At the side of this draw another rectangle and in it draw a closed loop.

Whole numbers from 1 to 20

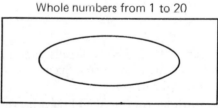

Now ask the children to come in turn to the blackboard and, from the numbers 1 to 20, write a multiple of 2 in the loop. They do this until all the multiples are shown within the loop. The numbers from 1 to 20 which are not multiples of 2 are written outside the loop, as below.

Whole numbers from 1 to 20

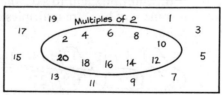

Using another rectangle on the blackboard, multiples of 3 are shown.

Whole numbers from 1 to 20

```
2  1    Multiples of 3    20  19
4        3        6
5   18                9        17
         15      12              16
7
    8   10    11    13    14
```

Now discuss with the children ways of showing both the multiples of 2 and the multiples of 3 in the same diagram. This will require much discussion before the diagram below is obtained.

Whole numbers from 1 to 20

```
Multiples of 2        Multiples of 3
    4   8  10    6
2                  3   9   15
    14  16  20  18  12
1    5    7    11    13    17    19
```

This is a helpful diagram as it shows:
  multiples of 2
  multiples of 3
  common multiples of 2 and 3
  numbers which are *not* multiples of 2
  numbers which are *not* multiples of 3
  numbers which are *not* multiples of 2 or of 3.
From it, too, the least common multiple of 2 and 3 can be picked out.

Note: A diagram like the one above is called a Venn diagram.

5   Repeat Activity 4 for other pairs of numbers (e.g. 3 and 4, 4 and 5, 2 and 5, 4 and 6).

6   Common multiples of three numbers can be found by using an extension of Activity 2. An example is shown below.

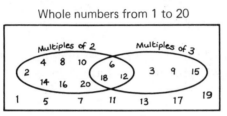

multiples of 2   2   4   6   8   10 12 14 16 18 20 22 24
multiples of 3   3   6   9 12 15 18 21 24 27
multiples of 4   4   8 12 16 20 24 28 32

12 and 24 are common multiples of 2, 3, and 4. The least common multiple is 12.

Other examples should be done by the children (2, 3, and 6; 2, 4, and 5). But care must be taken in choosing the three numbers. Otherwise the writing of the numbers becomes tedious.

7   Able children may be able to draw a diagram to show the multiples of three numbers, as in the example below. Some children, however, may find it too difficult.

Whole numbers from 1 to 24

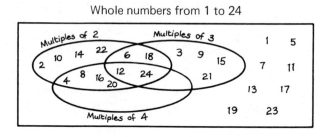

Factors

Children will have used the idea of a factor in multiplication and division but the word **factor** will probably not have been used. Ways of introducing this word are discussed below.

Activities

1   A good way to introduce the idea of a factor is to choose a particular number and find the different multiplications which give that number. For example, if 12 is the number chosen, then

$$1 \times 12 = 12 \qquad 2 \times 6 = 12 \qquad 3 \times 4 - 12$$
$$12 \times 1 = 12 \qquad 6 \times 2 = 12 \qquad 4 \times 3 = 12$$

These various multiplications can helpfully be shown in diagrams, as below:

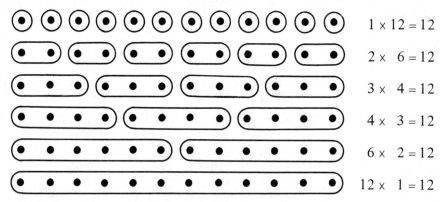

From these diagrams the children see that 12 objects can be arranged in ones, twos, threes, fours, sixes, and twelves. Each of the numbers 1, 2, 3, 4, 6, and 12 is a factor of 12. This activity should be repeated for many other numbers (e.g. 15, 18, 20, 14, 5, 8, 11, etc.).

2   From Activity 1 the children should see that if a number is divided by one of its factors there is no remainder. For example when 12 is divided, in turn, by each of its factors we have:

$$12 \div 1 = 12; \qquad 12 \div 2 = 6; \qquad 12 \div 3 = 4;$$
$$12 \div 4 = 3; \qquad 12 \div 6 = 2; \qquad 12 \div 12 = 1.$$

The children should use this idea to find the factors of a number. For example, using 24 we have

$24 \div 1 = 24$
$24 \div 2 = 12$
$24 \div 3 = 8$
$24 \div 4 = 6$
$24 \div 5$ has a remainder
$24 \div 6 = 4$
$24 \div 7$ has a remainder
$24 \div 8 = 3$
$24 \div 9$ has a remainder
$24 \div 10$ has a remainder
$24 \div 11$ has a remainder
$24 \div 12 = 2$
$24 \div 13$
to   } all have a remainder
$24 \div 23$
$24 \div 24 = 1$

The factors of 24 are 1, 2, 3, 4, 6, 8, 12, and 24. 24 has 8 factors.

Notes: a) With experience children find that there is no need to try all the numbers up to 24. They should first write down the factors 1 and 24, then try each number up to 12. After 12 there is no need to try 13 to 23 (each answer must be 1, with a remainder).

b) When the children find that, for example, 3 is a factor of 24, they should understand that 8 is also a factor ($3 \times 8 = 24$ and $8 \times 3 = 24$). The children should have plenty of practice in finding factors in this way.

3   When the children can find the factors of numbers they can go on to discuss the idea of common factors. For example, they know that:
     the factors of 12 are 1, 2, 3, 4, 6, and 12;
     the factors of 18 are 1, 2, 3, 6, and 18.
So
     the common factors of 12 and 18 are 1, 2, 3, and 6.
     The greatest of these is 6.
     So the **greatest common factor** of 12 and 18 is 6. (Some teachers use the phrase **highest common factor**.)
          Plenty of practice should be given in finding common factors and

greatest common factors of pairs of numbers. The extension to three or more numbers is straightforward if the basic ideas are understood.

Prime numbers

When we introduce the idea of prime numbers to children we must remember that, as discussed in 'Thinking about multiples, factors, and prime numbers', we are using the definition that 'A number which has two, and only two, different factors is called a **prime** number.'

Here are some activities for introducing this idea of a prime number.

Activities

1   The children first write down all the different factors of each of the numbers from, for example, 1 to 18, as started below.

Number	Factors
1	1
2	1, 2
3	1, 3
4	1, 2, 4
5	1, 5
6	1, 2, 3, 6

They then count the number of factors for each of the numbers. These can be shown on a table, as below.

Number	1	2	3	4	5	6	7	8	9	10	11	12	13	14	15	16	17	18
Number of different factors	1	2	2	3	2	4	2	4	3	4	2	6	2	4	4	5	2	6

It is also helpful to show these results by a graph, as below.

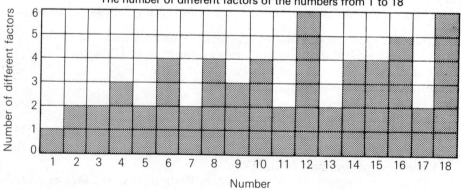

The number of different factors of the numbers from 1 to 18

From the table and from the graph the children see that some numbers have two, and only two, different factors, which are the number itself and one. These numbers are 2, 3, 5, 7, 11, 13, 17. These numbers are called **prime** numbers. It should be pointed out to the children that the number 1 is *not* a prime number. It does not have two different factors.

2   Each child is provided with a number-square, as shown. On this he lightly colours or shades each of the small squares which contains a prime number, as started on the right. This gives good practice in finding whether a number is prime.

1	2	3	4	5	6	7	8	9	10
11	12	13	14	15	16	17	18	19	20
21	22	23	24	25	26	27	28	29	30
31	32	33	34	35	36	37	38	39	40
41	42	43	44	45	46	47	48	49	50
51	52	53	54	55	56	57	58	59	60
61	62	63	64	65	66	67	68	69	70
71	72	73	74	75	76	77	78	79	80
81	82	83	84	85	86	87	88	89	90
91	92	93	94	95	96	97	98	99	100

The children look at their completed number squares (when they have been checked) and say what they notice. For example:

The only even number which is prime is 2.

All the other prime numbers are odd.

The coloured squares do not form a pattern.

The gaps between the prime numbers vary in length.

Discuss what they have to say.

3   An interesting activity which the more able children can do is described in steps below.

a)   Each child has a number-square, as shown. He colours or shades the small square which contains 1.

b)   Except for 2 itself he colours or shades all the small squares which contain a multiple of 2, as shown.

c)   Except for 3 itself, he colours or shades all the small squares containing a multiple of 3. (Some of these have already been coloured in dealing with multiples of 2.)

1	2	3	4	5	6	7	8	9	10
11	12	13	14	15	16	17	18	19	20
21	22	23	24	25	26	27	28	29	30
31	32	33	34	35	36	37	38	39	40
41	42	43	44	45	46	47	48	49	50
51	52	53	54	55	56	57	58	59	60
61	62	63	64	65	66	67	68	69	70
71	72	73	74	75	76	77	78	79	80
81	82	83	84	85	86	87	88	89	90
91	92	93	94	95	96	97	98	99	100

d)   All the multiples of 4 (including 4 itself) have been coloured in dealing with the multiples of 2. So no more multiples of 4 have to be coloured.

e)   Except for 5 itself, he colours or shades to show multiples of 5. (Some have already been done.)

f)   All the multiples of 6 (including 6 itself) have been coloured in dealing with the multiples of 2 and 3. No more need to be coloured.

1	2	3	4	5	6	7	8	9	10
11	12	13	14	15	16	17	18	19	20
21	22	23	24	25	26	27	28	29	30
31	32	33	34	35	36	37	38	39	40
41	42	43	44	45	46	47	48	49	50
51	52	53	54	55	56	57	58	59	60
61	62	63	64	65	66	67	68	69	70
71	72	73	74	75	76	77	78	79	80
81	82	83	84	85	86	87	88	89	90
91	92	93	94	95	96	97	98	99	100

g) Except for 7 itself, colour or shade all the multiples of 7. (Most of these have already been coloured.)

h) All the multiples of 8, 9, and 10 have been coloured in dealing with the multiples of 2, 3, and 5.

Ask the children what they notice about the numbers which have not been coloured. (They are the prime numbers less than 100.) Some of the children might be able to explain why the prime numbers are uncoloured.

Summary

When a child has completed the many activities in this chapter he or she should:

understand	the idea of a multiple, a factor, and a prime number
be able to find	multiples of a number
	common multiples of two numbers
	the least common multiple of two or more numbers
	the greatest common factor of two or more numbers
	whether or not a number is prime

Thinking about
operations with larger numbers

If children fully understand the ideas used in operations with numbers up to about one hundred and also know the number facts for each operation, they should be able to deal with larger numbers without too much difficulty. Unfortunately not all children are confident in both of these aspects of the operations and so the introduction and use of larger numbers creates more difficulties for them. The early stages are all important and the teacher should realize that some children need to spend more time on them before going on to further work.

There are, of course, other reasons why children make mistakes. Some of these are listed below.

1 Incorrect setting down
Two examples are given below.

$$\begin{array}{c}326 \\ +25 \\ \hline \end{array} \quad \text{instead of} \quad \begin{array}{c}326 \\ +\ \ 25 \\ \hline \end{array} \qquad \begin{array}{c}437 \\ -27 \\ \hline \end{array} \quad \text{instead of} \quad \begin{array}{c}437 \\ -\ \ 27 \\ \hline \end{array}$$

Mistakes like these arise from a lack of understanding of place-value or from untidy and careless setting down.

2 Mistakes in 'carrying' in addition and multiplication
In the addition on the right a child forgets to 'carry' the 1 *ten* from the units column to the tens column.

In the multiplication shown a child forgets to 'carry' the 3.

$$\begin{array}{c}4\ 5 \\ +3\ 8 \\ \hline 7\ 3 \end{array} \qquad \begin{array}{c}1\ 8 \\ \times\ \ 4 \\ \hline 4\ 2 \end{array}$$

Other mistakes of this kind arise when a child
a) uses the wrong 'carried' number;
b) uses the 'carried' number twice;
c) 'carries' a number when there is nothing to 'carry'.

These kinds of errors can easily arise if the teacher discourages the recording of the 'carried' number too early. It must be remembered that accuracy is more important than speed. Some children need to record the 'carried' number for a long time (as we ourselves sometimes do when dealing with complicated additions).

3 Mistakes in 'changing' in subtraction

In the subtraction shown a child uses one of the 6 *tens* and changes it to ten *units*. He forgets, however, to change the 6 to 5. This, again, can arise from not recording the 'changing'.

$$
\begin{array}{r}
6\ 5 \\
-1\ 8 \\
\hline
5\ 7 \\
\hline
\end{array}
$$

4 Mistakes in the addition of three numbers

In the addition of three numbers the total of the first two has to be kept in mind when adding the third. At times children use an incorrect total.

5 Mistakes with zero

Children say or write $7 \times 0 = 7$ or $0 \times 7 = 7$. Perhaps they confuse multiplication with addition. This type of error needs to be discussed and the children should be warned to be extra careful when a zero occurs in a multiplication.

In making up practice exercises teachers should always make sure that zeros occur in several of them.

6 Mistakes in division

It is easy to understand why many children find difficulties in division. For, in division, they have to be able to multiply and use the multiplication facts, and to subtract and use the subtraction facts. Any weaknesses which they might have in either of these operations will quickly show themselves, especially as much of the working has to be done in the head. A child might think he cannot do division when, in fact, his errors arise from mistakes in subtraction and multiplication.

In division, too, the idea of 'trying out' frequently has to be used. This is not easy for many children.

Chapter 19
Larger numbers: the four operations

Addition and subtraction with larger numbers. Multiplication by 10, 11 to 19, 20 (30, 40, . . .90), by any 2-digit number. Multiplication by any number. Division by 2-digit numbers. Division by numbers with 3 or more digits. Remainders in division. Divisions which require a decimal fraction in the answer. Short division.

In Chapters 9 to 13 we introduced ways of using place-value in the four basic operations $(+, -, \times, \div)$. Now we discuss ways of extending these methods when larger numbers are involved.

Addition

If the children

a)   fully understand place-value and its extension beyond hundreds,

b)   know the addition facts (to $9 + 9 = 18$),

then they should find no great difficulties in using addition for numbers involving hundreds, thousands, etc.

Any errors which occur will be mainly due to being not fully confident in a) and b) and at times to carelessness and poor setting down of the working.

Subtraction

As for addition children need to

a)   fully understand place-value,

b)   know the subtraction facts (up to $18 - 9 = 9$).

If they are confident in both of these then the children can move on to larger numbers without too many difficulties.

A subtraction such as $4000 - 273$, however, does need special consideration. Children can quickly become confused. Experienced teachers know that this happens so they should take great care to deal with corresponding types of examples in the earlier work.

At the first level this means that children should be confident in subtracting a 1-digit number from 10. At the next level children should have plenty of practice in subtracting from 100. Examples such as $100 - 5$, $100 - 30$, $100 - 35$ should be regularly *discussed* to help children to build up in their minds a picture of what they are doing. For $100 - 5$, some children will be able to give the answer (95) by some form of counting backwards (a very sensible approach) but may find difficulty in working through the steps used in written working. The use of apparatus might help some children.

For example, using straws or sticks, the 100 can first be shown as a big bundle of 10 *tens*.

H	T	U
1	0	0

To remove five straws the big bundle is first untied and shown as ten separate bundles of ten.

H	T	U
	10	0

One of these tens is then untied and shown as ten separate straws.

H	T	U
	9	10

Five straws are now removed from the ten separate straws.

H	T	U
	9	10
−		5
	9	5

The usual way of recording this untying of bundles is shown on the right.

H	T	U
1	0	0
−		5
	9	5

Note: It should be pointed out to the children that the writing of a '10' in any column is only done to help them to record what they are doing. Normally a '10' is never written in a column.

It is obvious that this kind of recording will be much better understood by children if it is based on practical activities such as the one described above. These activities, together with the necessary discussion, take time but it is time well spent. Some teachers may prefer to start with a subtraction such as $100-30$ (which involves only one untying) and then go on to $100-5$ and $100-35$, etc.

Subtractions from 100 can be followed by subtractions from 200, 300, . . ., 900. Then subtractions from 1000 can be dealt with in the ways described above. By this time, however, the children should be building up a good understanding of the method and should be able to apply it more easily to the larger numbers.

Multiplication

In Chapter 12, the multiplication of a 2-digit number by a 1-digit number was introduced and discussed. Now, the operation has to be extended to multiplication by 2-digit numbers, 3-digit numbers, etc. These extensions bring in some very important new ideas which need to be considered very carefully.

First we, as teachers, must agree that multiplication by two or more digits is based on:

a) multiplication by 10, 100, 1000, etc.;

b) the use of the idea of thinking of, for example,
57×45 as $(57 \times 40) + (57 \times 5)$;

c) the use of the idea that, for example,
$57 \times 40 = 57 \times (4 \times 10)$
$= (57 \times 4) \times 10$
or $57 \times 40 = 57 \times (10 \times 4)$
$= (57 \times 10) \times 4$

The use of a), b), and c) might be seen more clearly if we show the working of 57×45 in two of the ways normally used, as below.

57				57	
$\times$ 45				$\times$ 45	
2280	(57×40)	**OR**		285	$(57 \times \ 5)$
285	$(57 \times \ 5)$			2280	(57×40)
2565	(57×45)			2565	(57×45)

Notes: a) To multiply by 40 we multiply by 4 and put each digit in the answer one place to the left. That is, we multiply by 4 and then by 10.

b) The order of multiplication can, of course, be changed. We can first multiply by 40 and then by 5. Either order can be used.

A plan for introducing these ideas in steps to children

1 Multiplication by 10   This is the starting point. This step should not be hurried as it is the basis of all the work which follows.

a) *Multiplying a 1-digit number by 10*   The children are given more practice in multiplying a 1-digit number by 10 (e.g. 7 × 10). The answer is found by using repeated addition.

TU

$$7 \times 10 = 7 + 7 + 7 + 7 + 7 + 7 + 7 + 7 + 7 + 7$$
$$= 70$$

The multiplication can be recorded as on the right.

```
 TU
   7
x 1 0
─────
  70
```

From this and other examples (e.g. 6 × 10, 3 × 10), the children begin to see that, for example, when 7 is multiplied by 10 the 7 is moved to the *tens* column and there is a zero in the *units* column.

b) *Multiplying a 2-digit number between 10 and 20 by 10*   The answer to multiplications such as 16 × 10 is first found by repeated addition.

$$16 \times 10 = 16 + 16 + 16 + 16 + 16 + 16 + 16 + 16 + 16 + 16$$
$$= 160$$

The idea of thinking of 16 as (10 + 6) and writing the multiplication as (10 + 6) × 10 is introduced. This needs careful discussion. The working is shown as:

$$16 \times 10 = (10 + 6) \times 10$$
$$= (10 \times 10) + (6 \times 10)$$
$$= 100 + 60$$
$$= 160$$

In a vertical form the working is shown in two ways below.

HTU		HTU	
1 6		1 6	
× 1 0		× 1 0	
1 0 0	(10 × 10)	6 0	(6 × 10)
6 0	(6 × 10)	1 0 0	(10 × 10)
1 6 0	(16 × 10)	1 6 0	(16 × 10)

From this and other examples the children again see that when, for instance, 16 is multiplied by 10, the 1 and the 6 appear in the answer but each is one place to the left. There is a zero in the *units* place.

c) *Multiplying 20, 30, 40, . . ., 90 by 10*   Using 30 × 10 as an example, the answer is first found by repeated addition.

$$30 \times 10 = 30 + 30 + 30 + 30 + 30 + 30 + 30 + 30 + 30 + 30$$
$$= 300$$

Use is then made of $30 = 10 + 10 + 10$ to write the multiplication as:

$$30 \times 10 = (10 + 10 + 10) \times 10$$
$$= (10 \times 10) + (10 \times 10) + (10 \times 10)$$
$$= 100 + 100 + 100$$
$$= 300$$

From this and other examples (e.g. 40×10, 70×10) the children see, for instance, that when 30 is multiplied by 10 the 3 and the 0 appear in the answer but each is one place to the left. There is a zero in the *units* place.

d) *Multiplying any 2-digit number by 10*   Using 37×10 as an example we first use repeated addition.

$$37 \times 10 = 37 + 37 + 37 + 37 + 37 + 37 + 37 + 37 + 37 + 37$$
$$= 370$$

(*Note:*   The children see that repeated addition becomes increasingly long and tedious, and often gives rise to errors.)

The working is then shown as:

HTU

$$37 \times 10 = (30 + 7) \times 10$$
$$= (30 \times 10) + (7 \times 10)$$
$$= 300 + 70$$
$$= 370$$

$$
\begin{array}{ll}
3\,7 & \\
\times 1\,0 & \\
\hline
\,7\,0 & (\ 7 \times 10) \\
3\,0\,0 & (30 \times 10) \\
\hline
3\,7\,0 & (37 \times 10) \\
\hline
\end{array}
$$

In a vertical form the working is shown as on the right.

From this and many other examples (e.g. 24×10, 69×10), the children see that when any 2-digit number is multiplied by 10, the same two digits appear in the answer but each is one place to the left. There is a zero in the *units* place.

2 Multiplication by numbers from 11 to 19   An example such as 43×16 indicates an approach which can be used.

As for the earlier examples the multiplication should first be thought of as repeated additions. That is:

$$43 \times 16 = 43 + 43 + 43 + \ldots\ldots\ldots + 43 + 43 \ (16 \ \text{forty-threes})$$

These sixteen forty-threes can then be shown as:

$$43 + 43 + 43 + 43 + 43 + 43 + 43 + 43 + 43 + 43 \quad (43 \times 10)$$
$$43 + 43 + 43 + 43 + 43 + 43 \quad\quad\quad\quad\quad\quad (43 \times \ \ 6)$$

This will help the children to understand why multiplication by 16 can be done by multiplying by 10 and by 6 and adding the two results. It will also help children to understand the statements:

$$43 \times 16 = 43 \times (10 + 6)$$
$$= (43 \times 10) + (43 \times 6)$$
$$= 430 + 258$$
$$= 688$$

In vertical form the multiplication
can be recorded as on the right.

```
       HTU
        43
      x 16
      ─────
      430    (43 x 10)
      258    (43 x  6)
      ─────
      688    (43 x 16)
```

In the early stages the children should show in brackets, as above, the
two multiplications used in finding the answer. This is of great help to
the teacher in deciding whether a child understands what he is doing.
Much practice should be provided for this important step in multiplication.

3 Multiplication by 20, 30, 40, . . ., 90 Using as an example, 53 x 20, the
children should continue to think of the multiplication first as a repeated
addition. (The link between multiplication and repeated addition cannot be
over-emphasized. It helps many children who might otherwise be confused.)

$$53 \times 20 = 53 + 53 + 53 + \ldots \ldots + 53 \text{ (20 fifty-threes)}$$

The 20 fifty-threes can be shown as

$$(53 + 53 + 53 + 53 + \ldots) + (53 + 53 + 53 + \ldots) \text{ (10 fifty-threes + 10}$$

That is, $(53 \times 10) + (53 \times 10)$. So that: fifty-threes)

$$53 \times 20 = (53 \times 10) + (53 \times 10)$$
$$= 530 + 530$$
$$= 1060$$

This can also be shown as:

$$53 \times 20 = (53 \times 10) + (53 \times 10)$$
$$= (53 \times 10) \times 2$$
$$= (530) \times 2$$
$$= 1060$$

The repeated addition can also be shown as:

$$(53 + 53) + (53 + 53) + (53 + 53) + \ldots \ldots + (53 + 53) \text{ (ten times)}$$

That is:

$$53 \times 20 = (53 \times 2) \times 10$$
$$= (106) \times 10$$
$$= 1060$$

Each of these ways should be discussed fully with the children. Many other
examples of multiplication by 20 should then be discussed in the same way.
From these discussions the children should see that to multiply any number
by 20 they can:

first multiply the number by 10 and then multiply the result by 2
OR first multiply the number by 2 and then multiply the result by 10.

The children should then go on to multiplication by 30, 40, 50 . . ., 90.

4 Multiplication by any 2-digit number This brings together all the ideas and techniques which the children have gradually built up in their work so far. Using, as an example, 68×47, the children should now be able to think of this as

$$68 \times 47 = 68 \times (40 + 7)$$
$$= (68 \times 40) + (68 \times 7)$$
$$= 2720 + 476$$
$$= 3196$$

In a vertical form the multiplication can be shown as:

Th. HTU

```
     68
   × 47
```
   OR
```
   2720   (68 × 40)
    476   (68 ×  7)
   3196   (68 × 47)
```

Th. HTU

```
     68
   × 47
```
```
    476   (68 ×  7)
   2720   (68 × 40)
   3196   (68 × 47)
```

Much practice should be provided. The children, however, should not find this step difficult to understand if they have understood the earlier steps.

5 Multiplication by numbers with 3 or more digits This is a straight-forward extension of step **4**. It is based on multiplication by 100, 1000 etc. In the early stages the various multiplications should be shown in brackets, as in the vertical form for the example below.

$$347 \times 259 = 347 \times (200 + 50 + 9)$$
$$= (347 \times 200) + (347 \times 50) + (347 \times 9)$$
$$= 69\,400 + 17\,350 + 3123$$
$$= 89\,873$$

```
      347
    ×259
    3123   (347 ×   9)
   17350   (347 ×  50)
   69400   (347 × 200)
   89873   (347 × 259)
```

In all this work the children need to be fully confident in their knowledge of the multiplication facts.

Division

We need to make sure that the children are confident in multiplication and subtraction and fully understand the method used for division by a 1-digit number (as described on pages 127–31) before we go on to division by 2-digit and 3-digit numbers. We, ourselves, must also be sure that we understand how to deal with remainders, as discussed on page 61. In the discussions on division which follow the work is arranged, for convenience, in three sections. The first deals with divisions which can have remainders, the second with divisions which cannot have remainders, and the third with 'short' division.

1 Divisions which can have remainders

a) *Division by 2-digit numbers*

The approach is the same as for division by 1-digit numbers. This is illustrated by the working of $237 \div 13$, as shown on the right.

$$
\begin{array}{r}
8 \\
10 \\
13{\overline{)\,237}} \\
-\ 130 \quad (13 \times 10) \\
\hline
107 \\
-\ 104 \quad (13 \times\ 8) \\
\hline
3 \\
\end{array}
$$

Ten thirteens are first subtracted from 237. The children then have to decide how many thirteens can be subtracted from 107. They do this by 'trying out' possible numbers, or by writing down the multiples of 13 (13, 26, 39, 52, 65, 78, 91, 104). In the early stages children may be helped if the 10 and the 8 are written separately above the division line, as shown.

For a division such as $565 \div 13$, more than twenty thirteens can be subtracted from 565. This can be dealt with in one step or in several steps. Each way is shown below.

$$
\begin{array}{r}
3 \\
10 \\
10 \\
10 \\
10 \\
13{\overline{)\,565}} \\
130 \quad (13 \times 10) \\
\hline
435 \\
130 \quad (13 \times 10) \\
\hline
305 \\
130 \quad (13 \times 10) \\
\hline
175 \\
130 \quad (13 \times 10) \\
\hline
45 \\
39 \quad (13 \times\ 3) \\
\hline
6 \\
\end{array}
$$

$565 \div 13 = 43$, remainder 6

$$
\begin{array}{r}
3 \\
40 \\
13{\overline{)\,565}} \\
520 \quad (13 \times 40) \\
\hline
45 \\
39 \quad (13 \times\ 3) \\
\hline
6 \\
\end{array}
$$

$565 \div 13 = 43$, remainder 6

Each of the two ways should be discussed fully with the children and, in the early stages, the recording of the working should be as shown. This should help children to understand better what they are doing. The children think for themselves; they are not dependent on 'rules'. They use words and phrases which describe what they are doing.

b) *Division by whole numbers with 3 or more digits*

The method used is a straightforward extension of that used for 1-digit and 2-digit numbers. An example is shown on the right. The two subtractions of 247 x 10 can, of course, be done in the one step of 247 x 20.

$$
\begin{array}{r}
7 \\
10 \\
10 \\
\hline
247{\overline{\smash{\big)}\,6793}} \\
2470 \quad (247 \times 10) \\
\hline
4323 \\
2470 \quad (247 \times 10) \\
\hline
1853 \\
1729 \quad (247 \times 7) \\
\hline
124 \\
\end{array}
$$

$$6793 \div 247 = 27, \text{ remainder } 124$$

At this stage (and perhaps in the earlier stages) multiplication by 100 might be necessary, as in the example on the right. The two multiplications by 100 can, of course, be replaced by one multiplication by 200.

$$
\begin{array}{r}
275 \\
\hline
247{\overline{\smash{\big)}\,67930}} \\
24700 \quad (247 \times 100) \\
\hline
43230 \\
24700 \quad (247 \times 100) \\
\hline
18530 \\
17290 \quad (247 \times 70) \\
\hline
1240 \\
1235 \quad (247 \times 5) \\
\hline
5 \\
\end{array}
$$

$$67930 \div 247 = 275, \text{ remainder } 5$$

2 Divisions which cannot have remainders First it might be helpful to look at some completed divisions, as below. (The first division might arise from a question such as: 'A metal rod is 27 cm long. It is cut into five equal parts. How long is each?')

$27 \div 5$	$27 \div 4$	$27 \div 8$
5.4	6.75	3.375
5) 27	4) 27	8) 27
25 (5 × 5)	24 (4 × 6)	24 (8 × 3)
20 (tenths)	30 (tenths)	30 (tenths)
20 (5 × 4)	28 (4 × 7)	24 (8 × 3)
—	20 (hundredths)	60 (hundredths)
$27 \div 5 \doteq 5.4$	20 (4 × 5)	56 (8 × 7)
	—	40 (thousandths)
	$27 \div 4 = 6.75$	40 (8 × 5)
		—
		$27 \div 8 = 3.375$

From these examples we see that children must clearly understand:

i) place-value when it is extended to tenths, hundredths, and thousandths;

ii) the changing, for example, of 3 wholes to 30 tenths, 2 tenths to 20 hundredths, and 4 hundredths to 40 thousandths.

The type of division shown in the first example above can be introduced when the children understand decimal tenths and can divide by a 1-digit number. The changing of the 2 wholes to 20 tenths needs to be fully discussed. The children need to understand that the first 20 which appears in their working is 20 *tenths*. When these are divided into five equal parts each is 4 tenths. Many examples like this one (in which the division ends in the tenths) should be done by the children and fully discussed.

When the children are confident in the use of hundredths and thousandths they can go on to examples such as the second and third above.

At a later stage some divisions may have answers which are non-terminating decimals. For example, $27 \div 7 = 3.857142857. . ..$ Some children might be interested to go on with the division to see how the decimal recurs, but for practical purposes the answer needs to be given in a shorter form. For example:

$$27 \div 7 = 3.857 \quad \text{(correct to 3 places)}$$
or $\quad 27 \div 7 = 3.86 \quad \text{(correct to 2 places)}$
or $\quad 27 \div 7 = 3.9 \quad \text{(correct to 1 place)}$

These various forms of the answer should be fully discussed.

3 Short division   The recording of a division
in the shorter form, as shown in the example on
the right, demands that much of the working
be done in the head. So before this method is
introduced it is essential that children are very
confident in recording divisions the longer way. It may be unwise for the
less able children to attempt to use the shorter form. To do so might well
confuse them and destroy their confidence in using the longer form.

$$7\overline{)18361}$$
$$2623$$

Summary

When a child has completed the many stages and steps outlined in this
chapter he or she should:

understand   the use of place-value in addition, subtraction, multiplication,
  and division
  how to deal with larger numbers in the four operations
  the way of dealing with divisions in which there cannot be a
  remainder

be able to   use the four operations with large numbers

---

operations with fractions

Confusion and its causes

Children are more confused by operations with common fractions and decimal fractions than by any other topic in primary school mathematics. And, unfortunately, this confusion often stays with children right through the secondary school. Once they become confused it seems almost impossible to find a remedy.

The causes of this confusion are not difficult to find. They seem to be threefold.

1 The introduction of 'rules' too early. The children cannot understand them and apply them incorrectly. Here are some examples.

a) 'Turn upside down and multiply' or 'Invert and multiply'. Children can use this parrot-like for a division such as $\frac{2}{3} \div \frac{3}{4}$ but often cannot deal with $\frac{2}{3} \div 2$. (For this they are sometimes told to change the 2 to $\frac{2}{1}$. Yet another rule!)

b) 'To multiply by 10 move the decimal point one place to the right'. But when they were dealing with whole numbers they learned a rule such as 'To multiply by 10 add a zero'. So it is easy to understand why, in examinations at the secondary level, children mix up the two 'rules'.

2 The use of words and phrases which have little meaning to the children. For example:

a) 'cancel'. This word is all right if its meaning is understood. Often, however, it is not understood. This again shows itself at the secondary level in incorrect cancellings such as

$$\frac{a+b}{a} = \frac{\overset{1}{\cancel{a}}+b}{\cancel{a}_1} = 1+b \qquad \frac{7 \times 5}{2 \times 4} = \frac{\overset{2}{\cancel{7}}\overset{1}{\cancel{}}\times 5}{\cancel{2}_1 \times 4} = \frac{7 \times 5}{4} = \frac{35}{4} = 8\frac{3}{4}$$

To many children cancelling means crossing out anything at the top of a fraction which looks like something at the bottom of the fraction. That is all they know about it.

b) 'Find the L.C.M.' (Lowest Common Multiple). Why they have to find it in the addition and subtraction of fractions is often not clear to children. Some children do not even know what the L.C.M. is.

3   Some teachers themselves do not fully understand operations with fractions. All they can do is to introduce as quickly as possible 'rules' which they themselves learned at school. A real improvement in this work with fractions will be achieved only if:

a)   we ourselves understand the operations,

b)   we help the children as much as possible to understand each step;

c)   we use simple language to explain what we are doing. 'Rules' should come from the children's activities. They should not be imposed too early and with little understanding.

Chapter 20

Common and decimal fractions: the four operations

Common fractions: addition, subtraction, multiplication, and division. Planning the work. Understanding a working 'rule' for division. Decimal fractions: addition, subtraction, multiplication, and division. Quick ways of multiplying and dividing by 10, 100, 1000, etc. The idea of giving a decimal fraction to a specified number of places. Changing a common fraction to a decimal fraction.

Before starting to read this chapter teachers are advised to look again at 'Thinking about common fractions', 'Thinking about decimal fractions', and Chapters 8 and 14. This will help to link the work in this chapter with what has gone before.

Common fractions and decimal fractions are, of course, very closely related but for convenience and simplicity they are dealt with separately in this chapter. Whenever possible, however, the two should be linked as much as possible in discussions with the children.

Operations with common fractions

It is important that the new ideas and the activities should be arranged in carefully planned stages and steps. Suggestions for such a plan are given below.

1 Addition

a) Adding fractions of the same kind

Step i)　Each numerator is 1. Total less than 1.

$$\text{e.g. } \tfrac{1}{4} + \tfrac{1}{4} + \tfrac{1}{4} = \tfrac{3}{4} \qquad \tfrac{1}{8} + \tfrac{1}{8} + \tfrac{1}{8} + \tfrac{1}{8} + \tfrac{1}{8} = \tfrac{5}{8}$$

Step ii)　Some numerators greater than 1.

$$\text{e.g. } \tfrac{1}{8} + \tfrac{2}{8} = \tfrac{3}{8} \qquad \tfrac{1}{4} + \tfrac{3}{4} = \tfrac{4}{4} \qquad \tfrac{3}{4} + \tfrac{3}{4} = \tfrac{6}{4}$$

$$\tfrac{2}{5} + \tfrac{2}{5} = \tfrac{4}{5} \qquad\qquad = 1 \qquad\qquad = 1\tfrac{2}{4}$$

$$= 1\tfrac{1}{2}$$

Step iii)   As for *i)* and *ii)* with mixed numbers.

e.g. $1\frac{1}{4} + \frac{1}{4} = 1\frac{2}{4}$ $\qquad\qquad$ $3\frac{1}{8} + 2\frac{5}{8} = 5\frac{6}{8}$

$\qquad\qquad = 1\frac{1}{2}$ $\qquad\qquad\qquad\qquad = 5\frac{3}{4}$

Provided that children say the fractions in a proper way (for example, $\frac{2}{3}$ should be said as *two* thirds, with the emphasis on the *two*), they should have no great difficulties with this stage.

b) Fractions of different kinds (i.e. 'changing' is necessary)

Step i)   One fraction only is changed.

e.g. $\frac{1}{2} + \frac{1}{4} = \frac{2}{4} + \frac{1}{4}$ $\qquad\qquad$ $1\frac{1}{2} + 3\frac{5}{8} = 4 + \frac{4}{8} + \frac{5}{8}$

$\qquad\qquad = \frac{3}{4}$ $\qquad\qquad\qquad\qquad = 4 + \frac{9}{8}$

$\frac{1}{2} + \frac{3}{8} = \frac{4}{8} + \frac{3}{8}$ $\qquad\qquad\qquad\quad = 4 + 1\frac{1}{8}$

$\qquad\qquad = \frac{7}{8}$ $\qquad\qquad\qquad\qquad = 5\frac{1}{8}$

$1\frac{1}{2} + \frac{3}{8} = 1\frac{4}{8} + \frac{3}{8}$

$\qquad\qquad = 1\frac{7}{8}$

Step ii)   Both fractions are changed (common denominator found by inspection).

e.g. $\frac{1}{2} + \frac{1}{3} = \frac{3}{6} + \frac{2}{6}$ $\qquad\qquad$ $1\frac{2}{3} + 2\frac{1}{8} = 3 + \frac{16}{24} + \frac{3}{24}$

$\qquad\qquad = \frac{5}{6}$ $\qquad\qquad\qquad\qquad = 3 + \frac{19}{24}$

$\frac{2}{3} + \frac{1}{4} = \frac{8}{12} + \frac{3}{12}$ $\qquad\qquad\qquad\qquad = 3\frac{19}{24}$

$\qquad\qquad = \frac{11}{12}$ $\qquad\qquad$ $3\frac{3}{4} + 2\frac{2}{3} = 5 + \frac{9}{12} + \frac{8}{12}$

$\frac{3}{4} + \frac{1}{3} = \frac{9}{12} + \frac{4}{12}$ $\qquad\qquad\qquad\qquad = 5 + \frac{17}{12}$

$\qquad\qquad = \frac{13}{12}$ $\qquad\qquad\qquad\qquad = 5 + 1\frac{5}{12}$

$\qquad\qquad = 1\frac{1}{12}$ $\qquad\qquad\qquad\qquad = 6\frac{5}{12}$

When one fraction has to be changed the ideas involved need to be discussed fully. Using $\frac{1}{2} + \frac{1}{4}$ as an example, diagrams can first be used.

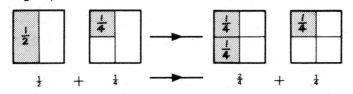

The many equivalent forms of $\frac{1}{2}$ should also be shown, as below.

$$\frac{1}{2} = \frac{2}{4} = \frac{3}{6} = \frac{4}{8} = \frac{5}{10} = \frac{6}{12} = \ldots \ldots$$

From these the idea of using $\frac{2}{4}$ is discussed. The children record the addition as

$$\frac{1}{2} + \frac{1}{4} = \frac{2}{4} + \frac{1}{4}$$
$$= \frac{3}{4}$$

Many other simple examples of this type should be discussed before the children go on to the other types of examples of *step i)*. When children are confident in changing one fraction in an addition they can go on to examples where both fractions are changed. Two examples are discussed below.

a) $\boxed{\frac{1}{3} + \frac{1}{4}}$

The equivalent forms of each fraction are first written down.

$$\frac{1}{3} = \frac{2}{6} = \frac{3}{9} = \frac{4}{12} = \frac{5}{15} = \frac{6}{18} = \frac{7}{21} = \frac{8}{24} = \frac{9}{27} = \frac{10}{30} = \frac{11}{33} = \frac{12}{36} = \ldots \ldots$$

$$\frac{1}{4} = \frac{2}{8} = \frac{3}{12} = \frac{4}{16} = \frac{5}{20} = \frac{6}{24} = \frac{7}{28} = \frac{8}{32} = \frac{9}{36} = \frac{10}{40} = \ldots \ldots$$

Pairs of fractions of the same kind are then linked, as below.

$$\frac{1}{3} = \frac{2}{6} = \frac{3}{9} = \boxed{\frac{4}{12}} = \frac{5}{15} = \frac{6}{18} = \frac{7}{21} = \boxed{\frac{8}{24}} = \frac{9}{27} = \frac{10}{30} - \frac{11}{33} - \boxed{\frac{12}{36}} = \ldots \ldots$$

$$\frac{1}{4} = \frac{2}{8} = \boxed{\frac{3}{12}} = \frac{4}{16} = \frac{5}{20} = \boxed{\frac{6}{24}} = \frac{7}{28} = \frac{8}{32} = \boxed{\frac{9}{36}} = \frac{10}{40} = \ldots \ldots$$

From these pairings the children see that both fractions can be changed to twelfths, twenty-fourths, or even smaller parts. To keep the numbers as low as possible, twelfths are chosen. The addition is recorded as

$$\frac{1}{3} + \frac{1}{4} = \frac{4}{12} + \frac{3}{12}$$
$$= \frac{7}{12}$$

It should be noted that the twelfths are found by inspection, not by the use of any kind of rule.

The changing of the two fractions can also be illustrated by diagrams:

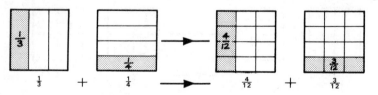

$$\frac{1}{3} \quad + \quad \frac{1}{4} \quad \longrightarrow \quad \frac{4}{12} \quad + \quad \frac{3}{12}$$

b) $\boxed{3\frac{3}{4} + 2\frac{2}{3}}$

To deal with this addition the children need to understand that $3\frac{3}{4}$ represents $3 + \frac{3}{4}$. This might seem to be an unnecessary statement to make. But it is suprising how some children in secondary schools do not understand this. (Probably because they have used too many rules without ever understanding the first ideas of fractions.)

The idea of first adding the whole numbers and then the fractions is discussed together with ways of setting down the addition tidily. One way of doing this is shown below.

$$3\frac{3}{4} + 2\frac{2}{3} = 3 + \frac{3}{4} + 2 + \frac{2}{3}$$
$$= 5 + \frac{3}{4} + \frac{2}{3}$$
$$= 5 + \frac{9}{12} + \frac{8}{12}$$
$$= 5 + \frac{17}{12}$$
$$= 5 + 1\frac{5}{12}$$
$$= 6\frac{5}{12}$$

Again, the kind of fraction to which the quarters and thirds are both changed is found by inspection. This helps the children to understand what they are doing and is the method used later in algebra. The introduction of the use of Least Common Multiples at this stage tends to confuse children and should not be necessary if small numbers are used for the denominators. After doing a number of examples some children will notice that the common denominator can be found by multiplying the denominator of the first fraction by that of the second. This does not always give the least common denominator but it is a method which can be usefully discussed.

Some teachers prefer to show $\frac{1}{3} + \frac{1}{4}$ as $\frac{4 + 3}{12}$. They say that it emphasizes that we are working in twelfths. If this method is used it is suggested that the two fractions are first written separately as twelfths.

2 Subtraction
a) Fractions of the same kind
Step i) No changing of whole numbers.

e.g. $\frac{3}{4} - \frac{1}{4} = \frac{2}{4}$
$= \frac{1}{2}$

$3\frac{5}{8} - 1\frac{2}{8} = (3 + \frac{5}{8}) - (1 + \frac{2}{8})$
$= (3 - 1) + (\frac{5}{8} - \frac{2}{8})$
$= 2 + \frac{3}{8}$
$= 2\frac{3}{8}$

Step ii)   Changing of whole numbers.

e.g. $1 - \frac{3}{5} = \frac{5}{5} - \frac{3}{5}$ $3\frac{1}{4} - 1\frac{3}{4} = 2 + \frac{1}{4} - \frac{3}{4}$

$\phantom{e.g.   1 - \frac{3}{5}} = \frac{2}{5}$ $\phantom{3\frac{1}{4} - 1\frac{3}{4}} = 1 + \frac{4}{4} + \frac{1}{4} - \frac{3}{4}$

$\phantom{3\frac{1}{4} - 1\frac{3}{4}} = 1 + \frac{2}{4}$

$\phantom{3\frac{1}{4} - 1\frac{3}{4}} = 1 + \frac{1}{2}$

$\phantom{3\frac{1}{4} - 1\frac{3}{4}} = 1\frac{1}{2}$

b) Fractions of different kinds (common fraction found by inspection)

Step i)   No changing of whole numbers.

e.g. $\frac{1}{2} - \frac{1}{3} = \frac{3}{6} - \frac{2}{6}$ $3\frac{1}{2} - \frac{1}{8} = 3 + \frac{4}{8} - \frac{1}{8}$

$\phantom{e.g.   \frac{1}{2} - \frac{1}{3}} = \frac{1}{6}$ $\phantom{3\frac{1}{2} - \frac{1}{8}} = 3 + \frac{3}{8}$

$\phantom{3\frac{1}{2} - \frac{1}{8}} = 3\frac{3}{8}$

Step ii)   Changing of whole numbers.

e.g. $1\frac{1}{2} - \frac{3}{4} = 1 + \frac{1}{2} - \frac{3}{4}$ $3\frac{1}{3} - \frac{3}{4} = 3 + \frac{4}{12} - \frac{9}{12}$

$\phantom{e.g.   1\frac{1}{2} - \frac{3}{4}} = 1 + \frac{2}{4} - \frac{3}{4}$ $\phantom{3\frac{1}{3} - \frac{3}{4}} = 2 + \frac{12}{12} + \frac{4}{12} - \frac{9}{12}$

$\phantom{e.g.   1\frac{1}{2} - \frac{3}{4}} = \frac{4}{4} + \frac{2}{4} - \frac{3}{4}$ $\phantom{3\frac{1}{3} - \frac{3}{4}} = 2 + \frac{7}{12}$

$\phantom{e.g.   1\frac{1}{2} - \frac{3}{4}} = \frac{3}{4}$ $\phantom{3\frac{1}{3} - \frac{3}{4}} = 2\frac{7}{12}$

$5\frac{1}{4} - 2\frac{2}{3} = 3 + \frac{1}{4} - \frac{2}{3}$

$\phantom{5\frac{1}{4} - 2\frac{2}{3}} = 3 + \frac{3}{12} - \frac{8}{12}$

$\phantom{5\frac{1}{4} - 2\frac{2}{3}} = 2 + \frac{12}{12} + \frac{3}{12} - \frac{8}{12}$

$\phantom{5\frac{1}{4} - 2\frac{2}{3}} = 2\frac{7}{12}$

If children have understood the various steps in the addition of fractions then the only new idea in subtraction is that of using one of the whole numbers and changing it to a fraction of the same kind as the other fractions. This idea can be introduced by discussing examples such as:

$$1 - \frac{1}{4} \quad 1 - \frac{3}{4} \quad 1 - \frac{2}{3} \quad 2 - \frac{1}{4} \quad 2 - \frac{3}{4} \quad 4 - \frac{1}{3} \quad 6 - \frac{2}{3}$$

In the last four of these examples only *one* of the whole numbers should be changed to a fraction. To change them all is unnecessary and complicates the working when large numbers are involved.

Examples such as those below should next be discussed.

$$2-1\tfrac{1}{4} \qquad 3-1\tfrac{3}{4} \qquad 5-2\tfrac{2}{3} \qquad 6-5\tfrac{1}{4} \qquad 4-2\tfrac{3}{4} \qquad 8-6\tfrac{1}{3}$$

In these examples the whole numbers are first subtracted. The subtractions **then become**:

$$1-\tfrac{1}{4} \qquad 2-\tfrac{3}{4} \qquad 3-\tfrac{2}{3} \qquad 1-\tfrac{1}{4} \qquad 2-\tfrac{3}{4} \qquad 2-\tfrac{1}{3}$$

An example such as $3\tfrac{1}{3} - 1\tfrac{3}{4}$ is then discussed. After dealing with the whole numbers the subtraction becomes $2 + \tfrac{1}{3} - \tfrac{3}{4}$. The two fractions are changed to twelfths to give $2 + \tfrac{4}{12} - \tfrac{9}{12}$. One of the whole numbers is is changed to twelfths, and the subtraction is written as $1 + \tfrac{12}{12} + \tfrac{4}{12} - \tfrac{9}{12}$. The two ways of dealing with the twelfths are now discussed.

$$\begin{aligned} \tfrac{12}{12} + \tfrac{4}{12} - \tfrac{9}{12} &= \tfrac{16}{12} - \tfrac{9}{12} \\ &= \tfrac{7}{12} \end{aligned} \qquad\qquad \begin{aligned} \tfrac{12}{12} + \tfrac{4}{12} - \tfrac{9}{12} &= \tfrac{12}{12} - \tfrac{9}{12} + \tfrac{4}{12} \\ &= \tfrac{3}{12} + \tfrac{4}{12} \\ &= \tfrac{7}{12} \end{aligned}$$

Each gives the answer $1\tfrac{7}{12}$ for the subtraction.

The children should understand and be able to use each of these two ways. Their ability to do so will indicate to the teacher whether they understand what they are doing. At the same time a teacher will appreciate that much thought is involved in dealing with these subtractions. The work should not be hurried and at each step it is helpful to get children to explain in their own words what they are doing.

3 Multiplication

We again start by giving a progression of stages and steps.

a) Multiplying a fraction by a whole number

Step i) $\quad \tfrac{1}{4} \times 3 = \tfrac{1}{4} + \tfrac{1}{4} + \tfrac{1}{4}$

$\qquad\qquad\quad = \tfrac{3}{4}$

Step ii) $\quad \tfrac{2}{3} \times 4 = \tfrac{2}{3} + \tfrac{2}{3} + \tfrac{2}{3} + \tfrac{2}{3}$

$\qquad\qquad\qquad = \tfrac{8}{3}$

$\qquad\qquad\qquad = 2\tfrac{2}{3}$

b) Multiplying a fraction by a fraction

Step i) The meaning of $\frac{1}{2} \times \frac{1}{2}, \frac{1}{3} \times \frac{1}{2}, \frac{2}{3} \times \frac{1}{2}, \frac{3}{4} \times \frac{2}{3}$, etc.

Step ii) The writing of $\frac{3}{4} \times \frac{2}{3}$ as $\frac{3 \times 2}{4 \times 3}$

Step iii) The idea of simplifying before multiplying, e.g.

$$\frac{4}{5} \times \frac{5}{6} = \frac{\cancel{4}^{2}}{\cancel{5}_{1}} \times \frac{\cancel{5}^{1}}{\cancel{6}_{3}}$$

$$= \frac{2}{3}$$

c) Multiplying mixed numbers

Step i) e.g. $1\frac{1}{2} \times \frac{3}{4} = \frac{3}{2} \times \frac{3}{4}$

$$= \frac{9}{8}$$

$$= 1\frac{1}{8}$$

Step ii) e.g. $1\frac{1}{2} \times 1\frac{3}{4} = \frac{3}{2} \times \frac{7}{4}$

$$= \frac{21}{8}$$

$$= 2\frac{5}{8}$$

Step iii) e.g. $2\frac{1}{4} \times 1\frac{1}{3} = \frac{9}{4} \times \frac{4}{3}$

$$= \frac{\cancel{9}^{3}}{\cancel{4}_{1}} \times \frac{\cancel{4}^{1}}{\cancel{3}_{1}}$$

$$= 3$$

Stage **a)** above requires only that children understand the meaning of multiplication. Repeated addition can be used for both the examples shown.

In the second example the children will quickly see that the working can be thought of as $\frac{2}{3} \times 4 = \frac{2 \times 4}{3}$. Plenty of practice should be given in this stage.

The first step in stage **b)** requires much discussion. One starting-point is to ask the children to copy and complete the set of multiplications shown on the right.

$$\frac{1}{2} \times 4 = \quad (2)$$
$$\frac{1}{2} \times 3 = \quad (1\frac{1}{2})$$
$$\frac{1}{2} \times 2 = \quad (1)$$
$$\frac{1}{2} \times 1 = \quad (\frac{1}{2})$$
$$\frac{1}{2} \times \frac{1}{2} = \quad (?)$$

The children should have no difficulty with the first four multiplications but they might not be able to give the answer to $\frac{1}{2} \times \frac{1}{2}$. To help them to give a meaning to this multiplication, discuss what each of the others stands for. The first, $\frac{1}{2} \times 4$, represents *four* halves. The next represents *three* halves. The next *two* halves. And $\frac{1}{2} \times 1$ represents *one* half. Using this pattern, $\frac{1}{2} \times \frac{1}{2}$ represents one *half* of one half.

The value of one *half* of one half can be shown by a diagram as below.

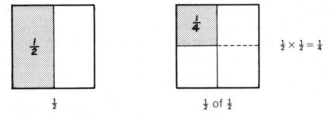

In the same way, $\frac{1}{2} \times \frac{1}{3}$ can be thought of as a *third* of one half and can be shown by a diagram such as that below.

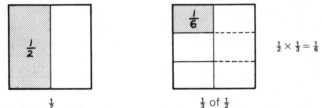

$\frac{1}{2} \times \frac{3}{4}$ can be thought of as *three-quarters* of one half and shown as below.

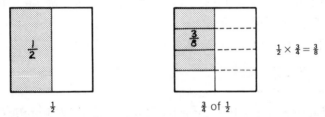

Many other multiplications, in which the numerator of the first fraction is 1, (e.g. $\frac{1}{3} \times \frac{1}{4}$, $\frac{1}{3} \times \frac{3}{4}$, $\frac{1}{5} \times \frac{2}{3}$, $\frac{1}{4} \times \frac{2}{5}$) should be dealt with in the same way. From their results the children should begin to see that, for example, the answer to $\frac{1}{2} \times \frac{3}{4}$ can be obtained from $\frac{1 \times 3}{2 \times 4}$. This is an important step and should be illustrated by many examples. Examples of multiplication in which the numerator of the first fraction is a number other than one should now be discussed. Using $\frac{3}{5} \times \frac{3}{4}$, the multiplication should be thought of as *three-quarters* of $\frac{3}{5}$. As before, this can be found from a diagram, as below.

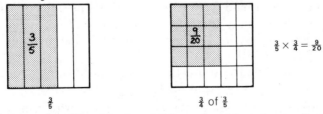

From many examples like this the children should again see that the answer can be found from $\frac{3 \times 3}{5 \times 4}$.

From an example such as that on the right $\frac{2}{5} \times \frac{3}{4} = \frac{2 \times 3}{5 \times 4}$ the children will find that the answer can be $= \frac{6}{20}$ simplified by dividing the top and the bottom numbers of the fraction by 2 (to give $\frac{3}{10}$). This can lead to a discussion as to whether this division by 2 could be done at an earlier stage. For example at the stage $\frac{2 \times 3}{5 \times 4}$ the top and the bottom can both be divided by 2 and shown as $\frac{1}{5} \times \frac{3}{2}$. It must be emphasized, however, that this way of showing the working is very difficult to explain and justify to children. There is a real danger that they will not understand what they are doing and will just be using a kind of rule. For this reason it might be best to delay this early simplification until much later.

The final stage in the multiplication of fractions involves mixed numbers. Provided that the children understand that, for example, $4\frac{2}{3}$ can be changed to $\frac{14}{3}$ and that $1\frac{1}{2}$ can be changed to $\frac{3}{2}$ this should present no difficulties. The multiplication $4\frac{2}{3} \times 1\frac{1}{2}$ can be changed to $\frac{14}{3} \times \frac{3}{2}$ and then worked in the same way as before.

It might be helpful to discuss other ways of finding the answer. For example, $4\frac{2}{3} \times 1\frac{1}{2}$ can be thought of as $(4\frac{2}{3} \times 1) + (4\frac{2}{3} \times \frac{1}{2})$.

The multiplication in the second bracket can then be thought of as $(4 \times \frac{1}{2}) + (\frac{2}{3} \times \frac{1}{2})$. In this way

$$4\frac{2}{3} \times 1\frac{1}{2} = (4\frac{2}{3} \times 1) + (4 \times \frac{1}{2}) + (\frac{2}{3} \times \frac{1}{2})$$
$$= \quad 4\frac{2}{3} \quad + \quad 2 \quad + \quad \frac{1}{3}$$
$$= 7$$

This kind of approach might appear to be unnecessarily complicated, but if children can sort out multiplication in this way then teachers can rightly feel that they have a very good understanding of fractions.

4 Division

The understanding of division by a fraction depends almost entirely upon whether children understand the idea and language of division. So before any work on division by a fraction is started a teacher needs to discuss the meaning of, for example, $21 \div 3$. This can represent 'How many sets of three objects can be formed from a set of twenty-one objects?' In simple language this is, 'How many threes make twenty-one?' The children should have much practice in saying, in their own words, what meaning can be given to $18 \div 2$, $24 \div 6$, $30 \div 5$, etc.

When they are able to do this they can begin to think about dividing by a fraction. Here is a suggestion for the stages and steps.

Note: In looking at the various stages it is important to remember that what we are discussing is division by a fraction. It is the number which comes *after* the division sign with which we are concerned.

a) Dividing by a fraction with 1 as numerator

Step i) e.g. $1 \div \frac{1}{4}$ $\quad 2 \div \frac{1}{4}$ $\quad 2 \div \frac{1}{3}$ $\quad 4 \div \frac{1}{3}$

Step ii) e.g. $\frac{1}{2} \div \frac{1}{4}$ $\quad \frac{3}{4} \div \frac{1}{4}$ $\quad \frac{1}{2} \div \frac{1}{3}$ $\quad \frac{2}{3} \div \frac{1}{6}$

b) Dividing by any fraction

Step i) e.g. $2 \div \frac{1}{4}$ $\quad 2 \div \frac{2}{4}$ $\quad 2 \div \frac{3}{4}$

$\qquad\qquad 3 \div \frac{1}{5}$ $\quad 3 \div \frac{2}{5}$ $\quad 3 \div \frac{3}{5}$ $\quad 3 \div \frac{4}{5}$

Step ii) e.g. $\frac{1}{2} \div \frac{1}{5}$ $\quad \frac{1}{2} \div \frac{2}{5}$ $\quad \frac{1}{2} \div \frac{3}{5}$ $\quad \frac{1}{2} \div \frac{4}{5}$

$\qquad\qquad 1\frac{2}{3} \div \frac{1}{4}$ $\quad 1\frac{2}{3} \div \frac{3}{4}$ $\quad 2\frac{3}{4} \div \frac{2}{3}$ $\quad 4\frac{1}{4} \div \frac{3}{5}$

c) Dividing by a mixed number

e.g. $1\frac{1}{2} \div 1\frac{2}{3}$ $\quad 4\frac{1}{3} \div 1\frac{2}{3}$ $\quad 2\frac{1}{2} \div 1\frac{1}{2}$ $\quad 3\frac{3}{4} \div 2\frac{1}{3}$

If children understand that, for example, $27 \div 3$ can represent, 'How many threes make twenty-seven?', they should not find it too difficult to give meanings to the divisions shown in the first step of stage **a)** above. For example, $1 \div \frac{1}{4}$ can be thought of as, 'How many quarters make one whole?' They should quickly be able to give the answer, four.

In the same way, $2 \div \frac{1}{3}$ can be thought of as, 'How many thirds make two wholes?' Knowing that three thirds make one whole, the children can give the answer, six. From many examples of this kind the children should begin to see that they can quickly give the answer to a division of a whole number by a fraction with 1 as its numerator. Even for a division such as $19 \div \frac{1}{15}$ they should be able to give the answer, 19×15 (i.e. 285). This is an important step as it introduces the use of multiplication in finding the answer to a division by a fraction.

The first two examples in step *ii)* of stage **a)** are straightforward if the right kind of language is used. For example, $\frac{1}{2} \div \frac{1}{4}$ should be thought of as, 'How many quarters make one half?' The third example, $\frac{1}{2} \div \frac{1}{3}$, should be discussed fully. There are various ways in which the answer to 'How many thirds make one half?' can be found. These are given below.

1 Three thirds make one whole. So $1\frac{1}{2}$ thirds make one half.

2 Change both fractions to sixths. The division is now $\frac{3}{6} \div \frac{2}{6}$. This can be thought of as 'How many *two*-sixths in *three*-sixths. The answer is $1\frac{1}{2}$.

3 By drawing a diagram such as:

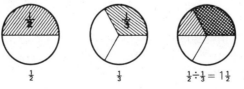

$\frac{1}{2}$ $\qquad\qquad$ $\frac{1}{3}$ $\qquad\qquad$ $\frac{1}{2} \div \frac{1}{3} = 1\frac{1}{2}$

When children are confident in dividing by a fraction with 1 as its numerator they can go on to discuss divisions such as $3 \div \frac{3}{4}$. The starting-point is the known result $3 \div \frac{1}{4} = 12$. In words this can be expressed as, 'There are twelve quarters in three wholes'. We need to find how many *three*-quarters make three wholes. This we can do by dividing 12 by 3. A diagram such as the one below might help to understand this approach.

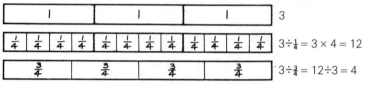

$3 \div \frac{1}{4} = 3 \times 4 = 12$

$3 \div \frac{3}{4} = 12 \div 3 = 4$

When the children have done several examples of this type, in which the answer is a whole number, it is helpful to discuss a set of divisions such as:

$$4 \div \frac{1}{5} \qquad 4 \div \frac{2}{5} \qquad 4 \div \frac{3}{5} \qquad 4 \div \frac{4}{5}$$

Using diagrams these can be shown as:

$4 \div \frac{1}{5} = 4 \times 5 = 20$

$4 \div \frac{2}{5} = \frac{20}{2} = 10$

$4 \div \frac{3}{5} = \frac{20}{3} = 6\frac{2}{3}$

$4 \div \frac{4}{5} = \frac{20}{4} = 5$

The answer to each of these divisions is clearly seen from the diagram except for $4 \div \frac{3}{5}$. For this division there is not a whole number of three-fifths. The two-fifths at the end of the diagram do not form a complete three-fifths. There are only two fifths instead of three. Together they form two-thirds of three-fifths. So the answer to $4 \div \frac{3}{5}$ is $6\frac{2}{3}$. This kind of fractional answer needs much discussion.

Children should have plenty of practice in dealing with sets of divisions such as the one shown for fifths above. From these they should gradually see that they can quickly write down the answer to any division by a fraction. For example, the answer to $8 \div \frac{5}{6}$ is obtained by first multiplying 8 by 6 and then dividing the result by 5.

This can be shown as $\frac{8 \times 6}{5}$ or as $8 \times \frac{6}{5}$. This leads to a working rule such as, 'To divide by a fraction we invert the fraction and multiply (instead of dividing)'.

When this is fully understood division by a mixed number is straight-forward. The mixed number is changed to a fractional form and the division is done in the same way as before.

Operations with decimal fractions

Operations with decimal fractions are less complicated than those with common fractions (which are sometimes called vulgar fractions). The methods used are extensions of those used for whole numbers. To understand these extensions, however, and to be able to use them children must:

a) understand place-value and its extension to decimal fractions;

b) understand the decimal notation;

c) be confident in dealing with operations involving whole numbers;

d) know the addition, subtraction, multiplication, and division facts.

Weaknesses in any of these aspects of number work will result in lack of success in using operations with decimal fractions.

1 Addition and subtraction

Measuring activities can form a good introduction to addition and subtraction with decimal tenths. Two examples are given below.

a) Two lines are drawn, as shown. The length of each is measured, in centimetres and millimetres. The measurements are shown on the drawing, as in the example, and questions are asked such as:

4.7cm

6.2cm

i) What is the total length of the two lines?

ii) What is the difference between the lengths of the two lines?

Various ways of finding the total length should be discussed and set down, as below.

cm	mm		mm		cm
4	7		47		4.7
+ 6	2		+ 62		+ 6.2
10	9		109		10.9

The children should understand each of these forms and should be able to move easily from one to another.

In this example no carrying from the tenths is necessary but examples should be provided in which this does occur, as below.

cm	mm		mm		cm
5	8		58		5.8
+ 7	6		+ 76		+ 7.6
13	4		134		13.4

The various ways of finding the difference between the lengths of the two
line segments need to be fully discussed (e.g. adding on, subtraction). When
subtraction is used the working should be shown in various ways, as for
addition.

cm	mm		mm		cm
6	2		62		6.2
− 4	7		− 47		− 4.7
1	5		15		1.5

Note: In each of these subtractions of measures the same method that
was introduced and used for numbers should be used for dealing with the
'2 − 7' step. If 'decomposition' is used with numbers it should be used with
measures. Using a mixture of methods will confuse the children. To many
of us the advantages of decomposition are even more clearly seen when we
come to deal with measures.

b) A stop-watch is used to measure the times taken by two children to run
a given distance. These times are recorded in seconds and tenths of seconds.
They are then used for additions and subtractions as for the lengths of the
two line segments. For example:

seconds	tenths		tenths		seconds
21	4		214		21.4
− 19	8		− 198		− 19.8
1	6		16		1.6

When addition and subtraction with tenths and hundredths are introduced,
as much use as possible should be made of activities involving money. It
might be necessary, however, to discuss in more detail the way in which the
decimal notation is used for money. For example, many children will think
of £2.45 as 2 pounds 45 pence. They might not have thought of it as 2
1-pound bank notes, 4 10-pence coins, and 5 1-pence coins. They will also
need to understand that the value of a 10-pence coin is 1-tenth of the value
of a 1-pound note.

2 Multiplication and division

To understand multiplication and division with decimals and to be competent
in their calculations, children must be able to multiply and divide by 10,
100, 1000, etc. Without this ability they will find it very difficult to understand what they are doing.

From their work with whole numbers the children should already
know that when a whole number is *multiplied* by 10 the same digits appear

in the answer but each is one place to the left. A zero is put in the empty *units* column.

For division by 10 we need to show that a kind of opposite movement takes place. That is, when a number is *divided* by 10 the same digits appear in the answer but each is one place to the right.

Similar results also need to be established for multiplication and division by 100 and then by 1000.

We should remember the importance of these special multiplications and divisions when we come to them in our teaching.

We now look at each of these operations (multiplication and division) in more detail.

Multiplication

An outline of the suggested stages and steps is given below, with examples.

Stage a)   Multiplication of a decimal number by a whole number

Step i)   Multiplication by a single digit number.

e.g. 2.3 x 6   0.9 x 7   12.8 x 5   206.4 x 9
      2.36 x 6   0.92 x 7   12.87 x 5   206.43 x 9

Step ii)   Multiplication by 10.

e.g. 2.6 x 10   56.7 x 10   0.8 x 10   674.1 x 10
      2.64 x 10   56.78 x 10   0.83 x 10   674.17 x 10

Step iii)   Multiplicatiqn by a 2-digit number.

e.g. 3.4 x 14   4.2 x 24   0.6 x 35   219.3 x 62
      3.46 x 14   4.27 x 24   0.69 x 35   219.32 x 62

For the first step an example such as 2.3 x 6 should be discussed and set down in two ways as shown below. The first uses place-value and column headings. The second uses place-value without column headings. The multiplication 0.3 x 6 can be thought of as 3-tenths x 6. This gives 18-tenths. That is, 1 whole and 8-tenths. This is written as 1.8.

```
        T U t
          2 3                              2.3
    x     6                        x       6
        ------                            ------
        1 2      (2   x 6)           12       (2   x 6)
          1 8    (0.3 x 6)            1.8     (0.3 x 6)
        ------                            ------
        1 3 8    (2.3 x 6)           13.8     (2.3 x 6)
```

When the children have done many examples like this and understand the method used, they can go on to an example such as 2.36 x 6. Again the working should be set down in two ways as below.

```
  T U t  h
    2 3 6                                    2.36
 x    6                                  x     6
  ───────                                ─────────
    1 2      (2    x 6)                      12      (2    x 6)
      1 8    (0.3  x 6)                      1.8     (0.3  x 6)
        3 6  (0.06 x 6)                      0.36    (0.06 x 6)
  ───────                                ─────────
    1 4 1 6  (2.36 x 6)                    14.16     (2.36 x 6)
  ═══════                                ═════════
```

The new step in this example is 0.06 x 6. Thinking of 0.06 as 6-hundredths, this give 36-hundredths. These can be changed to 30-hundredths and 6-hundredths. The 30-hundredths are then changed to 3-tenths. So 0.06 x 6 is equal to 0.36.

Many examples like this should be discussed. For each it is essential that the working should be set down neatly with each numeral in its correct place.

The working for 2.36 x 6 can, of course, be done in the order shown below. This order is helpful when the working is set down in a shorter form, as shown. Practice in using this shorter form is necessary at this stage, as it is used when multiplication by 2-digit numbers is introduced.

```
    2.36                                      2.36
 x    6                                    x    6
  ────────                                 ─────────
     .36    (0.06 x 6)                        14.16
    1.8     (0.3  x 6)
   12       (2    x 6)
  ────────
   14.16    (2.36 x 6)
  ════════
```

Multiplication by 10 can be introduced by discussing in detail the two examples below. For each the working is set down as for multiplication by a 1-digit whole number.

```
    3.7                                       3.74
 x 10                                      x 10
  ──────                                   ────────
   30       (3    x 10)                      30       (3    x 10)
    7       (0.7  x 10)                        7      (0.7  x 10)
  ──────                                        .4    (0.04 x 10)
   37       (3.7  x 10)                    ────────
  ══════                                     37.4     (3.74 x 10)
                                           ════════
```

The multiplication 0.7 x 10 can be done by thinking of 0.7 as seven-tenths. Multiplying this by 10 gives 70-tenths, that is, 7 units.

It can also be shown as: $\frac{7}{10} \times 10 = \frac{70}{10}$

$$= 7$$

In the same way, $0.04 \times 10 = \frac{4}{100} \times 10$

$$= \frac{40}{100}$$

$$= \frac{4}{10}$$

$$= 0.4$$

After many examples like these the children should see that when a decimal number is multipled by 10 the same digits appear in the answer but each is one place to the left. (This is the same 'rule' as the one we use with whole numbers.)

Multiplication by 2-digit numbers between 10 and 20 should then be discussed. Two examples are shown on the right. From these it will be seen that it is necessary to be able to:

	3.4		3.46	
	x 14		x 14	
	34	(3.4 x 10)	34.6	(3.46 x 10)
	13.6	(3.4 x 4)	13.84	(3.46 x 4)
	47.6	(3.4 x 14)	48.44	(3.46 x 14)

a) multiply by 10;

b) multiply by a 1-digit number and set down the working in the short form.

Before going on to multiplication by other 2-digit numbers, multiplication by 20, 30, 40, etc. needs to be looked at again. The children dealt with these multiplications earlier with whole numbers, but they might need reminding that, for example, to multiply by 20, they can:

    either multiply by 2 and then by 10

    or   first multiply by 10 and then by 2.

Examples such as 9.4 x 20, 3.7 x 30, 32.6 x 40, 62.85 x 60, etc. should be discussed and the working shown.

A multiplication such as that shown on the right can now be introduced and discussed. When this is understood the children should do many other examples, such as those shown in *Step iii*) on page 225.

	4.7	
x	23	
	94	(4.7 x 20)
	14.1	(4.7 x 3)
	108.1	(4.7 x 23)

Stage b) Multiplication by a decimal number (with tenths only)

e.g. 4.3 x 1.6   8.9 x 5.8   0.7 x 8.3   67.4 x 21.7
      4.37 x 1.6   8.98 x 5.8   0.75 x 8.3   67.44 x 21.7

Multiplication by a number such as 2.3 can be done by first multiplying by 2, then by 0.3, and adding the two results. This involves the new idea of multiplying by 0.3. To do this we can think of 0.3 as $\frac{3}{10}$ and find the result of the multiplication by first dividing by 10 and then multiplying by 3 (*or* by first multiplying by 3 and then dividing by 10). But an alternative method, described below, is also helpful, especially as it gives a direct lead to the quick method children will later use for multiplying by decimal numbers. This method makes use of the children's knowledge of ways of calculating the area of a rectangle.

A rectangle is drawn on cm/mm graph paper, as shown. Ways of calculating its area, in cm², are then discussed. Using millimetres, the area is 43 x 29 mm². Using centimetres, the area is 4.3 x 2.9 cm² or $4\frac{3}{10} \times 2\frac{9}{10}$ cm².

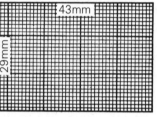

The working for these multiplications is shown below.

Using cm

$4.3 \times 2.9 = 4\frac{3}{10} \times 2\frac{9}{10}$

$= \frac{43}{10} \times \frac{29}{10}$

$= \frac{43 \times 29}{100}$

$= \frac{1247}{100}$

$= 12\frac{47}{100}$

$= 12.47$

Area $= 12.47$ cm²

Using mm

43
x 29
―――
860
387
―――
1247
―――

Area $= 1247$ mm²

$= \frac{1247}{100}$ cm²

$= 12\frac{47}{100}$ cm²

$= 12.47$ cm²

Looking at these two ways of working the children should see that they can find the value of 4.3 x 2.9 by first multiplying 43 by 29 and then dividing the result by 100.

Many other examples of the same kind should be worked in these two ways. For each the children should see that they can multiply as for whole numbers and then divide by 100.

Stage c) **Multiplication by a decimal number (with tenths and hundredths only)**

e.g. 5.8 $\times$ 2.48   9.4 $\times$ 6.95   0 3 $\times$ 21.69   84.4 $\times$ 36.93
5.89 $\times$ 2.48   9.41 $\times$ 6.95   0.38 $\times$ 21.69   84.07 $\times$ 36.93

To introduce stage **c)** a multiplication such as 5.8 $\times$ 2.48 is discussed with the children. The setting down of the working is shown below.

$$5.8 \times 2.48 = 5\tfrac{8}{10} \times 2\tfrac{48}{100}$$
$$= \tfrac{58}{10} \times \tfrac{248}{100}$$
$$= \tfrac{58 \times 248}{1000}$$
$$= \tfrac{14384}{1000}$$
$$= 14.384$$

```
   248
 ×  58
 12400
  1984
 14384
```

The changing of $\tfrac{384}{1000}$ to a decimal form might need to be discussed. One way of doing this is to write the fraction as:

$$\tfrac{300}{1000} + \tfrac{80}{1000} + \tfrac{4}{1000}$$

These fractions can be changed to

$$\tfrac{3}{10} + \tfrac{8}{100} + \tfrac{4}{1000}$$

i.e. 0.3 + 0.08 + 0.004.

So, $\tfrac{384}{1000}$ = 0.384

Many children will see this changing, however, as an extension of the changing of, for example, $\tfrac{67}{100}$ to 0.67, which was discussed in detail in an earlier chapter.

For the multiplication (5.8 $\times$ 2.48) the answer to 58 $\times$ 248 is first found. The result is then divided by 1000.

The reason for dividing by 1000 in this example, instead of by 100 as in the earlier examples, should be discussed. In 5.8 there are tenths, so there is a 10 at the bottom of the fraction. In 2.48 there are tenths and hundredths so there is a 100 at the bottom of the fraction. So we have 10 $\times$ 100, which is 1000, in the denominator of the fraction.

When they have done other examples such as 5.89 $\times$ 2.48 the children should begin to notice that if they count the number of digits after the decimal point in each of the two numbers in a multiplication and add them, the result gives the number of digits after the decimal point in the answer to the multiplication. This leads to a quick way of doing a multiplication which involves decimal fractions. For example, for 56.8 $\times$ 34.96, the quick way is:

a) multiply 568 by 3496   (1 985 728);

b) count the number of digits after the decimal point in each of the two numbers and add the two results $(1 + 2 = 3)$;

c) insert a decimal point in the answer so that there are 3 digits after the decimal point.

The answer is 1 985.728.

It should be emphasized that this working rule should emerge from the children's own experiences and their own thinking. The children should *not* be given the rule and told to use it without understanding.

It must also be emphasized that *before* children start to find the answer to a multiplication in which decimal fractions appear they should look at the two numbers and quickly work out an approximate answer.
For example:

$$1.9 \times 2.1 \quad \approx \quad 2 \times 2$$
$$\approx \quad 4$$

$$8.4 \times 0.2 \quad \approx \quad 8 \times \tfrac{2}{10}$$
$$\approx \quad \tfrac{16}{10}$$
$$\approx \quad 1.6$$

$$7.85 \times 0.9 \quad \approx \quad 8 \times 1$$
$$\approx \quad 8$$

$$86.67 \times 0.89 \approx 87 \times 0.9$$
$$\approx 87 \times \tfrac{9}{10}$$
$$\approx \tfrac{783}{10}$$
$$\approx 78.3$$
$$\approx 78$$

The children will then be able to check that their calculated answer is sensible. This will help to avoid errors arising from putting the decimal point in the wrong position.

Stage d)   Extensions of a), b), and c)   Multiplication by 100. Then by a 3-digit number. Multiplication by a decimal number (with tenths, hundredths, and thousandths).

The stages in the multiplication of decimals discussed in **a)**, **b)**, and **c)** are probably more than enough for most children in primary schools. If there is a real need to extend the work, however, this should cause no difficulties provided the children understand what they have done so far.

Division

The use of decimals to give the answer to a division by a 1-digit number (e.g. $27 \div 4$) was introduced and discussed on page 208. At that stage the examples were chosen so that for each division there was an exact answer. Division by a 1-digit number for which there is not an exact answer now needs to be introduced. This leads to the idea of a recurring decimal (an understanding of this idea is essential when changing common fractions to decimal fractions). When division by any 1-digit whole number is understood there should be no difficulty in extending the work to division by

2-digit and 3-digit numbers.

The special results obtained from divisions by 10, 100, and 1000 then need to be discussed. This can lead to a helpful working rule.

The children should now be ready for the introduction of ways of dealing with a divsion by a decimal number (e.g. division by 1.2, 2.6, 0.8).

There are obviously several important ideas and techniques to be introduced in this section. Suitable stages and steps are listed below.

Stage a) **Divisions by a whole number for which there is not an exact decimal answer**

e.g. $13 \div 3 = 4.3333 \ldots \ldots$

$17 \div 6 = 2.8333 \ldots \ldots$

$19 \div 7 = 2.714285 \ldots \ldots$

The first of these two examples should be done on the blackboard with the children, as below.

```
      4.3333
   3 )13
      12
      __
       10      (tenths)
        9
       __
        10     (hundredths)
         9
        __
         10    (thousandths)
          9
         __
          10   (ten thousandths)
           9
          __
           1
```

The children quickly see that the division goes on and on. Explain that the decimal part of the answer is called a recurring decimal. The 3 recurs. To avoid writing down many threes a special notation is used. We write:

$4.3333 \ldots \ldots$ as $4.\dot{3}$

The dot over the 3 tells us that the 3 recurs. The children then do other divisions for which there is a recurring answer. For example:

$19 \div 9 = 2.1111 \ldots \ldots \quad (2.\dot{1})$

$16 \div 6 = 2.6666 \ldots \ldots \quad (2.\dot{6})$

$20 \div 9 = 2.2222 \ldots \ldots \quad (2.\dot{2})$

For each of them the children show the answer in the short form. The division $17 \div 6$ is now worked and discussed with the children. The way of showing the recurring 3 in the answer needs to be explained carefully ($17 \div 6 = 2.8\dot{3}$).

The division $19 \div 7$ can also be worked with the children, and the way of showing the answer in a short form when several digits recur can be introduced ($19 \div 7 = 2.\dot{7}1428\dot{5}$, the dots above the 7 and the 5 indicating that all the six digits from the 7 to the 5 recur). However the main purpose at this stage is to introduce children to decimal answers which do not terminate. There is a danger of confusing the children if too much is done on recurring decimals.

What is more important is that the children should be introduced to ways of writing decimals (both terminating and non-terminating) to a specified number of places. The use of a practical situation helps in explaining the idea. For example: 'A piece of thin wire, 100 cm long, is cut into seven equal pieces. How long is each?'

By division the children find that $100 \div 7 = 14.2857 \ldots \ldots$
That is, the length of each piece is $14.2857 \ldots \ldots$ cm.
The '2' represents 2-tenths of a cm. That is, 2 mm.
The '8' represents 8-hundredths of a cm. That is, 0.8 mm.
For practical purposes we need to go no further. In fact it is generally sufficient for our purpose to give the result to the nearest millimetre. In this case the length to the nearest millimetre is 14.3 cm (since 2.8 mm is nearer to 3 mm than to 2 mm). An example like this provides a reason for using only the first few digits after the decimal point.

The children need practice in writing a decimal fraction to a specified number of places. For example:

$$14.2857 \ldots \ldots = 14.3 \quad \text{(to 1 place)}$$
$$14.2857 \ldots \ldots = 14.29 \quad \text{(to 2 places)}$$
$$14.2857 \ldots \ldots = 14.286 \quad \text{(to 3 places).}$$

The idea of increasing the last digit required by one if the number following is 5, or more, will need to be discussed.

Stage b)   Changing a common fraction to a decimal fraction

Step i) The link between a fraction and a division.   As teachers we know that we can change a fraction such as $\frac{3}{8}$ to a decimal fraction by dividing 3 by 8. But this is not obvious to children. It needs to be discussed.

The explanation should be kept simple. It does not help to over-explain. A simple approach is to draw a strip on the blackboward as below.

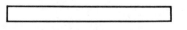

COMMON AND DECIMAL FRACTIONS: THE FOUR OPERATIONS

Then say, 'I am going to divide this strip into five equal parts. How can I show what I am going to do?' After discussion write $1 \div 5$ on the blackboard.
Mark the strip as shown.

Ask, 'What fraction of the whole is each part?' (1-fifth)
Show this:

Discuss the relationship between $1 \div 5$ and $\frac{1}{5}$.
That is, $1 \div 5 = \frac{1}{5}$.
(The children should already know this result but they may not have seen it shown in this form.)
Now draw two strips as below.

2 wholes

Divide these into five equal parts and show as:

$2 \div 5$

Also show as:

$\frac{2}{5}$

The shaded part shows $2 \div 5$.
It is also $\frac{2}{5}$ of one strip.
So $2 \div 5 = \frac{2}{5}$.
In the same way $3 \div 5 = \frac{3}{5}$ and $4 \div 5 = \frac{4}{5}$.
    From this example (and others if necessary) the children see that, for example, the fraction $\frac{2}{5}$ is the value of $2 \div 5$.

Step ii) Changing a common fraction to a decimal fraction.   Using the example in step *i)* the children start with $\frac{2}{5}$ and change it to $2 \div 5$.
They divide 2 by 5 as shown and obtain the result 0.4. They repeat this changing for $\frac{3}{5}$ and $\frac{4}{5}$.

$$5 \overline{\smash{)}2\,0} \quad \text{(tenths)}$$
$$\,0.4$$
$$2\,0$$

    Now discuss, for example, the fraction $\frac{3}{8}$. The children make use of the previous examples and decide that this is linked to the division $3 \div 8$ (if necessary, this can be demonstrated by dividing 3 strips into 8 equal parts).

The division is then done,
as shown. The children
write the result as:

$$\frac{3}{8} = 3 \div 8$$

$$= 0.375$$

Several other fractions
should be dealt with in
this way (in some of
these, recurring decimals will appear).

$$\begin{array}{r} 0.375 \\ 5\overline{\smash{)}3\ 0} \\ 2\ 4 \\ \hline 60 \\ 56 \\ \hline 40 \\ 40 \\ \hline \end{array}$$

(tenths)

(hundredths)

(thousandths)

Stage c)   Division by 10   Division by 10 (and later, by 100, 1000, etc.) is
very important in dealing with decimals.
    Division by 10 can be introduced using, for example, the division
$75 \div 10$. The working can be shown in two ways.

$$\begin{array}{r} 7.5 \\ 10\overline{\smash{)}75} \\ 70 \\ \hline 50 \\ 50 \\ \hline \\ \hline \end{array}$$

(tenths)

$$75 \div 10 = 7\frac{5}{10}$$

$$= 7.5$$

Several examples like this should be done by the children (e.g. $84 \div 10$,
$69 \div 10$, $137 \div 10$, etc.).
An example such as $27.3 \div 10$ can then be discussed.

$$\begin{array}{r} 2.73 \\ 10\overline{\smash{)}27.3} \\ 20 \\ \hline 73 \\ 70 \\ \hline 30 \\ 30 \\ \hline \\ \hline \end{array}$$

(tenths)

(hundredths)

From this and many other examples of the same kind (including examples
such as $15.37 \div 10$) the children begin to see that when a number is divided
by 10 the same digits appear in the answer but each is one place to the right.

For example, $27.3 \div 10 = 2.73$

$2.73 \div 10 = 0.273$

$0.273 \div 10 = 0.0273$

It might be helpful at this stage to remind the children of what they found out about multiplication by 10.

e.g.

$27 \times 10 = 270$

$2.7 \times 10 = 27$

$0.27 \times 10 = 2.7$

$0.027 \times 10 = 0.27$

Stage d)   Dividing by a decimal number   We, as teachers, know that we deal with a division such as $1.82 \div 1.3$ by multiplying both the 1.82 and the 1.3 by 10. This changes the division to $18.2 \div 13$. We now have to divide by 13 and this we can do. We need to think very carefully about how we can best introduce this idea to children.

One way of doing this is to write down a set of simple divisions such as: $6 \div 2$ $12 \div 4$ $24 \div 8$ $48 \div 16$ $96 \div 32$
The children find that the answer to each of these is 3. They then look at the numbers in the divisions and say what they notice. Most children will quickly say that as they go from one division to the next on its right, each of the two numbers in the division is doubled (multiplied by 2). Some of the children will also see that the two numbers in the third division ($24 \div 8$) can be obtained by multiplying each of the two numbers in the first division ($6 \div 2$) by 4. Others will notice multiplication by 8 ($48 \div 16$) and by 16 ($96 \div 32$).

Other sets of divisions which all have the same answer are then discussed in the same way.

A division such as $10 \div 2$ is now written on the blackboard and each child writes down a set of other divisions which have the same answer. This is repeated for further divisions.

From these activities the children begin to see that the answer to a division is unchanged if both the numbers of the division are multiplied by the same number.

Another approach which can be used is to link a division with a fraction. For example $6 \div 2$ and $\frac{6}{2}$ both have the same value. The first can be thought of as 'How many twos make six?', the second as '*Six* halves'. These both have the same value—three. Examples like this help the children to understand why a division such as $128 \div 16$ can be written as $\frac{128}{16}$.

A division such as $1.2 \div 0.4$ is now discussed. The children know how to divide by a whole number so if the 0.4 were changed to 4 they could do the division. This they can do by multiplying the 0.4 by 10. At the same time they *must* multiply the 1.2 by 10. So the division is changed to 12 ÷ 4.

This changing of the division can also be illustrated by using the fractional form $\frac{1.2}{0.4}$. Knowing that the value of a fraction is unchanged if both the top and bottom numbers are multiplied by the same number, the children will see that multiplication by 10 changes $\frac{1.2}{0.4}$ to $\frac{12}{4}$.

From this and other examples the children should begin to understand the method used for division by a decimal number.

The first step in divisions such as 27 ÷ 0.3, 15.9 ÷ 1.5, 2.345 ÷ 7.9, etc. is to change the divisor to a whole number by multiplying *both* numbers in the division by 10.

For divisions such as 24.76 ÷ 2.45, 60 ÷ 3.02, 1.462 ÷ 0.56, etc. the first step is to change the divisor to a whole number by multiplying *both* numbers in the division by 100.

When the divisor has been changed to a whole number the division follows the usual pattern.

During this stage division by 100 and 1000 can be discussed. For each a simple working rule can be formulated. These should be compared with the working rules for multiplying by 100 and by 1000.

Summary

When a child has worked through the stages and steps in this chapter and has had plenty of practice, he or she should:

understand	the ways in which the four operations are used with common fractions and decimal fractions
	the quick method for multiplying and dividing by 10, 100, 1000, etc.
	the idea of a division which does not have an exact answer
	the idea of writing a decimal fraction to a specified number of places
be able to	use the four operations with common and decimal fractions
	write a decimal fraction to a specified number of places
	change a common fraction to a decimal fraction.

Thinking about π

More than 2000 years ago men discovered a relationship between the circumference and the diameter of a circle. They used it in designing their buildings. At first they used the approximate relationship:

$$C = D \times 3$$

Then more exact relationships were used, such as:

$$C = D \times 3\tfrac{10}{71}$$

For centuries people tried to find the correct value of the fraction. But they did not succeed, and when they used decimals they found that the decimal did not terminate, but went on and on. For example, they found that:

$$C = D \times 3.141\ 592\ 653\ 589\ 793\ 238\ 46 \quad \cdots \cdots$$

With a computer the number has now been found to thousands of places of decimals.

To avoid such complicated decimals, a symbol is used for the number. The symbol is π. It is called **pi**.

Using π, the relationship is: $\qquad C = D \times \pi$

This can be written as: $\qquad\qquad C = \pi \times D$

More briefly, this is written: $\qquad C = \pi D$

For everyday calculations, 3.14 is often used for π ($\pi \approx 3.14$).

As $0.14 \approx \tfrac{1}{7}$, the value $3\tfrac{1}{7}$ is sometimes used for π ($\pi \approx 3\tfrac{1}{7}$).

Using r for the radius, we can write:

$$D = 2r$$

So the relationship $C = \pi D$ becomes:

$$C = \pi \times (2r)$$

This can be written as:

$$C = 2\pi r$$

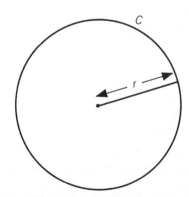

Chapter 21

Measuring and measures: all the measures

Length·(kilometres; perimeters; circumference of a circle). Area (use of grids; areas of irregular shapes; use of cm^2; conservation of area; areas of triangles, parallelograms, and circles; ares and hectares). Volume and capacity (volume of irregular objects; volumes of cubes and cuboids; volumes of prisms and cylinders; litres and millilitres). Time (the 24-hour clock). Angles (a complete turn; fractions of a turn; direction; degrees; measuring angles; acute, obtuse, and reflex angles; angle sum of a triangle). Mass (kilograms and grams).

Before reading this chapter it might be helpful to look again at 'Thinking about standard measures' on page 140. For convenience, the various aspects of measures (length, area, etc.) are dealt with in turn in this chapter. But it should not be assumed that each should be completed before going on to another. For example, the many activities on area should be spread over the last two or three years in the primary school.

Length

1 The kilometre

The introduction of the use of metres and centimetres was discussed in Chapter 15. It was also suggested that the millimetre should be introduced when the need arose to measure more accurately or to measure small lengths.

When the unit for longer lengths is introduced it should be remembered that the idea of a kilometre can be very unreal to children unless they themselves have marked out, along a path or road, a length of 1 kilometre. This can be done in various ways. For example, the children could use a piece of string of length 25 m. Forty of these lengths along a road give 1 kilometre. A child could also find how many strides he takes, in covering a marked length of 100 m on the compound or along a path. Multiplication of this number by 10 gives the number of strides for 1 kilometre. If a child now makes this number of strides along a road he will have, at least, some idea of a kilometre. He or she will remember the activity and will think about it when dealing with other activities which bring in kilometres.

2 Perimeters of shapes with straight edges

The idea of the perimeter of a shape is not difficult for children to understand. The mathematically interesting aspect of the topic is the various ways in which the perimeter of a rectangle can be found. For example, the perimeter of the rectangle below can be calculated from:

a) $5 + 3 + 5 + 3$

b) $(5 + 3) \times 2$

c) $(5 \times 2) + (3 \times 2)$

5cm

3cm

Each of these should be discussed and the more able children can go on to write down the perimeter when letters are used for numbers. For the rectangle shown, the perimeter in cm can be written as:

a) $l + w + l + w$

b) $(l + w) \times 2$

c) $(l \times 2) + (w \times 2)$

l cm

w cm

3 The circumference of a circle

The introduction and the use of π in finding the circumference of a circle is an important step for children. It brings in for the first time a fraction which cannot be written either as a common fraction or as an exact or recurring decimal fraction. To avoid possible confusion we need to think carefully about the way in which we introduce this new idea. We must not go into too much detailed explanation but at the same time we must make clear that the numerical values we use for π are only approximate. These values are usually, however, good enough for the purpose for which we use them.

As far as possible the children should build up their ideas of π through their own activities. For these they need a good supply of objects such as cylindrical tins, plates, bicycle wheels, coins, buckets, etc. For each of these they measure the diameter and the circumference of the circles which form part of them.

The *diameter* of a circle can be measured by:

a) moving a ruler across the circle until the maximum measurement is obtained;

b) placing the circular object between two books standing upright on a table, and measuring the distance between the books;

c) using calipers, as shown below.

Method (c) usually gives the most accurate measurement.

The *circumference* can be measured by:

a) Using the method shown in the diagram below.

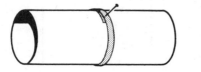

This involves wrapping a strip of paper around the circular object, leaving an overlap. A pin is pushed through the overlap.

The strip is then laid flat on a table and the distance between the two pin-holes measured.

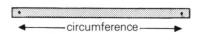

This distance gives the circumference of the circle. Some children, however, may not immediately see the connection between this distance and the circumference. To demonstrate that the two lengths are the same, the strip should be cut at the pin holes, and then wrapped again around the circular object. The two ends of the strip should just meet.

b) Wrapping a piece of string or thread several times around the circular object. The length of the string is measured and then divided by the number of complete turns it made around the object.

c) Rolling the circular object along the ground, in the way described below.

i) Stand the object on a straight line marked on the floor.

ii) Mark, with chalk, the object and the floor where they touch.

iii) Roll the object along the line until the chalk mark again touches the floor.

iv) Measure the distance between the two chalk marks on the floor. This length is the circumference of the circle.

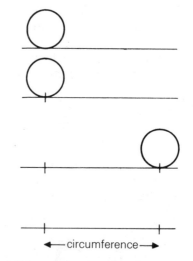

Using methods such as these, the children measure the diameter and the circumference of many circular objects, and list the results. For each pair of results they divide the circumference by the diameter. They find that the answer to each division is a little more than 3. The children should then use the value of 3 to find the approximate value of the circumferences of other circles, by measuring the diameter and multiplying by 3. They should understand, however, that the answers obtained are not exact; the actual value of each circumference will be a little more than the calculated value.

At this stage the fraction which has to be added to the 3 needs to be discussed. A short account, as in 'Thinking about π', of the way in which men have tried to deal with this difficulty may interest the children and help them to understand why the symbol π was introduced.

We need to be careful to introduce 3.14 as the value of π to 2 places of decimals before using the value of $3\frac{1}{7}$. If the latter is introduced first children will think of it as the exact value. They will then think of 3.14 as a decimal approximation of $3\frac{1}{7}$.

Area

1 Areas of irregular shapes

When asked what they understand by *area* many adults can think only of a rectangle (with *length multiplied by width*) or of a half-forgotten formula about the area of a circle. This seems to be a poor return for the many hours they spent on the topic at school. We need to give a better understanding of the idea of area and to avoid introducing rules too quickly or too early.

One way of doing this is to use duplicated grids of squares, rectangles, triangles, and other shapes. For example, each child is provided with a duplicated sheet on which shapes are drawn on a grid of rectangles, as below.

The children answer questions such as:

a) Which of the shapes are the same size?
b) Which is the largest shape?
c) Which is the smallest shape?
d) How many times bigger than A is:
  i) B?   ii) C?   iii) D?   iv) E?

Here is another example for which the children answer the same questions.

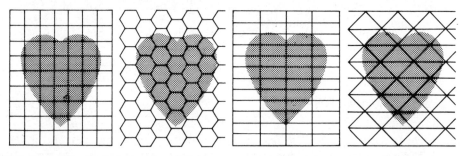

A duplicated sheet is then provided for each child on which the same shape is drawn on four different grids, as below.

For the grid of triangles the children count the number of whole triangles covered by the shape and then discuss how to deal with the *parts* of, triangles. They estimate how many whole triangles these parts would make. Then they write down the number of triangles altogether.

  The children repeat this activity for each of the other three grids. They discuss their four answers and also decide which of the four grids is the easiest to use. (Usually they say the grid of squares is the easiest.)

  It might also be helpful to discuss the following method for dealing with parts of shapes:

  If the part is less than a half, ignore it;

  If the part is greater than a half, count it as a whole shape.

Using this method the children should quickly repeat their counting for each grid to see what differences, if any, there are in their results.

  Another helpful activity is to provide each child with two leaves (of about the same area) as in the example below.

Sycamore leaf Peach leaf

The children are asked to say which is the larger of the two leaves. Some will choose the peach leaf as it is longer than the sycamore leaf. Some will choose the sycamore leaf as it is wider than the peach leaf. Other children may suggest measuring the perimeter of each leaf to see which is the longer. Some children, of course, will realize that it is the surface of each leaf which has to be measured. Discuss ways of doing this. Lead to the idea of placing each leaf on a grid of squares and drawing around it. Then the number of squares covered by each leaf can be counted and the two numbers compared.

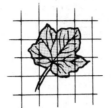

If a grid of centimetre squares is used for these activities then the idea of *a square centimetre* can be introduced as the amount of space covered by one of the squares. The symbol, cm^2, can also be introduced. The children should be provided with many activities which involve the use of a grid of squares in finding area. To make the checking of the children's results easier, sheets on which shapes are drawn on a grid can be prepared and duplicated. An example is shown below.

The children will soon discover that there are quick ways of counting the squares for a rectangle such as the one on the sheet. Instead of counting them one by one they will find that if they count the number in a row and then the number of rows, then the total number of squares can be found by multiplying the first number by the second. This will eventually lead to the idea of multiplying the number of centimetres in the length by the number in the width, but the introduction of a rule should not be necessary at this stage.

2 Conservation of area

During these many activities the teacher should try to make sure that the children understand the important idea of the conservation of area. One way of illustrating this is to provide each child with a supply of paper 1 cm squares. With these the child makes a variety of shapes using the same number of squares for each. For example, using eight squares, shapes such as those shown below can be made. The children should realize that the area of each of the shapes is 8 cm².

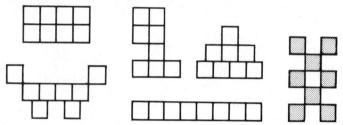

Half-squares can also be used for making shapes such as:

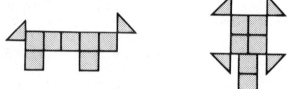

Again the children should be able to say that the area of each shape is 8 cm².

3 Quick ways of finding the areas of common shapes

When the children have a good understanding of the idea of area and the conservation of area, they can go on to establish quick ways of finding the areas of other common shapes such as a triangle, a parallelogram, and a circle. Some activities for each of these are given below.

a) The area of a triangle

1   The children draw a rectangle with the length and width each a whole number of centimetres (the use of squared paper is helpful). They find the area of the rectangle.
A diagonal is drawn, as shown. The rectangle is then cut out, and the two triangles formed by cutting along the diagonal are placed one on top of the other to show that they are the same size. The idea that the area of each of the two triangles is one half of the area of the rectangle is discussed.

2   The children draw a right-angled triangle on 1 cm squared paper, as in the example on the right. The two dotted lines are drawn to form a rectangle. The area of the rectangle is found and, by dividing the result by two, the area of the triangle is calculated.

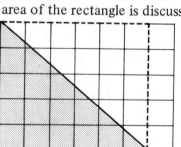

3 When the children have done several examples, as in Activity 2, they should have built up the idea of finding the area of a right-angled triangle by multiplying the number of centimetres in the length of the base by the number in the height and dividing the result by two. This gives the number of square centimetres in the area. The children now go on to find the area of each of several right-angled triangles drawn on plain paper. The checking of their results is made easier if the sheet of triangles is duplicated so that all the children are dealing with the same set of triangles.

4 The children draw a triangle on 1 cm squared paper, as in the example on the right. (*Note*: each of the three angles should be less than a right-angle.) They discuss ways in which its area can be found. From the previous activities some children will

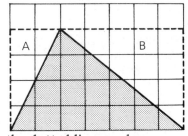

suggest forming a rectangle by drawing the dotted lines as shown.
　　　This rectangle is cut out. The triangles marked A and B are cut off. These two triangles are then placed on the shaded triangle and are found to cover it exactly. So, again, the shaded triangle is half the rectangle. Its area is half the area of the rectangle. Repeat this activity for several triangles.

5 Using the ideas introduced in Activity 4, the children now go on to find the area of a triangle drawn on plain paper, such as that shown on the right. To do this they have to measure the height of the triangle. An easy way of doing this is to cut out the triangle and place it, as shown, on a sheet of cm/mm graph paper. The height can then be read from the graph paper. If this kind of graph paper is not available then it might be helpful to use triangles whose heights are a whole number of centimetres. Then centimetre graph paper can be used. Alternatively a corner of a book can be used as a kind of set square (if a proper set square is not available).

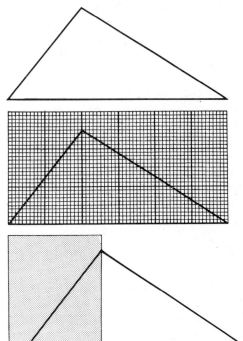

The areas of several triangles drawn on plain paper should be found. Again it is helpful to provide a duplicated sheet of these triangles.

6 From the above activities the children should have consolidated the idea that they can find the area of a triangle by measuring its base and the corresponding height, finding the product of these two measurements, then dividing by two. Care should be taken, however, to make sure that the children understand that any one of the three edges of the triangle can be used as the base. This idea can be introduced by providing each child with a paper triangle, with, for example, edges of length 5 cm, 6 cm, and 7 cm. The children are asked to find the area of the triangle.

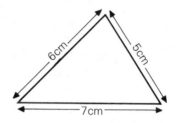

Using the established methods some children will use the 5 cm edge as the base, other will use the 6 cm edge, while others will use the 7 cm edge. When they have all found the area of the triangle, the various ways used by the children should be discussed. The results should, of course, all be approximately the same (the measurements and the calculations for results which are very different should be checked). This activity should be repeated for another triangle (e.g. edge lengths of 6 cm, 7 cm, and 9 cm) but now each child should use each edge, in turn, as the base.

For obtuse-angled triangles, use the edge opposite the obtuse angle as the base to avoid complications.

b) The area of a parallelogram
Some children might be interested in discussing how to find the area of a parallelogram. For a parallelogram *ABCD*, as shown, the simplest way is to draw the line *BD*.

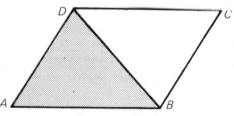

(This is called a *diagonal*.) By cutting out the parallelogram and then cutting along *BD*, the children should check that the two triangles *ABC* and *BCD* fit exactly on top of each other (i.e. they are *congruent*).

The children know that the area of the triangle *ABD* is obtained from $\frac{1}{2}$ (base × height).
The area of the parallelogram is twice the area of triangle *ABD*.
That is, the area is given by *base* × *height*.

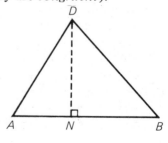

It is wise to check that all the children understand clearly what is meant by the height of a parallelogram. Children who do not fully understand sometimes multiply one edge length by the other to find the area, as for a rectangle. This kind of misunderstanding can often be clarified by discussing the areas of a set of parallelograms as shown below.

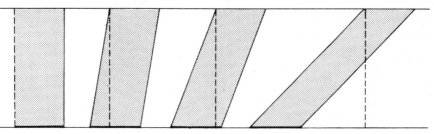

The parallelograms all have the same base length and the same height (each should be a whole number of centimetres for simplicity). The children draw a line to show the height of each parallelogram. They should see that although the slant edge gets longer the height remains the same and that all the parallelograms have the same area.

c)   The area of a circle

At the primary school level it is not possible to prove that the area of a circle is πr^2. The use of πr^2 can only be shown to be reasonable. Some activities which can be used for this purpose are given below.

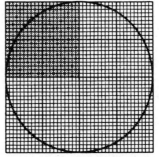

1   The children draw a circle on cm/mm graph paper, as shown. (A whole number of centimetres should be used for the radius.) The area of the circle is found by counting the squares.

The children then find the area of the shaded square. (This can be done by straightforward multiplication.) The area of the circle is then divided by the area of the square. The answer should be a little more than three. This activity is repeated several times using different radii (or several children can each use a different radius). For each of these different radii the children should find that the area of the circle is a little more than three times the area of the square. This result can then be linked with the results they obtained when they found the circumference of circles. The children can now be told that this number which is a little more than three is again the number which we represent by π.

A formula can be introduced to represent the results. Using the drawing on the right, the area of the shaded square is $(r \times r)$ cm^2. This can be written as r^2 cm^2. So if A cm^2 represents the area of the circle, we can write $A = r^2 \times \pi$. This can be written as $A = \pi \times r^2$ or as $A = \pi r^2$.

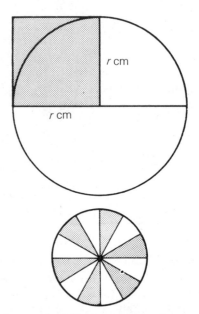

2   For this activity each child needs a circle divided into a number of equal parts. An example is shown on the right. (These circles can be duplicated by the teacher or drawn by the children themselves if they can use a protractor.)

The paper circle is then cut along the marked lines and the pieces arranged as shown below (one piece of the circle should be folded and then cut into two equal parts to provide the two end pieces in the diagram).

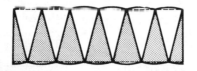

Arranged in this way, the pieces approximately form a rectangle.

The length of the rectangle is approximately half the circumference of the circle. So, if r cm is the radius of the circle, the length $\approx \frac{1}{2}(2\pi r)$ cm.

That is, the length $\approx \pi r$ cm.

The width of the rectangle $\approx$ the radius of the circle.

That is, the width $\approx r$ cm.

The area of the circle $\approx$ the area of the rectangle.

That is, the area $\approx (\pi r \times r)$ cm^2.

So, the area of the circle $\approx \pi r^2$ cm^2.

This is an interesting activity in that the use of approximate lengths and widths for the rectangle gives the exact answer for the area of the circle. (This needs to be discussed so that the children understand that we do not usually get an exact answer for a multiplication when we use approximate measurements.) This activity demands more understanding than the first and is probably only suitable for able children.

4 Ares and hectares

The various units for measuring larger areas should be discussed with the children, but activities should not at this stage involve complicated calculations. It is sufficient if they have an idea of the size of a *square metre*, an *are*, and a *hectare*.

A square of one metre edge length can be drawn on the floor or on the blackboard (if it is large enough). It can also be made from one or two sheets of newspaper stuck together. From this the children get some idea of its size. They can then go on to find the approximate area of the classroom floor, the walls, etc., in square metres. Outside, the areas of rectangular shapes such as the football pitch can also be found. The symbol m^2 should be introduced.

For the football pitch the children will find that the answer is a large number of square metres. This can lead to a discussion about the need for a unit larger than a square metre. The idea of an **are** is introduced. This is the area of a square of 10 m edge length. Using pegs and string, an are should be marked on the ground outside. The children should quickly see that:

1 are = 100 square metres.

Using the symbol *a* for are, this is written as:

$$1a = 100 \text{ m}^2.$$

By dividing the number of square metres by 100, the children can go on to change the area of the football pitch to ares. For example, if the edge lengths of the pitch are 80 m and 45 m, then:

$$\text{area} = 80 \times 45 \text{ m}^2$$
$$= 3600 \text{ m}^2$$
$$= 36 \, a$$

For larger areas the **hectare** (100 ares) is used. This is not easy for children (or adults) to visualize. One way of getting some idea of its size is by reference to something like a football pitch. For example, the pitch discussed above is 36 ares. So 100 ares are about three pitches put side by side. This gives an approximate idea of a hectare. This is enough for the children's needs at this stage.

Volume and capacity

The word *volume* is usually used when we are thinking about the amount of space which an object takes up. *Capacity* is usually used when we are thinking about how much a container will hold. For example, we use phrases such as, 'the volume of a concrete block' and 'the capacity of a motor car petrol tank'.

Capacity can be measured directly. We can use a litre measure to fill, for example, a bucket with water and count the number of litres required. We cannot, however, measure volume directly. We have to use indirect methods. Two of these are described below.

Volume

1 Using displacement

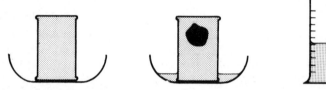

A tin is put in an empty dish and filled with water. An object (e.g. a stone or a piece of metal) is put into the water. Some of the water overflows. The amount which overflows is collected and measured, in millilitres, using a graduated vessel. The volume of the water is the same as the volume of the object. This description gives the basic idea of the method. To obtain more accurate results other ways of collecting the water are needed. One way is shown in the diagram below.

The spout on the side of the can enables the water to be collected without going down the sides of the can.

The object can also be put directly into a measuring vessel and the change in the water level noted.

If an object floats in water, some method of making it sink has to be used. (For example, by pushing it down with a long pin.)

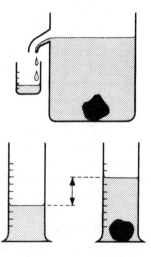

2 By calculation

It is possible to calculate the volume of many shapes which have some regularity. At the primary level these include the cube, the cuboid, the prism, and the cylinder. Formulae can be established which provide quick ways of finding these volumes but these should be introduced through appropriate activities. Without these activities the children will quickly become confused. They will have little understanding of the ideas on which the formulae are based. Some helpful activities are listed below. For many of these a good supply of wooden cubes is essential. In the early stages large cubes are easier to handle but eventually the children will need to handle and use centimetre cubes.

Cuboids and cubes

1   Each child (or group) needs a good supply of identical cubes. With these they build shapes of their own choice. For each they write down how many cubes are used.

2   Using cubes, the children build cuboids. They write down how many cubes are used for each. Some children will count the cubes one by one, others will begin to see quick ways of finding the number used. For example, the cuboid on the right has eight cubes in the bottom layer and there are two layers. So altogether there are sixteen cubes.

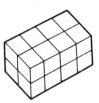

3   The children make more cuboids but now the idea of building them in layers is emphasized. For example, the children make the bottom layer as shown on the right. They count the number of cubes used (15). They then put on a second layer and write down the number of cubes used altogether (15 × 2 = 30). They continue in this way (15 × 3 = 45, 15 × 4 = 60, etc.)

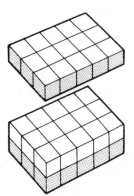

This is an important activity as it forms the basis of the approach used for finding the volumes not only of cuboids but also of prisms and cylinders.

4 At this stage the children begin to make statements about quick ways of finding the volume of a cuboid. For example, using the cuboid shown on the right, the children say, 'There are five cubes in a row. There are three rows in the bottom layer. So altogether there are fifteen cubes in the bottom layer. There are four layers, so there are sixty (15 × 4) cubes altogether in the cuboid.'

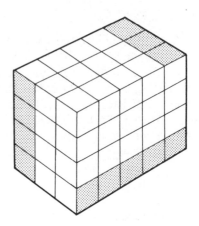

Using centimetre cubes, the length of the cuboid is 5 cm, the width is 3 cm, and the height is 4 cm. The volume is (5 × 3 × 4) cm³.

During this activity explain to the children that the volume of a cube, of edge length 1 cm, is called *one cubic centimetre*. A short way of writing cubic centimetre is **cm³**. It might be helpful to relate this to the use of cm² and to try to explain the use of the 3 and the 2.

This explanation can be based on the number of measurements made, as below.

Length	1 measurement	**cm**
Area	2 measurements	**cm²**
Volume	3 measurements	**cm³**

5 In Activities 1–4 each edge of the cuboid has been a whole number of centimetres. The children now need to have experience of dealing with cuboids for which fractions of a centimetre appear in some of the measurements.

A first step can be to discuss a cuboid such as that shown on the right. When this is built up with centimetre cubes, there will be 8 cubes in the bottom layer. In the second layer there will also be 8 cubes. But only 4 cubes are needed for the third layer if each of these is cut in half. So altogether 20 cubes are needed. This, again, can be obtained from 4 × 2 × 2½. The volume is 20 cm³.

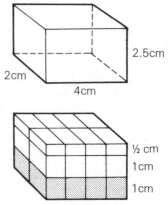

For the cuboid shown on the right, the number of cubes which are needed for the bottom layer needs first to be discussed. A drawing of the base of the cuboid shows that 8 whole cubes and 2 half- cubes are needed to form the bottom layer. Another way of thinking of this is to say that $4\frac{1}{2}$ cubes are needed for each of the two rows in the bottom layer. So, altogether, nine ($4\frac{1}{2}$ × 2) cubes are needed for the layer. There are two and a half layers so, for the whole cuboid, $9 \times 2\frac{1}{2}$ cubes are needed. This multiplication comes from (4.5 × 2) × 2.5.

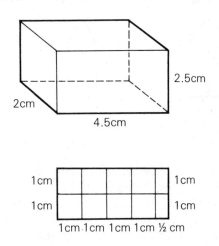

This kind of approach can be extended to deal with the cuboid shown on the right. A drawing of the base of the cuboid shows that 8 whole cubes, 6 half-cubes, and 1 quarter-cube are needed for the bottom layer, that is, $11\frac{1}{4}$ cubes (or 11.25 cubes).

Again, this result can be obtained by thinking of the number of cubes in a row ($4\frac{1}{2}$) and multiplying by the number of rows ($2\frac{1}{2}$). Using decimals this is 4.5 × 2.5. There are 2.5 layers, so the volume of the cuboid is (4.5 × 2.5) × 2.5 cm³.

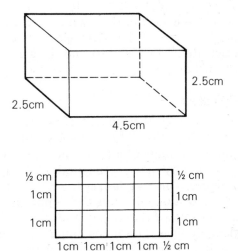

The children should now understand that the number of centimetre cubes needed for the bottom layer is the same as the number of centimetre squares needed to cover the base of the cuboid (i.e. the area of the base). They know how to find the area of any rectangle, so they can find the volume of any cuboid by calculating the area of the base and multiplying the number of square centimetres by the number of centimetres in the height. This gives the volume, in cm³.

Prisms

base is a
right-angled
triangle

base is an
equilateral
triangle

base is a
regular
hexagon

base is an
L shape

When the children understand the ideas and methods discussed in Activity 5 they should, if necessary, be able to go on to find the volume of any prism. The idea of using the area of the base and the height for a prism is a direct extension of the method used for a cuboid. The only difficulty which might arise is in finding the area of the base of some of the prisms.

For example, the children cannot at this stage calculate the area of a regular hexagon. They will need to draw the hexagon (full size or to scale) and then divide it into six triangles as shown. If they measure the height of one of these triangles they can calculate its area, and so find the area of the hexagon.

Cylinders

A cylinder can be thought of as a special prism. So if the children understand how to find the volume of a prism they should find no difficulty in using the method for a cylinder. This emphasizes the earlier statement in this section regarding the importance, throughout the work on cuboids and prisms, of thinking of the area of the base and the height when finding their volumes. Too much emphasis on length, width, and height may hinder children from seeing the general approach which applies to all of these shapes.

Capacity

The capacity of any container can be measured in cubic centimetres. But, in everyday life, *litres* and *millilitres* are often used. A litre can be introduced as the amount of liquid which will fill a cube such as that described on page 144.

The use of the cube also helps children to understand that a cubic centimetre and a millilitre are identical in size.
When the cube is filled with water we know that the amount of water can be described as either

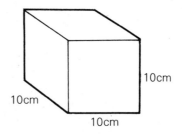

1000 cm³ or 1 litre

A millilitre is one-thousandth of a litre. But 1 cm³ is also one-thousandth of a litre.
So 1 cm³ and 1 ml both describe the same amount of water.

When this relationship is understood the children might be helped in building up some ideas about millilitres if they collect medicine bottles and other containers on which the amount of liquid they hold is marked. For example, a bottle might have marked on it 'Contents 98 ml'. Another bottle might have 'Contents 150 cm³' on it. The use of these two types of marking helps to reinforce the link between 1 cm³ and 1 ml. The children also see the amount of liquid represented by 98 ml and 150 cm³.

They can then go on to find how many times they have to fill one of the bottles with water to obtain one litre. This should check the marking on the bottle (for example, the '98 ml' bottle should need to be filled about ten times to obtain one litre of water). This kind of activity also helps the children to remember the relationships 1000 ml = 1 litre and 1000 cm³ = 1 litre.

The children should also be introduced to the decimal forms of these relationships. For example:

$$1 \text{ ml} = \tfrac{1}{1000} \text{ litre} = 0.001 \text{ l}$$

$$1 \text{ cm}^3 = \tfrac{1}{1000} \text{ litre} = 0.001 \text{ l}$$

The children may find these decimal forms useful in their science lessons.

Time

Ways of introducing the use of *past* and *to* were discussed on page 146. Most children quickly become confident in using these words to tell the time, but some children do not find it easy and often become confused. It is a good idea to make regular checks to find which children need more help. Each day they can be asked what time is shown on the classroom clock. This helps the teacher to discover each child's difficulties. These can then be discussed individually.

The use of a diagram is helpful in introducing the ideas of a.m. and p.m.

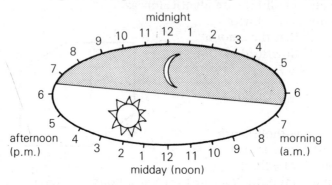

The diagram also helps when children have to calculate the amount of time from, for example, 10.35 a.m. to 2.17 p.m. They can use the marked curve as a kind of number line. If necessary they can draw part of the curve and mark the two times:

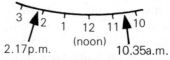

From this kind of diagram some children will see that the amount of time is 3 hours plus 25 minutes plus 17 minutes. That is, 3 hours and 42 minutes. Other children will think of 25 minutes (to 11.00 a.m.), 1 hour (to 12 noon), 2 hours (to 2 p.m.), and 17 minutes (to 2.17 p.m.). That is, 3 hours 42 minutes altogether. Other children will probably suggest different ways of finding the amount of time. These should all be discussed.

This curved number line is also useful when introducing the 24-hour clock. If the children think of the curved line being cut at midnight and then pulled into a straight line, they should have no difficulty in seeing that the line will then look like the one shown below.

	a.m.								midday			p.m.					midnight		
1	2	3	4	5	6	7	8	9	10	11	12	1	2	3	4	5	6	7	8	9	10	11	12

A zero can be inserted at the left-hand point of the line to indicate that the day starts there.

To avoid confusion which might arise from the repetition of the two sets of numbers from 1 to 12, the idea of using the numerals from 0 to 24 can be shown on a second line, below the first, as below.

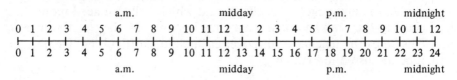

The children should find this kind of diagram very helpful in interchanging 12-hour times and 24-hour times.

To give practice in showing 24-hour times the children can make an interesting piece of apparatus. Using thick paper or thin card they first mark, and then cut out, four strips and a rectangle, as shown below. The rectangle has to be slit along the marked lines.

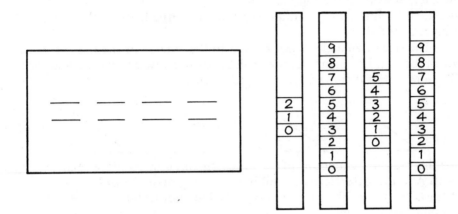

To show a 24-hour time, for example 15.26, the strips are put through the slits in the rectangle, as shown below.

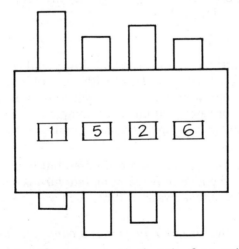

One advantage of using this apparatus is that the four strips emphasize that in *all* 24-hour times four numerals have to be used. (For example, 17 minutes past midnight is written as 00.17)

Before teachers discuss the *calendar* and *leap years*, they might find it helpful to look again at pages 40–1.

Measuring and drawing angles

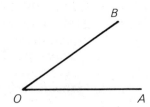

On page 52 an angle was defined as
'Two straight lines with a common
end-point'. To *measure* an angle we
use the idea of turning. For example,
the angle shown on the right is
measured by finding the amount OA must be turned, about the point O, to
bring it over OB.

The size of an angle is not related to the lengths of the line segments
which form it. For example, the angles shown below are all the same size.
(The amount of turning is the same for each.)

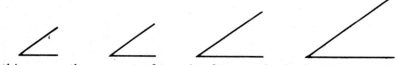

For this reason the amount of turn is often emphasized more than the angle
itself. And this often leads to children thinking of angles *only* as amounts
of turn. We need to be careful in our teaching not to build up this kind of
thinking about angles.

The idea of turning is, however, more interesting and more linked with
the everyday activities of children than the idea of an angle, so it is usual to
introduce the work on angles through activities involving turning. Some
suitable activities are given below.

Activities

1   The teacher stands facing the class and slowly makes a complete turn.
The phrase *a complete turn* is discussed with the children. The teacher then
makes several complete turns and the children count how many. This
activity is repeated for various numbers of complete turns.

The children then stand up and make complete turns as told by the
teacher.

2   The teacher again stands facing the children but now makes only half
of a complete turn. The idea of *half a complete turn* is discussed. The
children then stand and make various turns such as $\frac{1}{2}$, $1\frac{1}{2}$, $2\frac{1}{2}$, $3\frac{1}{2}$, etc. of a
complete turn.

3   In a similar way the idea of *a quarter of a complete turn* is introduced.

4   It is important that children make complete turns, half-turns, and
quarter-turns from different starting positions. These turns should be made
in a clockwise direction and also in an anti-clockwise direction.

5   If the ideas of direction have not been introduced to the children in
their geography lessons, then it might be helpful to discuss them at this

stage. The drawing below shows an interesting and helpful activity which the children can do on a day when the sun shines.

A pole is put in the ground in an upright position. Starting early in the morning, two children mark, with a short stick or cane, the position of the end of the shadow of the pole. They do this every half an hour, until about 4.0 p.m. (At various times the other children go out and look at what the two children are doing.)

The children notice that during the day the length of the shadow first gets shorter and then gets longer. They decide which small cane marks the shortest shadow. The children then tie a piece of string around the pole and pull it straight so that it touches the small cane, as in the drawing on the right.

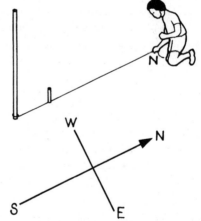

If a child stands at the pole and looks along the string he or she is looking towards the north. (This may be only an approximation but it is good enough at this stage.) The positions of S, E, and W are then marked (using paint if possible).

It is a good idea to mark the approximate directions of N, S, E, and W in chalk in a convenient place on the floor of the classroom.

6   A child stands and looks to the north. He then makes a quarter-turn, in a clockwise direction, and says in what direction he is now looking. The activity is recorded as on the right.

The child starts again, looking to the north. He then makes a half-turn in a clockwise direction and says in what direction he is now looking. The activity is recorded as shown. The child repeats the activity again, but now makes three-quarters of a turn.

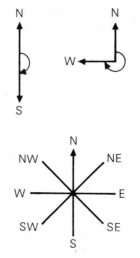

7   Activity 6 is repeated but the turns are now made in an anti-clockwise direction.

8   The directions NE, SE, SW, and NW can be introduced by using a half of a quarter-turn. These can be shown on a diagram as on the right.

9   The children should have practice in, for example, looking in the direction SE and then making turns, half-turns, and quarter-turns in clockwise and anti-clockwise directions. For each they say in what direction they are looking when they have finished turning.

10   The children should now be ready for the introduction of the use of a degree as a unit of measure. This avoids the use of fractions of complete turns and also enables turns to be measured more accurately.

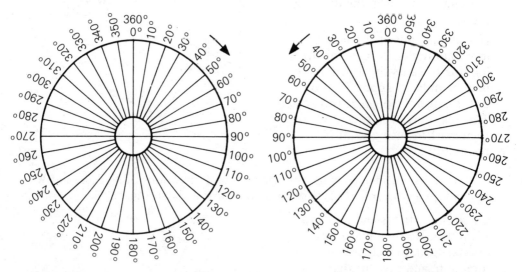

First the children should be shown a complete turn divided into 360 equal parts, as shown above. The word *degree* and the small symbol should be discussed.

This kind of diagram helps the children to see that a quarter-turn is 90°, a half-turn is 180°, etc. It is important that the children should also be shown a complete turn with the degree markings shown for anti-clockwise turns, as shown. (This prepares them for the two sets of markings on a commercial protractor.)

11 If 360° protractors are available the children should be introduced to the ways of using them to measure turns shown on a piece of paper. Some examples are indicated below.

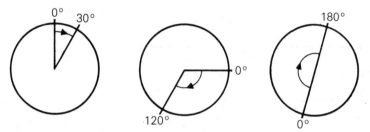

For each, they should place the 0° line on the protractor along the line of the initial direction and then read the protractor to find how much turning is needed to reach the second direction.

Much practice should be provided.

It is *very important* that, from the start, the teacher should insist, before any measurement is made, that the children **estimate** (and write down) the amount of turn. This will help the children to avoid reading a protractor wrongly and giving answers which are obviously wrong.

12 If 360° protractors are not available then the children will have to use 180° protractors. If possible these should have only one set of markings on them as shown below left.

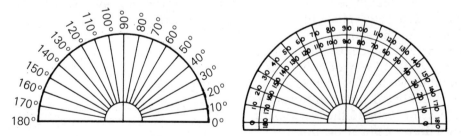

If only standard commercially produced protractors are available (as above right), then the way in which they are used must be fully discussed. Many children are often confused by the two sets of markings. With each type of protractor much practice should be provided in measuring amounts of turn. To simplify the checking of the children's work it is helpful to duplicate a set of angles as in the example shown on the next page.

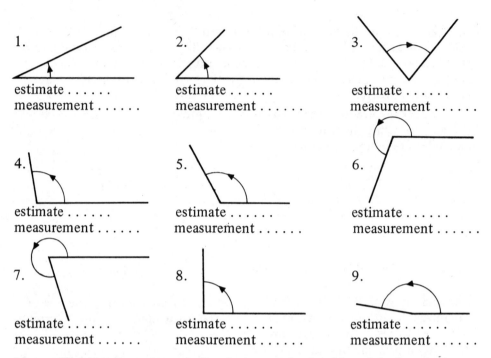

1.

estimate . . . . . .
measurement . . . . . .

2.

estimate . . . . . .
measurement . . . . . .

3.

estimate . . . . . .
measurement . . . . . .

4.

estimate . . . . . .
measurement . . . . . .

5.

estimate . . . . . .
measurement . . . . . .

6.

estimate . . . . . .
measurement . . . . . .

7.

estimate . . . . . .
measurement . . . . . .

8.

estimate . . . . . .
measurement . . . . . .

9.

estimate . . . . . .
measurement . . . . . .

Note: The two line segments forming an angle should each be longer than the radius of the protractor.

For each angle, the children write down their estimate of its size before measuring it. This should help them to give sensible answers.

For examples 6 and 7 on the sheet the angle cannot be measured directly with a 180° protractor. The children have to measure the unmarked turn and subtract the result from 360°.

13   The children go on to draw angles of given sizes (e.g. 40°, 72°, 110°, 170° , 215°, etc.) Much practice is usually needed.

The use of the names *acute, obtuse,* and *reflex* can be introduced at this stage. A useful way of doing this is to draw two lines at right-angles on the blackboard and then to fasten a piece of string to the blackboard by a drawing pin at the point *O*.

The string is pulled tightly along *OA* and is then turned about *O* in an anti-clockwise direction. Lines are drawn from *O* along the string for various amounts of turn. Each of these forms an angle with the line *OA*.

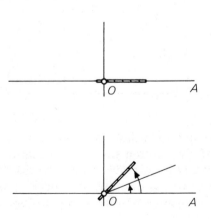

When the string has turned through one right-angle several angles will have been drawn, as shown. Each of these is called an **acute angle**. (Reference can be made to a meaning of the word acute—sharp or pointed.)

The chalk lines should be rubbed off (except for the two original lines at right-angles) before the turning of the string is continued. (This avoids having too many lines on the drawing.)

When the string has been turned through two right-angles several angles will have been drawn, as shown. Each of these is called an **obtuse angle** (obtuse can mean 'not sharp').

When the string has turned exactly through two right-angles, the angle formed is called a *straight angle*.

The turning of the string is continued from two right-angles to four right-angles. Each of the angles formed is called a *reflex angle*.

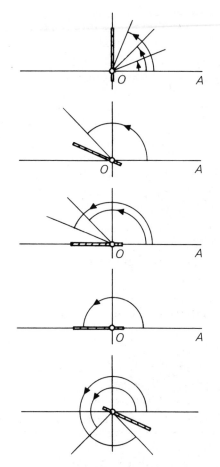

This activity should be repeated, again starting with the string along *OA*, but with the turning in a clockwise direction. The results can be linked with degrees and summarized as below.

Acute angles	between 0° and 90°
Right-angle	90°
Obtuse angles	between 90° and 180°
Straight angle	180°
Reflex angles	between 180° and 360°
Complete turn	360°

The sum of the angles of any triangle can also be investigated at this stage. Three helpful activities are shown on pages 264–5.

1 Draw a square on the blackboard. Discuss the sum of the four angles of the square (4 right-angles).

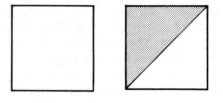

Insert a diagonal and colour or shade one of the resulting triangles.
Discuss the two triangles (are they congruent?). If necessary, demonstrate the congruency by using a large cardboard square and cutting along one of the diagonals.

Now discuss the sum of the three angles of each triangle (one half of 4 right-angles). Repeat this activity with a rectangle.

2 Each child draws a large triangle on paper or card.
The three angles are marked or coloured.

The triangle is torn or cut, as shown.

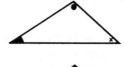

The three pieces are rearranged, as shown.
They can be retained in this position by sticking them onto another piece of card or thick paper.

The children discuss the sum of the three angles. They see that together they make half a complete turn (two right-angles; 180°). It is advisable to get the children to repeat this activity with a second paper triangle, without any further discussion, because very often the novelty of the tearing-off of the corners tends to obscure the mathematical objective. Using a second triangle also helps in generalizing the results. This generalizing is emphasized by the fact that the triangles drawn by the children are all different. But the same result is obtained for each.

3 Each child has a duplicated copy of a tessellation of scalene triangles:

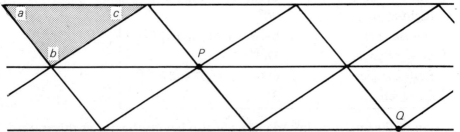

The angles of one triangle (shaded in the drawing) are marked *a, b, c*. This triangle is cut out. The children check that this triangle fits exactly onto each of the other triangles of the tessellation. They then use it to mark the angles at the points P and Q, as below.

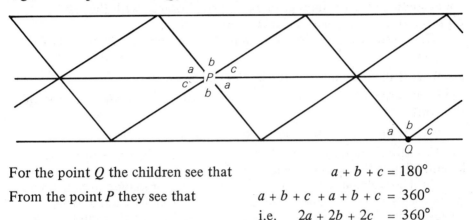

For the point Q the children see that $\qquad$ $a + b + c = 180°$

From the point P they see that $\qquad$ $a + b + c + a + b + c = 360°$

i.e. $\quad 2a + 2b + 2c = 360°$

i.e. $\quad a + b + c = 180°$.

These two results show that the sum of the three angles of the shaded triangle is $180°$.

Mass

In Chapter 15, the uses of a kilogram and of simple fractions of a kilogram ($\frac{1}{2}$ kg, $\frac{1}{4}$ kg) were discussed. At some stage the idea and use of a gram also needs to be introduced. This is not easy from a practical point of view as a gram is a very small unit and an accurate balance is needed.

The children will understand, however, that a kilogram is too large a unit for accurate measurement or for measuring the mass of a small object, and that a unit even smaller than a $\frac{1}{2}$ kg or a $\frac{1}{4}$ kg is needed. They already know that, to provide a smaller unit for measuring capacity, a litre is divided into a thousand equal parts, so it will seem sensible to divide a kilogram also into a thousand equal parts. Each of these is called a **gram**. This can be emphasized by discussing the relationship between a millilitre of water and a gram. To show this relationship, an open watertight 1 cm cube made of thin card is filled with water. The volume of the water is 1 cm^3 or 1 ml. The mass of the water is 1 gram (strictly the water should be at a temperature of 4°C, but within the limitations of the demonstration, this can be ignored). The symbol, g, for gram should also be introduced.

Children must have some experience of using grams in weighing before they start doing calculations which involve mass. To do this a variety of 'weights' are needed. These can be of the commercially produced metal type or they can be made from clay, or other suitable material, if one set of standard weights is available. Using these weights the children can find the masses of various objects by using a balance. The use of a spring balance could then be introduced. As a first exercise the children could compare the readings given on a spring balance with the results obtained from an ordinary balance, using weights.

Their results can be used for simple calculations involving mass. For example:

a) What is the total mass of the book and the bottle?

b) What is the difference between the mass of the book and the mass of the bottle?

c) What is the mass of six books like the one you weighed?

d) The strip of metal you weighed is divided into five strips of the same length. What is the mass of each?

In these calculations the children use grams, or kilograms and grams. When necessary they change 1000 g to 1 kg, or 1 kg to 1000 g. When, however, they understand the decimal notation up to thousandths, the writing of the masses in a decimal form should be introduced. To understand this the children must first understand that:

a) 1 g is $\frac{1}{1000}$ kg and can be shown as 0.001 kg;

b) 67 g is $\frac{67}{1000}$ kg and can be shown as 0.067 kg;

c) 254 g is $\frac{254}{1000}$ kg and can be shown as 0.254 kg.

It has already been mentioned in various places in this book that children often find difficulties in the kind of changing required in (b) and (c). These difficulties should be anticipated by discussing several examples of the same type before children attempt them. For example:

for (b), $\frac{67}{1000}$ can be thought of as $\frac{60}{1000} + \frac{7}{1000}$

The $\frac{60}{1000}$ can then be changed to $\frac{6}{100}$.

So, using place-value and column headings,

$\frac{67}{1000}$ can be written as on the right.

U	t	h	th
0	0	6	7

Without column headings the fraction is written as 0.067.

for (c), $\frac{254}{1000}$ is first written as $\frac{200}{1000} + \frac{50}{1000} + \frac{4}{1000}$.

This is then changed to $\frac{2}{10} + \frac{5}{100} + \frac{4}{1000}$.

Using the decimal notation the fraction is then written as 0.254. Much practice is needed in the type of changing used for (b) and (c). The children can then go on to calculations (involving $+$, $--$, $\times$, $\div$) in which the masses are in kilograms and decimal fractions of a kilogram.

Summary

When a child has completed the many activities in this chapter he or she should:

understand   the ideas of perimeter, area, volume, and capacity
the idea of π
the idea and use of the 24-hour clock
the idea of an angle and the ways in which angles are measured
the naming of angles
the idea of direction
the ways in which the sum of the angles of a triangle can be established
the use of grams in measuring mass

be able to   calculate perimeters
calculate the circumference of a circle
find the area of an irregular shape
calculate the areas of rectangles, triangles, parallelograms, and circles
find the volume of an irregular object
calculate the volumes of cuboids, prisms, and cylinders
relate 12-hour clock times and 24-hour clock times
measure angles in degrees
name angles
use the angle sum property of a triangle
relate grams and kilograms in weighing activities

Chapter 22
Shapes: properties of 2-D shapes, scale

Sorting and naming plane shapes (triangles, quadrilaterals, and other polygons). Regular polygons. Fitting shapes together (tessellations). Line symmetry. Congruence. Similarity. Forming shapes. Drawing shapes. Simple geometrical constructions.

Some of our first ideas about shapes and ways in which they can be introduced to children were discussed in the section 'Thinking about shapes' and in Chapter 5.

    The aim of this further work on shapes is to provide the children with a background of ideas and knowledge which will be helpful in everyday life and which will form a good foundation for developing geometrical ideas and techniques in their mathematical work in the secondary school. There are many ideas involved. But, unlike addition and subtraction, for example, there is not a definite step-by-step progression in developing them. Each forms part of the background of knowledge being built up but they do not necessarily have to be dealt with in a given order. For this reason each topic is discussed separately below.

Sorting and naming plane shapes

Sorting a set of shapes in various ways helps children to become familiar with the shapes and, through looking at the ways in which they are alike or different, they build up a knowledge of the properties of the various shapes.

Activities

1   Each child or small group is provided with a set of shapes such as that shown below.

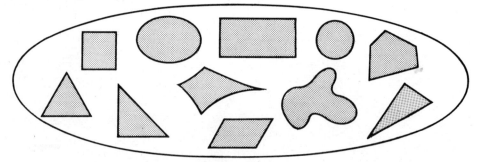

The children sort them in various ways. For example, they might pick out, in turn, the shapes:

a) with only straight edges;

b) with only curved edges;

c) with straight and curved edges;

d) with three edges;

e) with three straight edges;

f) with four edges;

g) with all their edges the same length.

The shapes obtained for each sorting should be fully discussed. Where appropriate the shapes should be named (e.g. triangles, quadrilaterals).

2   Each child or small group is provided with a set of large triangles, such as that shown below.

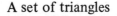

A set of triangles

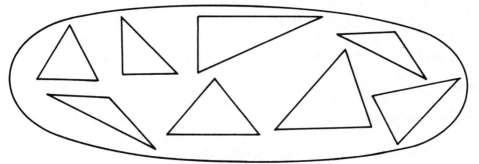

The children pick out, in turn, the triangles:

a) with three edges the same length;

b) with two edges the same length;

c) with no edges the same length.

If the children know about angles they might pick out the triangles:

d) with one angle a right-angle;

e) with one angle greater than a right-angle;

f) with all three angles less than a right-angle.

During these activities the names *equilateral, isosceles, scalene,* and *right-angled* can be introduced. Special attention should be given to the spelling of these names. Otherwise some children will always be unsure when they have to write them later.

3   Each child or small group of children is provided with a set of large quadrilaterals, such as those shown on the next page.

A set of quadrilaterals

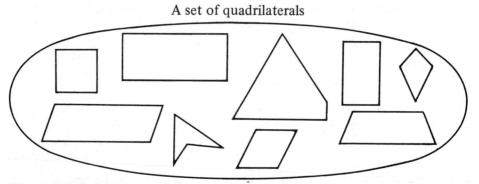

The children pick out, in turn, the quadrilaterals:

a) with all four edges the same length (square and rhombus);

b) with the opposite edges the same length (square, rectangle, rhombus, parallelogram);

c) with each angle a right-angle (square, rectangle);

d) with all four edges the same length and each angle a right-angle (square).

If the children have not already been introduced to the idea of *parallel* lines it could be discussed at this stage, but no formal definition is required. It is sufficient to point out and discuss sets of lines in the classroom which are parallel. For example: a set of lines in an exercise book; the opposite edges of a page of a book; the opposite edges of a table top; etc. When the children understand this idea they can use it to pick out from their set of quadrilaterals those:

a) with a pair of opposite edges parallel (square, rectangle, trapezium, parallelogram);

b) with both pairs of opposite edges parallel (square, rectangle, rhombus, parallelogram);

c) with only one pair of opposite edges parallel (trapezium).

4   Working in small groups the children are provided with sets of shapes with straight edges such as those shown below. The shapes should be made from thin card and large enough for the edge-lengths and angles to be easily measured.

A set of triangles   A set of quadrilaterals

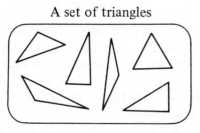 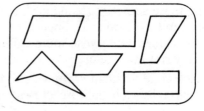

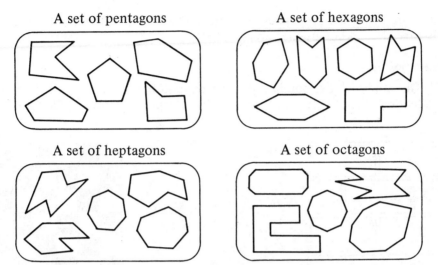

The children look at each set of shapes in turn. The names for each set (depending on the number of edges) can be introduced and the general name **polygon** can also be discussed and used. The children discuss the edge-lengths and the angles of each shape and, where necessary, check their observations by measuring. From these activities the children should find that in each set there is one shape which has all its edges the same length and all its angles the same size. A polygon which has these two properties is said to be a **regular** polygon. Sometimes children think that only one of these properties is necessary. The need for both can be emphasized by referring to two hexagons such as those below.

The first has all its edges the same length, but all the angles are not the same size. It is not regular. The second shape is a regular hexagon.

During these activities the names *quadrilateral, square, rectangle, parallelogram, rhombus, trapezium* should be introduced and spelt. When the children have completed Activities 1, 2, 3, and 4 above they should be able to recognize and name the plane shapes which they see in everyday life and should have built up a knowledge of their properties.

Fitting shapes together

On page 56 the idea of fitting 3–D shapes together so that there are no gaps was introduced. We now go on to discuss ways for fitting 2–D shapes together so that there are no gaps or overlaps. These ideas of space filling have many applications in everyday life. They are also helpful in finding out more about the properties of shapes and are very useful in introducing the first ideas of congruence and similarity.

Activities

1   The children look around the classroom and the school to find examples of identical shapes fitted together. Three examples are shown below.

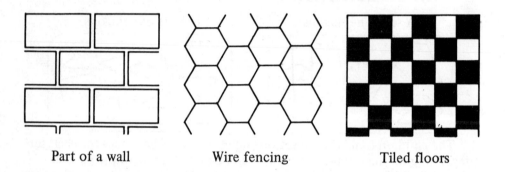

| Part of a wall | Wire fencing | Tiled floors |

The children sketch the patterns and say what shape is used in each.

2   Each child is provided with a cardboard shape, such as a rectangle and, by repeatedly drawing around the shape, makes a pattern in which there are no gaps or overlaps. Three examples of patterns are shown below.

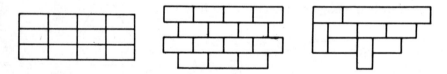

Encourge them to draw as many different patterns as they can, provided there are no gaps or overlaps. Some children like to colour their patterns.

3   The children repeat Activity 2 with shapes such as those shown below.

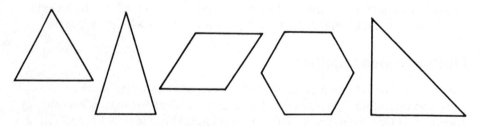

The use of the word *tessellation* can be introduced for the patterns made.

4 Forming a tessellation with a scalene triangle or any quadrilateral is not as straightforward as for the shapes in Activities 2 and 3, and the children may need some guidance. The drawings show how each shape can be used.

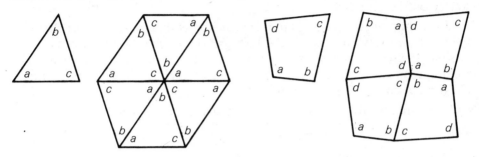

Note: i) For the tessellation of scalene triangles, at the point where six triangles meet, $a + b + c + c + b + a = 360°$

i.e. $$a + b + c = 180°$$

This shows that the sum of the three angles of a triangle is 180°.

  ii) For the tessellation of quadrilaterals, at the point where four quadrilaterals meet, $a + b + c + d = 360°$

This shows that the sum of the four angles of a quadrilateral is 360°.

Symmetry

Symmetrical forms occur frequently in nature and in everyday life, and use is made of symmetry in many creative activities (architecture, design, art, etc.). It is a topic which appeals to many children. At the primary level the ideas of line symmetry can be introduced and used. The activities described below are essentially practical and need a good supply of paper, scissors, drawing pins, and coloured pens or crayons.

Activities

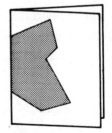

1 Each child has a piece of paper. (This can be of any shape.) The child folds the paper and on it draws a shape of his own choice, with one edge along the fold line, as shown. Keeping the paper folded the child cuts out the shape. He opens out the cut-out shape and marks the fold line.

  This activity is repeated several times. The children are encouraged to make their shapes as interesting as possible. Some children may like to colour their shapes. A selection of the opened-out shapes can be displayed.

The phrase *a line of symmetry* can be introduced to describe the fold line for each shape. From these activities the children should begin to see that if a shape is folded about a line of symmetry then the two parts fit exactly onto each other.

2   Each child or group of children is provided with a set of cut-out shapes, such as those shown on page 268. (To make the preparation as easy as possible, the set of shapes can be drawn on a sheet and duplicated. The children then cut out the shapes.) The children then try to find, by folding, which shapes have a line of symmetry.

3   Each child is provided with a duplicated sheet of shapes, as shown.

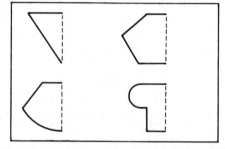

Each shape is half a shape, for which the dotted line is a line of symmetry. The children draw the other half of the shape.

4   Each child folds a piece of paper twice and, in the position shown, draws a shape. Keeping the paper folded he or she then cuts out the marked shape. The cut-out shape is then unfolded and the fold lines on it are marked. By folding 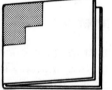 along these fold lines in turn the child finds that the shape has two lines of symmetry. This activity should be repeated several times, with different shapes drawn on the twice-folded paper. The various shapes should be coloured and a selection displayed in the classroom.

5   The children are provided with a duplicated sheet of shapes, as shown.

The children cut out the shapes and, for each, find the number of lines of symmetry. For the circle there are very many lines of symmetry.

6   From the activities listed above the children write down all they have found out about each of the shapes. For example:

a)   two angles of an isosceles triangles are the same size;

b)   the three angles of an equilateral triangle are all the same size;

c)   the diagonals of a rhombus cut each other into two equal parts (i.e. they bisect each other).

These results can, of course, be discussed when each shape is dealt with.

Congruence and Similarity

Congruence and similarity are two important ideas in everyday life. For example: in industry and commerce many identical shapes are made; for technical drawings and maps the ideas of similarity are used. Activities which lead to the first ideas of both of these topics can be provided for children in primary schools. Some of these are listed below.

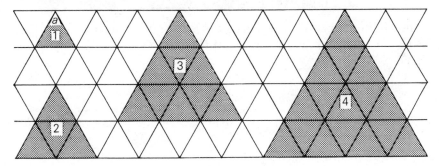

Activities

1   Each of the children has a duplicated copy of the tessellation of equilateral triangles shown above. The children then cut out the small shaded triangle, marked '1', and check that it fits exactly onto each of the other triangles in the tessellation (i.e. all the small triangles are congruent). They also measure the length of each edge of this triangle. By using the angle marked '*a*' and fitting it in turn onto each of the angles of one of the other triangles they should find that the three angles of each triangle are the same size. The children then shade or colour the other three shaded triangles shown above, marked 2, 3, and 4.

The children discuss these three triangles and say all they can about them. For example, for triangle 2,

a)   the edges of triangle 2 are equal in length;

b) the edges of triangle 2 are each twice as long as those of triangle 1;

c) the three angles of triangle 2 are equal in size and are the same as those of triangle 1;

d) the area of triangle 2 is four times the area of triangle 1.

Some children may also notice that the edge-lengths of triangle 4 are twice those of triangle 2 and that the area of triangle 4 is four times the area of triangle 2.

2 Repeat Activity 1 for each of the tessellations shown below, and for tessellations of isosceles triangles.

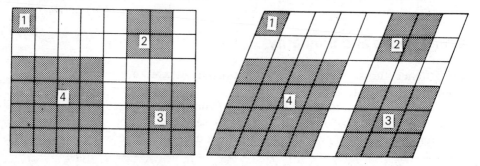

3 The children each draw a triangle *ABC*, of their own choice. They measure the edge-lengths and angles of the triangle.

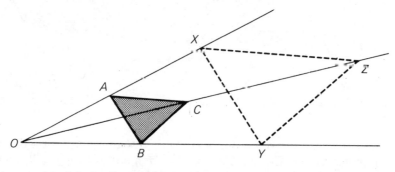

Approximately in the positions shown the children mark a point, *O*, and through *O* draw straight lines through *A, B,* and *C*.

On *OA* they mark a point, *X*, such that the length of *OX* is twice the length of *OA*.

In the same way, points *Y* and *Z* are marked on *OB* and *OC*.

XY, YZ, and *ZX* are then drawn.

The children now measure the edge-lengths and angles of the triangle *XYZ*. They should find that the edge-length of each edge of triangle *XYZ* is twice that of the corresponding edge-length of triangle *ABC*. The corresponding angles of the two triangles should be equal in size.

4   Activity 3 is repeated but now the points X, Y, and Z are marked so that the lengths of OX, OY, and OZ are three times the lengths of OA, OB, and OC. (This may need a larger sheet of paper.)

5   Activity 3 is repeated with the points X, Y, and Z marked so that the lengths of OX, OY, and OZ are one-half of the lengths of OA, OB, and OC.

6   The children draw a triangle and then, using a straight edge and compasses, make an identical copy of it. (This is discussed below.)

From these activities the children should begin to get their first ideas of:
i) *congruence* (a shape fits exactly onto another shape);
ii) *similarity* (a shape is an enlargement or reduction of another shape).

Drawing and copying shapes

Most children enjoy drawing activities, especially when new and interesting shapes are produced. Many find satisfaction in making neat and accurate drawings and in colouring them. In mathematics this kind of enjoyment should be encouraged and, at the same time, simple technical skills in the use of instruments should be developed. The ability to make a neat accurate drawing is very helpful in everyday life, in some trades and professions and in later mathematical work.

a) Forming shapes
These activities give practice in using a pencil, a straight edge (ruler), and compasses. Encourage the children to colour their shapes.

Activities

1   The children draw two straight lines OA and OB, as in the diagram. Starting from O, they mark a set of equally spaced points (1 cm is convenient) along each. These are numbered, as shown. Straight lines are then drawn to join pairs of points with the same number. A curved shape emerges. This can be coloured. Good drawings can be displayed in the classroom.

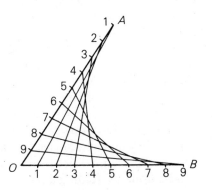

An interesting alternative to drawing the line joining pairs of points is to use a needle and coloured thread or thin wool. A small hole is made at each numbered point on the two lines and, in turn, the threaded needle is taken through them to form each of the lines. It is better to use thin card rather than ordinary paper when the activity is done in this way.

2   For this activity each child needs a circle drawn on paper or card, with 36 equally spaced points on it, as shown. If the children can use a protractor they can draw round the curved outline to produce a semicircle. A second semicircle can then be drawn to make a full circle. The 10° markings on the protractor can be used in marking the equally spaced points.

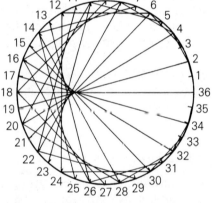

If the children are not familiar with a protractor the easiest alternative is to provide duplicated sheets of marked circles. The equally spaced points are labelled 1 to 36, as shown, The children then draw straight lines to join the following pairs of points: $1 \rightarrow 2; 2 \rightarrow 4;$ $3 \rightarrow 6; 4 \rightarrow 8; 5 \rightarrow 10;$ etc. That is, each point is joined to the point whose number is twice that of the first point. Going on in this way the children come to $18 \rightarrow 36$. They then try to deal with $19 \rightarrow 38$. But there is no point labelled 38. They can, however, think of 38 as being $36 + 2$ (that is, a complete turn and 2 more spaces). So $19 \rightarrow 2$. In the same way $20 \rightarrow 4, 21 \rightarrow 6$, etc. The last few points to be joined are $34 \rightarrow 32, 35 \rightarrow 34, 36 \rightarrow 36$. As the children draw the line segments

a curve emerges, as shown. This curve is called a **cardioid**. Again, coloured thread can be used to join the points. Most children enjoy this activity.

3   The children draw two lines, XY and PQ, at right-angles to each other, as shown. (If necessary, this can be done by folding a piece of paper twice.) A strip of firm cardboard or thin wood, $ABCD$, is then placed so that point A is on OP and point B is on OY. A line is drawn along the side of the edge AB.

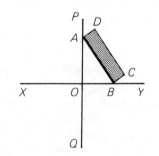

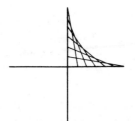

A is then moved to another position on *OP*, making sure that *B* is still on *OY*, and another line drawn. This activity is repeated for many positions of *A* and *B* on *OP* and *OY*. A curved shape is formed as shown.

The strip is then placed in the top left region and the activity repeated. Then, in turn, the two bottom regions are used. The complete closed curve formed is called an **astroid.**

b) Drawing shapes

Activities

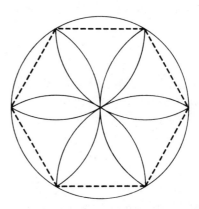

1   The children practise using compasses to draw circles. (Many children need this practice in order to learn how to hold and use the compasses.)

When they are competent in drawing circles they can go on to make simple designs, as shown.

By joining the points on the circle with straight lines they can also draw a regular hexagon, as shown by the dotted lines. Most children enjoy colouring their designs.

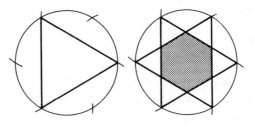

2   The six points on the circle in Activity 1 can be used to produce other shapes and designs, as in the two examples shown.

3   This is an important activity as it is the basis of many of the drawing activities which follow.

The children draw a straight line, *AB*, of length 6 cm.
With centre *A* and radius 5 cm they draw a circle.
With centre *B* and radius 4 cm they draw another circle.
The points of intersection of the two circles are labelled *P* and *Q*.
The children then discuss what they know about the point *P*. (It is 5 cm from *A* and 4 cm from *B*.) In the same way they discuss the point *Q*.
By drawing the lines *AP* and *BP* the children then form a triangle, *ABP*, whose edges are 6 cm, 4 cm, and 5 cm.

They can then go on to draw an identical triangle *ABQ*. (The two triangles can be shown to be identical by either cutting out the two triangles and placing one on the other, or by cutting out the shape *APBQ* and folding it along the line *AB*.)

4   The children repeat Activity 3, using various values for the lengths of *AB* and various radii for the two circles. During these drawing activities the children should notice that:

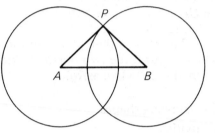

a) When the radii of the two circles are the same, the triangle *APB* is isosceles.

b) When the radii of the two circles are each equal to the length of *AB*, the triangle *APB* is equilateral.

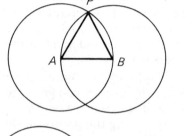

c) When the sum of the two radii is less than the length of *AB*, the two circles do not intersect. No triangle can be formed.

d) When the sum of the two radii is equal to the length of *AB*, the two circles touch each other.

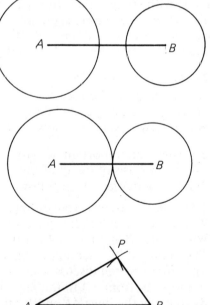

5   The children use the ideas of Activity 4 to draw triangles of given edge-lengths. They should quickly realize that there is no need to draw the whole of the two circles. Two small arcs are sufficient, as shown on the right.

If the children can use protractors they should measure the three angles of each triangle they draw. This gives practice in measuring angles and helps to lead to the idea that the sum of the three angles is 180°.

6 When the children can use protractors they can go on to draw triangles using given values of:

a) one edge-length and two angles;

b) two edge-lengths and the included angle.

7 The drawing of regular polygons can be introduced by first considering a regular hexagon. For example, the children draw a circle and, keeping the same radius, step off equal lengths along it to form a hexagon, as shown. By measuring the edge-lengths and the angles the children check that it is a regular hexagon.

They then join each vertex of the hexagon to the centre, as shown. The six triangles formed are discussed and the fact that they are all identical equilateral triangles should be established. The children now look at the six angles at the centre of the circle. Each is one-sixth of a complete turn. That is, each is 60°.

The finding of the value of each of these angles provides another starting point for drawing a regular hexagon, as discussed below. A circle is drawn, with centre *O*. Angles of 60° are then drawn as shown. The lines *AB*, *BC*, *CD*, *DE*, *EF*, and *FA* are then drawn to form a regular hexagon.

A regular pentagon should be drawn using the same method. If necessary, practice should be given in drawing other regular polygons in the same way.

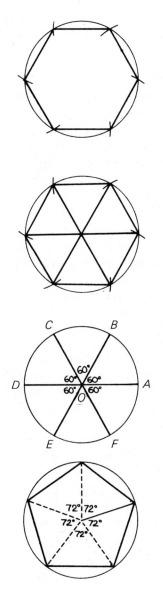

c) Simple geometrical constructions

The following geometrical constructions, using only compasses and a straight edge, are discussed in the activities which follow:

i) drawing the perpendicular bisector of a straight line;

ii) drawing, from a point, a line at right-angles to a given line;

iii) bisecting an angle;

iv) drawing angles of 60°, 30°, 90°, and 45°.

Each construction should be fully discussed, so that the children not only are able to use it but also can understand why the particular method is used.

Activities

1   The children draw a line AB. With centres A and B and the same radius they draw arcs of circles to intersect at P and Q.
They discuss the lengths of AP, BP, AQ, and BQ.

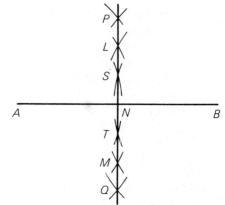

They repeat the activity using various radii and obtain a set of points of intersection (L and M; S and T; etc.).

Looking at this set of points they see that they are all on a straight line. They draw the line. The point where the line intersects AB is labelled N.

Using compasses the children check that any point on the line PQ is the same distance from A as it is from B. In particular they find that the length of the line NA is the ·same as the length of the line NB. That is, N is the midpoint of the line AB.

By measuring or by folding the paper along AB and then along PQ, the children find that the four angles at N are all the same size. That is, each is a right-angle. So the line PQ bisects the line AB and is also at right angles to it; PQ is the *perpendicular bisector* of AB.

The children then discuss the fact that only the points P and Q are needed in order to draw the line PQ.

2   The children draw a straight line AB and mark a point P, as shown. To draw a line from P perpendicular to AB they use the ideas of Activity 1.

Knowing that any point on
the perpendicular from *P* to *AB*
is equidistant from two points on
AB, they draw, with centre *P* and
a convenient radius, arcs to
intersect *AB* at *L* and *M*, as shown.
With centres *L* and *M* and a
convenient radius they then draw
two arcs to intersect at *Q*.

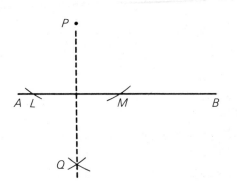

The children draw the line
PQ. From their construction the
children know that the lengths
of the lines *LP* and *MP* are equal·
and that the lengths of the lines
QL and *QM* are also equal. So the line *PQ* is the perpendicular bisector of
the line *LM*. That is, the line *PQ* is *perpendicular* to the line *AB*.

3   The children draw an angle,
BAC, as shown. With centre *A*
and a convenient radius they
draw two arcs to intersect *AC*
at *P* and *AB* at *Q*. Then with
centres *P* and *Q* and a convenient
radius they draw two arcs to
intersect at *T*. The line *AT* is
then drawn. By cutting out

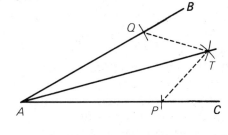

the shape *APTQ* and folding along *AT*, the children find that the two
triangles *APT* and *AQT* are identical. In particular, the two angles *TAP* and
TAQ are equal. That is, the line *AT bisects the angle PAQ.* Instead of
folding along *AT* the children can cut out the two triangles *APT* and *AQT*
and show that they are identical by placing one on the other.

4   To construct an angle of
60° the children need only to
draw an equilateral triangle,
using compasses and a straight
edge.

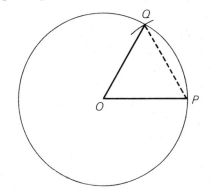

Another helpful way is to
draw a circle as shown. Then,
with centre *P* and radius equal
to the radius of the circle, they
draw an arc to intersect the
circle at *Q*. The lengths of the
line segments *OP, OQ,* and *PQ*
are all the same, so triangle *OPQ* is equilateral. That is, angle *POQ* is 60°.

By bisecting the angle *POQ* an angle of 30° is obtained.

An angle of 90° can be drawn by using the constructions described in Activities 1 and 2.

By bisecting an angle of 90°, an angle of 45° can be obtained.

Summary

When a child has completed the many activities in this chapter he or she should:

understand	how polygons are named
	the idea of a regular polygon
	the idea of a tessellation
	the idea of line symmetry
	the ideas of congruence and similarity
	how to draw shapes and to copy simple shapes
	the ideas underlying simple geometrical constructions
be able to	name all the common plane shapes
	make and use simple tessellations
	find lines of symmetry
	decide whether two shapes are congruent or are similar
	enlarge or reduce a shape
	copy a shape
	use simple geometrical constructions

Thinking about
percentages

Many intelligent children (and some teachers) experience difficulties when they have to deal with percentages. The reasons for this are not difficult to find. In their early work on percentages they went too far too quickly. They did not understand the basic idea of a percentage. They did not see the links between common fractions, decimal fractions, and percentages. 'Rules' were imposed on them which they did not understand and could not use correctly.

Children would find percentages much easier to deal with if–from the start–they thought of a percentage as a special kind of fraction. Nothing more and nothing less. All they have to understand is that, instead of using common fractions of various denominations such as $\frac{1}{2}, \frac{1}{4}, \frac{1}{25}, \frac{3}{5}, \frac{9}{10}$, or decimal fractions such as 0.5, 0.25, 0.04, 0.6, and 0.9, we change them all to hundredths. So the fractions listed above become $\frac{50}{100}, \frac{25}{100}, \frac{4}{100}, \frac{60}{100}, \frac{90}{100}$.

Thinking of the fractions in this way has several advantages:

a) All the fractions are of the same kind so we can easily compare them.

b) We can think of each fraction as a point on a 0 to 100 scale, so we can quickly get a good idea of its size.

c) It is the number of hundredths in which we are interested. This is usually 'rounded off' to a whole number. So effectively we are dealing with whole numbers instead of fractions. (But, of course, we have to understand that these are whole numbers of hundredths.)

The use of the special way of writing a percentage (e.g. 65% for $\frac{65}{100}$) is helpful in recording but in the early stages it can confuse children if they do not fully understand it.

Apart from the introduction and use of this new symbol there is nothing new in percentages. The only ability required is to change a common fraction to hundredths. In a few cases this can be done by simple equivalence (e.g. $\frac{1}{4} = \frac{25}{100} = 25\%$). In other cases the easiest method is to think of the whole as 100 hundredths. Then, for example, $\frac{5}{7}$ of the whole is $\frac{5}{7}$ of 100 hundredths. That is:

$$\frac{5}{7} = \frac{5}{7} \text{ of 100 hundredths}$$

$$= \frac{5}{7} \times 100 \text{ hundredths}$$

$$= \frac{500}{7} \text{ hundredths}$$

$$= 71.4 \text{ hundredths (to 1 place)}$$
$$= 71.4\% \text{ (to 1 place)}$$

Note: If the fraction is given in a decimal form the same method can be used. For example:

$$0.375 = 0.375 \text{ of } 100 \text{ hundredths}$$
$$= 0.375 \times 100 \text{ hundredths}$$
$$= 37.5\%$$

There is no real need for 'rules' when dealing with percentages.

Chapter 23
Percentages: everyday life

Comparing fractions by changing them to hundredths. Changing any fraction to hundredths. The use of the word 'percentage' and the symbol '%'. Profits and losses as percentages. Interest.

In 'Thinking about percentages' we saw that in introducing percentage we need to emphasize that a percentage is only a special kind of fraction. All that is involved is changing fractions to hundredths.

It is the notation used which causes children to think that percentages are different and more difficult. We need to delay the introduction of this notation until the children are confident in changing a fraction to hundredths. And when we do introduce the symbol '%' for hundredths we need to explain it carefully and help the children to understand why it is used. Some suitable stages and steps are outlined below.

Stage 1 Comparing fractions by changing to hundredths

The use of shapes can be helpful in this step. For example, various fractions of a square can be coloured or shaded, as in the diagram below.
The children are asked questions such as, 'What fraction of each square is coloured?' ($\frac{2}{5}$, $\frac{3}{10}$, $\frac{7}{20}$, $\frac{18}{50}$, $\frac{37}{100}$); 'Which square has most colour on it?' 'Which has least?' They are then asked to arrange the squares in order according to the amount of colour on them. (The children might not find this very easy.)

The squares are then shown again, with the same fraction of each coloured, but now each is divided into a hundred small squares, as below.

The above questions are now repeated and the children find that they can give the answers quickly as each square is divided into the same number (100) of small squares.

The children record:

$$\frac{2}{5} = \frac{40}{100} \qquad \frac{3}{10} = \frac{30}{100} \qquad \frac{7}{20} = \frac{35}{100} \qquad \frac{18}{50} = \frac{36}{100} \qquad \frac{37}{100} = \frac{37}{100}$$

This kind of activity is repeated for other fractions of the large squares. (These should be chosen so that each is a whole number of small squares.)

Stage 2 Changing any fraction to hundredths

Step i) Fractions which are equivalent to an exact number of hundredths.

The children are asked, for example, to colour $\frac{3}{5}$ of a square. They have to decide how many small squares have to be coloured. That is, they have to find $\frac{3}{5}$ of 100.

A simple way of doing this is to first find $\frac{1}{5}$ of 100 (i.e. 20) and then to multiply 20 by 3 (to get 60). They colour 60 squares and record

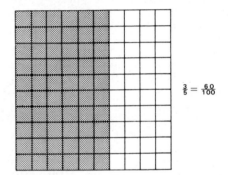

$$\frac{3}{5} = \frac{60}{100}$$

$$\frac{3}{5} = \frac{60}{100}$$

They repeat this activity for many other fractions such as

$$\frac{4}{5}, \quad \frac{9}{10}, \quad \frac{3}{20}, \quad \frac{13}{20}, \quad \frac{7}{25}, \quad \frac{21}{25}.$$

(The denominators of each of these should each be a factor of 100.)

It is very important that, in turn, each of these should be recorded as below.

$$\frac{4}{5} = \frac{80}{100} \qquad \frac{9}{10} = \frac{90}{100} \qquad \frac{3}{20} = \frac{15}{100} \qquad \frac{13}{20} = \frac{65}{100} \qquad \frac{7}{25} = \frac{28}{100} \qquad \frac{21}{25} = \frac{84}{100}$$

Without the recording the activity will lose much of its value.

Step ii) Fractions for which the number of hundredths involves a terminating decimal.

The children are asked to colour $\frac{1}{8}$ of a square. The number of small squares they have to colour can be found in several ways.

$$\begin{array}{r} 12 \\ \hline 8)\,100 \\ 80 \\ \hline 20 \\ 16 \\ \hline 4 \\ \hline \end{array} \qquad \begin{array}{r} 12.5 \\ \hline 8)\,100 \\ 80 \\ \hline 20 \\ 16 \\ \hline 40 \\ 40 \\ \hline \end{array} \qquad \begin{array}{l} \text{Using } \tfrac{1}{4} = \tfrac{25}{100} \\[4pt] \tfrac{1}{8} = \tfrac{1}{2} \text{ of } \tfrac{1}{4} \\[4pt] = \tfrac{1}{2} \text{ of } \tfrac{25}{100} \\[4pt] = \tfrac{12\frac{1}{2}}{100} \end{array}$$

In the first way there is a remainder of 4 (small squares). These have to be divided into 8 equal parts. Each of these 8 parts is one half of a small square.

$$\text{So } \tfrac{1}{8} = \tfrac{12\frac{1}{2}}{100}$$

In the second way the answer is given as a decimal:

$$\text{Again } \tfrac{1}{8} = \tfrac{12.5}{100}$$

In the third way the known fact $(\tfrac{1}{4} = \tfrac{25}{100})$ is used, together with the knowledge that $\tfrac{1}{8}$ is one-half of one-quarter.

$$\text{Again } \tfrac{1}{8} = \tfrac{12\frac{1}{2}}{100}$$

Each of these methods should be discussed carefully.

The children are now asked to colour $\tfrac{3}{8}$ of a square. To find the number of small squares which need to be coloured two ways can be used.

a) The children know that $\tfrac{1}{8} = \tfrac{12\frac{1}{2}}{100}$

$$\text{So } \tfrac{3}{8} = \tfrac{12\frac{1}{2} \times 3}{100}$$
$$= \tfrac{37\frac{1}{2}}{100}$$

Using decimal fractions the recording is:

$$\tfrac{3}{8} = \tfrac{12.5 \times 3}{100}$$
$$= \tfrac{37.5}{100}$$

b) The children find $\tfrac{3}{8}$ of 100 without using the known fact that $\tfrac{1}{8}$ of $100 = 12\tfrac{1}{2}$. To do this the equivalence of 'of' and '×' is used (as discussed earlier in the section on multiplying by a fraction).

They write $\frac{3}{8}$ of $100 = \frac{3}{8} \times 100$

$$= \frac{3 \times 100}{8}$$

$$= \frac{300}{8}$$

$$= 37.5$$

```
     . 37.5
8 )300
   240
   ───
    60
    56
   ───
    40
    40
   ───
    ──
```

Both ways should be discussed fully. This is a very important step. The fractions $\frac{5}{8}$ and $\frac{7}{8}$ should be dealt with in the same way.

Step iii) Fractions for which the number of hundredths involves a non-terminating decimal fraction.

The children are asked to colour $\frac{1}{3}$ of a square. To find the number of small squares which have to be coloured, 100 has to be divided by 3. Two ways of doing this are shown.

```
      33                          33.33 . . .
3 )100                      3 )100
   9                           90
  ──                          ──
  10                          10
   9                           9
  ──                          ──
   1                          10
  ──                           9
                             ──
                             10
                              9
                             ──
                              1
                             ──
```

In the first way there is a remainder of 1 (small square). This has to be divided into 3 equal parts. Each of these is one-third of a small square.

So $\frac{1}{3} = \frac{33\frac{1}{3}}{100}$

In the second way a recurring decimal is obtained.

$\frac{1}{3} = \frac{33.\dot{3}}{100}$

Each of these methods needs to be discussed fully. Other fractions of this kind should now be changed to hundredths. For example:

$\frac{2}{3}$ ($\frac{66\frac{2}{3}}{100}$ or $\frac{66.\dot{6}}{100}$); $\frac{1}{6}$ ($\frac{16\frac{2}{3}}{100}$ or $\frac{16.\dot{6}}{100}$); $\frac{5}{6}$ ($\frac{83\frac{1}{3}}{100}$ or $\frac{83.\dot{3}}{100}$)

For a fraction such as $\frac{1}{7}$ the fractional form of the answer is $\frac{14\frac{2}{7}}{100}$. The decimal form is $\frac{14.2857}{100}$. For this decimal form the answer should be given to 1 place or 2 places of decimals.

That is, $\frac{1}{7} = \frac{14.3}{100}$ (to 1 place)

$\frac{1}{7} = \frac{14.29}{100}$ (to 2 places)

Much practice in changing fractions of all kinds (e.g. $\frac{2}{11}, \frac{3}{7}, \frac{5}{9}, \frac{8}{13}$) to hundredths should be given.

Stage 3   Introducing the use of the word 'percentage' and the symbol '%'

It is helpful if the children first discuss words in which the idea of a hundred appears. For example:

a *century* in cricket

a *centime* as one-hundredth of the French franc and *cent* as one-hundredth of a dollar .

a *centenarian* as a man of age 100 years

cent as the name for 100 in the French language.

The use of 'per cent' is now introduced.

For example, explain that for $\frac{7}{100}$ the phrase '7 per cent' is used. '7 per cent' can be thought of as '7 out of 100'.

Relate this to the colouring of squares by discussing the relationship between 7 small squares of the large square and 7 out of the 100 small squares.

The children then practise using this new phrase.

They record many examples such as: $\frac{12}{100}$ is called 12 per cent, $\frac{43}{100}$ is called 43 per cent, etc.

Finally the symbol for 'per cent' is introduced. Explain that a short way of writing 'per cent' is often used. This is the symbol '%'. It might help to mention that the symbol '%' can be thought of as a rearrangement of the three numerals 1, 0, and 0 of 100.

The children practise using this new symbol as in the examples below.

$\frac{7}{100}$ =   7 per cent =   7%

$\frac{13}{100}$ = 13 per cent = 13%

$\frac{69}{100}$ = 69 per cent = 69% etc.

The children should also record some of their easier earlier results using percentages. For example:

$$\tfrac{1}{5} = \tfrac{20}{100} = 20\%$$

$$\tfrac{1}{2} = \tfrac{50}{100} = 50\%$$

$$\tfrac{1}{8} = \tfrac{12.5}{100} = 12.5\%$$

Stage 4 Everyday uses of percentages

When children are able to interchange fractions and percentages they should be able to deal with any everyday activity which brings in the idea of percentage (e.g. interest, profit and loss). The essential needs are to be able to understand the question or situation and to realize that a percentage is only a special kind of fraction. There is no need to introduce 'rules'. They tend to confuse rather than help.

a) Profit and loss   The first step is to provide examples of buying and selling in which either a profit or a loss is made. For each example the children decide whether a profit or a loss is made, and find the amount of this from the difference between the cost price and the selling price. Examples such as the one below are then discussed.

'A dealer bought a bicycle for £40 and sold it for £55.
Another dealer bought a table for £60 and sold it for £80.
Which dealer made the better profit? Which dealer made the better use of his money?'

The children quickly see that the first dealer made a profit of £15 and the second a profit of £20. So the second dealer made more profit than the first.

The second question brings in the idea of relating a profit to the amount of money used:

The first dealer used £40 and made a profit of £15. His profit was $\tfrac{15}{40}$ (or $\tfrac{3}{8}$) of the money used.

The second dealer used £60 and made a profit of £20. His profit was $\tfrac{20}{60}$ (or $\tfrac{1}{3}$) of the money used.

The two fractions, $\tfrac{3}{8}$ and $\tfrac{1}{3}$, can be compared by changing them both to twenty-fourths ($\tfrac{3}{8} = \tfrac{9}{24}$; $\tfrac{1}{3} = \tfrac{8}{24}$).

The profit, as a fraction of the money used, was better for the first dealer than the second.

We were able to compare these two fractions easily by changing them to twenty-fourths. But often the comparison becomes complicated. To avoid this and to use always the same kind of fraction, we change the fractions to percentages. For the two fractions above:

$\frac{3}{8} = \frac{3}{8}$ of 100%　　　　　　　　$\frac{1}{3} = \frac{1}{3}$ of 100%

$\quad = \frac{300}{8} \%$　　　　　　　　　　　$= \frac{100}{3} \%$

$\quad = 37.5\%$　　　　　　　　　　　　$= 33\frac{1}{3}\%$ (or 33.3%)

From these percentages we quickly see that the first dealer made the better use of his money. This is usually expressed by saying that the *profit* of the first dealer was 37.5% of the *cost price* of the article he bought. The profit of the second dealer was $33\frac{1}{3}\%$ of the cost price.

Note:　Sometimes in business transactions the profit is reckoned as a percentage of the *selling price*. Using this method:

the profit of the first dealer　　$= \frac{15}{55}$ of 100%

$\qquad\qquad\qquad\qquad\qquad = \frac{3}{11}$ of 100%

$\qquad\qquad\qquad\qquad\qquad = \frac{300}{11} \%$

$\qquad\qquad\qquad\qquad\qquad = 27.27\%$ (to 2 places)

the profit of the second dealer　$= \frac{20}{80}$ of 100%

$\qquad\qquad\qquad\qquad\qquad = \frac{1}{4}$ of 100%

$\qquad\qquad\qquad\qquad\qquad = 25\%$

In calculating a percentage profit it is most important that the children should always show whether the percentage is of the cost price or of the selling price. In the early stages it is better to use the cost price as the basis of percentage profit. Otherwise some children might become confused. In the same way, when losses and percentage losses are being calculated, it must be clearly shown whether the cost price or the selling price is being used.

b) Interest　The introduction of the idea of interest should be based on examples from everyday life. For example:

 i) when we borrow money from a bank we have to pay for the use of the money;

 ii) when we lend money to a bank, we are paid for the use of our money by the bank;

iii) when we put money in the Post Office Savings bank we are paid for the use of our money;

iv) when we borrow money from a Building Society to buy a house we have to pay for the use of the money.

The amount that is paid for the use of the money, by us or by a bank, is called the **interest** on the money. The interest is usually stated as a percentage of the money borrowed. For example, when we borrow money from a bank we might have to pay interest at the rate of 10%. This means that for each £100 we borrow we have to pay 10% of £100 = £10 interest each year. For a loan o f£700 we have to pay £70 each year.

After a discussion such as that outlined above the children's understanding of the topic can be checked and extended in the following steps.

i) Finding the interest on a whole number of hundreds of pounds at various rates of interest.

ii) As for (i) but with amounts such as £50, £75, £120, £625, etc.

iii) Finding the interest rate when the amount borrowed and the yearly interest are known (e.g. £300 borrowed; interest for year is £27: what is the interest rate?).

iv) Finding the amount borrowed when the interest for the year and the interest rate are known (e.g. interest for one year is £48; interest rate is 12%; how much was borrowed?).

v) Finding the interest for a number of months (e.g. £420 borrowed at 9% for 5 months: how much interest must be paid?).

Complicated calculations involving the idea of compound interest are not appropriate at the primary level. But the idea of getting interest on the interest after one year can usefully be discussed. For example, a man puts £600 in a bank when the interest rate is 5%. At the end of the year his interest is £30. He leaves this in the bank so that during the second year he is paid interest on £630. The children can calculate this interest. Several examples of this kind are sufficient to give the first ideas of compound interest.

Summary

When a child has completed the many activities in this chapter he or she should:

understand   the idea of comparing fractions by changing them to hundredths
the use of the word 'percentage' and the symbol '%'

be able to   change any fraction to a percentage
apply the use of percentages to everyday situations involving profit and loss, interest, etc.

Thinking about
ratio, proportion, and scale

This is a short section in which two topics are discussed which do not conveniently fit into any of the other chapters. Both enter into everyday activities and to a certain extent there is a direct connection between them.

Ratio and proportion

Ratio

There are several ways of comparing two quantities. For example, using the lengths of the two lines shown on the right, we can say:

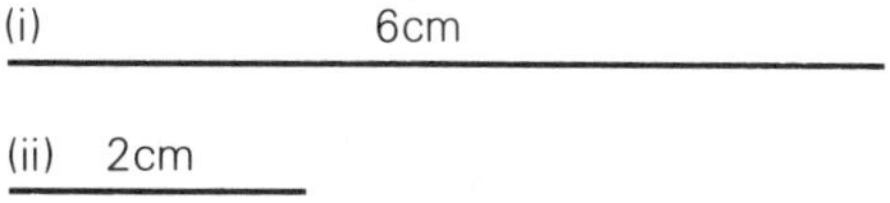

(i) _____ 6cm

(ii) 2cm _____

a) Line (i) is 4 cm longer than line (ii);
b) Line (ii) is 4 cm shorter than line (i);
c) The length of line (ii) is $\frac{1}{3}$ of the length of line (i);
d) The length of line (i) is three times the length of line (ii).

Another way of making the last statement is to use the language of ratio and say or write:

The ratio of the lengths of line (i) and line (ii) is $3:1$.

In the same way statement (c) can be expressed by saying:

The ratio of the lengths of line (ii) and line (i) is $1:3$.

There is, of course, a very close link between a fraction and a ratio.

For the rectangle shown we can write the relationship between the length and the width as:

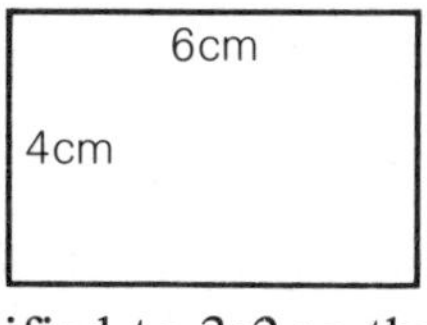

the ratio of the length to the width is $6:4$.

or   length : width $= 6:4$.

As for a fraction, the ratio $6:4$ can be simplified to $3:2$ so that length:width $= 3:2$. The $3:2$ could be changed to $1\frac{1}{2}:1$, but in writing ratios we usually try to avoid the use of fractions. It is easier to think of $3:2$ than $1\frac{1}{2}:1$.

In dealing with ratios we must remember that:

a) we can only compare quantities of the same kind. For example, a week and a day are both quantities of time so we can compare them. We cannot, however, compare 1 day (time) with 4 kilograms (mass).

b) we must have both quantities in the same units. For example, to compare a day and a week we change them both to days.

When we introduce the idea of ratio to children we should make use of as many different types of quantities as we can, for example, length, area, volume, mass, time, money, capacity. The examples should be chosen to help the children to see that they can only compare quantities of the same kind and that the same units must be used for each.

There are two uses of ratio which might require some discussion when they are first introduced.

1 The idea of showing a change in a quantity by a ratio

For example, if a man has £7 and is then given another £2, we can say that his money has increased by £2 or, using ratio, we can say that:

the ratio of the two amounts of money is 9:7.

Another way of saying this is:

his money has *increased* in the ratio 9:7.

If the man had started with £7 and then spent £2 we would say that:

his money has *decreased* in the ratio 5:7.

In using a ratio in this way we must remember to write it in a form to represent

new amount : original amount.

2 The idea of using ratio in taking samples

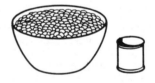

This is illustrated by the example below.
A bowl of beans is shown on the right.
We want to find the number of beans
without counting them all. We can do
this by first filling (level) a small tin with beans from the bowl and counting them. Then we can find how many tin-fulls we can get from the beans in the bowl.

If, for example, there are 24 tin-fulls, then we can say that:

number of beans in bowl : number in tin = 24:1

If there are 62 beans in a tin-full, then the number of beans in the bowl is 62 × 24.

Children need to understand and be able to use the first ideas of ratio for they are used extensively in dealing with similar shapes and later in Trigonometry.

Proportion

Sometimes we have to compare more than two quantities. For example, a farmer has 60 cattle and wishes to share them among his three sons, Jimmy, Bill, and Gary, so that for every one Jimmy has, Bill has two and Gary has three. To find how many each son has the farmer can think:

for every six cattle $(1 + 2 + 3)$, Jimmy has 1, Bill has 2, and Gary has 3.
So Jimmy has $\frac{1}{6}$, Bill $\frac{2}{6}$, and Gary $\frac{3}{6}$ of the 60.
$\frac{1}{6}$ of 60 = 10, $\frac{2}{6}$ of 60 = 20, and $\frac{3}{6}$ of 60 = 30.
Jimmy has 10, Bill has 20, and Gary has 30.

To show this kind of sharing we write:

A farmer shares 60 cattle among his sons in the **proportion** 1:2:3.

Here is another example in which the relationships between more than two quantities occur. 'The perimeter of a triangle is 39 cm. The lengths of the three edges are in the *proportion* 6:4:3. Find the lengths of the three edges.'

The starting-point for finding the answer is to find the total of 6, 4, and 3 (i.e. 13). We then write the proportion as $\frac{6}{13} : \frac{4}{13} : \frac{3}{13}$. This leads to thinking of the longest edge as $\frac{6}{13}$ of the perimeter, the second edge as $\frac{4}{13}$ of the perimeter, and the shortest edge as $\frac{3}{13}$ of the perimeter, that is, $\frac{6}{13}$ of 39 cm, $\frac{4}{13}$ of 39 cm, and $\frac{3}{13}$ of 39 cm. From this the edge-lengths are 18 cm, 12 cm, and 9 cm $(18 + 12 + 9 = 39)$.

Another approach is again to start by finding the total of 6, 4, and 3. From the result we can say that if the perimeter were 13 cm, the edge lengths would be 6 cm, 4 cm, and 3 cm. But the perimeter is 39 cm. This is three thirteens so the edge-lengths are (6×3) cm, (4×3) cm, and (3×3) cm. That is, 18 cm, 12 cm, and 9 cm.

Many examples such as these two should be provided for the children, using as many different kinds of quantities as possible. In particular, use should be made of recipes in cooking, mixes used in industry (e.g. concrete), and the many other examples of proportion which occur in everyday life.

Scale

The idea and use of scale enter into many everyday activities. When a child makes his or her first drawings use is made of the idea of scale, even though the child may not think of it as such. Photographs and pictures usually involve the use of scale. Maps are always drawn 'to scale'. Plans of buildings have the scale written on them. When drawing various graphs we often have to decide what scale to use.

So, like graphical work, it is probably best not to set out to teach the topic on its own, but to develop and use the various aspects of the topic as they occur or are required in other topics.

Generally children do not find the idea of scale difficult to understand. They can, for example, measure to the nearest metre, the length and width of the floor of a room (e.g. 12 m, 8 m), and then draw a rectangle on paper to represent the floor. They will themselves often realize that some sort of scale should be used. For this example they might well decide to represent 1 m by 1 cm. They should, however, discuss the possibility of using other scales. For example, $\frac{1}{2}$ cm to represent 1 m or 2 cm to represent 1 m. From the start they should, of course, always record the scale used.

The idea of scale comes into the drawing of many graphs, though in the early stages the children might not think of it as such. They can usually use 1 cm intervals along each of the two axes. Later they might have to use $\frac{1}{2}$ cm intervals along both axes in order to show the numbers involved. There will be occasions however when they need to show, for example, 0–10 along one axis and 0-100 along the other. Then the idea of using different scales along the two axes will need to be carefully discussed. The way in which the choice of scale affects the size of the graph also needs to be discussed and illustrated by examples. The children should always be encouraged to make full use of the piece of graph paper they are using.

As far as possible scale drawing by the children should be based on measurements which they themselves have made. The floor of a room has already been mentioned. The blackboard, the top of a desk, and windows can also be measured and shown by a scaled drawing.

Outside the classroom, the football pitch, a tennis court, a netball pitch can also be measured and drawn to a suitable scale. Later, when the children can measure angles, they can make a scaled drawing of an irregular piece of land.

In the reading of maps and obtaining of distances from them, the children's main difficulty is often that of understanding what the scale means and then being able to use it. The scale often involves large numbers and various ways are used to show it. For example, the same scale can be shown in the three ways below.

$$1 : 1000 \qquad\qquad \frac{1}{1000} \qquad\qquad 1 \text{ mm represents } 1 \text{ m}$$

In this case the third way is more easily understood by children than the first or second. But often the scale is given only in the first form. Children need help in understanding and using this way of stating the scale. Using even larger numbers the scale might be given as 1:100 000. This can be explained by reference to a length of 1 cm on the map. From the stated scale we can say that the distance on the ground which this 1 cm represents is 100 000 cm.

This can first be changed to metres (1 cm represents 1000 m).

The 1000 m can then be changed to kilometres (1 cm represents 1 km).
    The children can use this form of the scale. Much practice should be given in this kind of changing. Children should realize that drawings of very small objects are sometimes made larger than the actual object. For example, a drawing of a fly is shown on the right. The scale is:

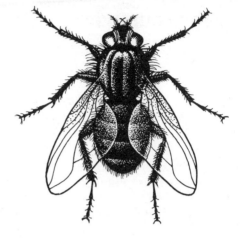

    10 cm represents 1 cm.

    This could also be shown as 10:1.

    From a drawing such as this the lengths of small parts of the fly can be measured and the actual lengths worked out.

Thinking about
negative numbers

In the early stages in primary school mathematics we do not attempt to deal with subtractions such as 4 − 7, 2 − 8, etc. We simply say that we cannot give an answer (Children say, for example, 'I cannot take 7 from 4'). But for mathematicians this was not very satisfactory. They wanted to be able to give answers to subtractions of this kind. So they introduced some new numbers. These numbers are not, however, linked with physical objects. They are given names and can be shown as points to the left of zero on a number line but that is all that is known about them. For example, to take 7 from 4 a number line is used as below.

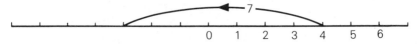

Starting at the point for 4, we move 7 spaces to the left. The point at which we arrive is 3 spaces to the left of zero. The name **negative three** is given to this point and the symbol ⁻3 is used for it.

Note: The name and symbol used need careful discussion. For many years the point, for example, four spaces to the left of zero was called *minus four* and the symbol −4 (with the bar halfway up the 4) was used for it. This was unfortunate in that children associated the '−' of −4 with the symbol for subtraction. To them the two 'minus' symbols in a statement such as 7 − (−4) were identical in some way. They did not appreciate the dual use and quickly became confused. They were not helped either when they were taught that 'two minuses make a plus' or that 'a minus times a minus is a plus'. In an attempt to help children and to overcome deep-seated confusion in the minds of some teachers, the '−' is now put in a higher position relative to the numeral (e.g. ⁻4) and the term 'negative four' is used instead of 'minus four'.

All other points to the left of zero on the extended number line can be given names in the same way so that the number line can be shown as below.

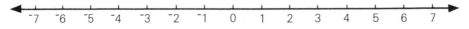

Now we can give answers to all the subtractions for which we could not previously give answers.

Children do not find difficulty in understanding this extension of the number line to the left of zero and it can well be introduced in the primary school. The children can also go on to deal with additions, using a number line, such as ‾3 + 5, ‾5 + 8, ‾1 + 9. Using ‾3 + 5 as an example, the children start at the point for ‾3 and move to the right 5 spaces. They come to the point for 2. So that, ‾3 + 5 = 2.

It is doubtful, however, whether more than this should be attempted. Operations with negative numbers (e.g. 3 + ‾2, 3 − ‾4, ‾4 × 4, ‾7 × ‾6, etc.) involve much deeper thinking and are best left until the secondary stage.

From what has been said above it is suggested that the introduction of negative numbers to children is best based on the use of a number line. The use of situations such as going up and down stairs, bank overdrafts, temperature, etc. might help but are not linked with earlier activities (as the number line is) and might confuse the children.

Chapter 24

Organizing the mathematical work in a school

The need for a plan for the school. Helping each child: individual, group, and class activities.

A plan for the school

We would all agree that the mathematical work in a school needs to be planned. Each teacher needs to be able to see how his or her work fits into the scheme for the whole primary course. Each teacher needs to know what the children have done before they come to him and what they will be doing in the next year. Each teacher needs to know what methods should be used for particular topics (e.g. for subtraction, for division). Each teacher needs to know what words and phrases should or should not be used (e.g. in subtraction, in dealing with fractions). Each teacher needs to know what methods of setting down and recording are to be used in various topics (e.g. are four nines to be recorded as 4 x 9 or as 9 x 4?). If a teacher does not have this knowledge then different methods of working, different words and phrases, and different ways of recording might be used as a child moves through several classes. This will not help the children and will certainly confuse the less able.

A plan for the school should cover all of these aspects of teaching mathematics. It should, of course, also indicate the various stages and steps in teaching each topic. This need not necessarily be done on a yearly basis. For if the stages are clearly listed then a teacher can easily indicate to the member of staff who is taking his class the following year, the stage he has reached in each topic.

Ideally, the planning should be done together by the head teacher and his staff, so that the plan can be well discussed and understood by all the teachers concerned. The agreed plan should be recorded in detail and each teacher should have a copy. When a new teacher comes to the school, time should be spent discussing the plan with him or her.

All the above would seem to be sensible and obvious to all of us. But, unfortunately, far too often a teacher is provided with no guidance of this kind. Many schools do not have an overall plan (or if they have one, it is not used). This can be a handicap to both the teacher and the children.

Helping each child

Throughout this book it has been emphasized that children can best build up an understanding of mathematical ideas and techniques through their own activities and their own thinking. As teachers, our job is to provide the activities and to encourage each child to think about what he or she is doing, to look for relationships which may emerge, and to build up a store of mathematical techniques.

We must also remember that, for most children, the understanding of a new mathematical idea usually starts with a practical experience. For example, children are helped to build up their first ideas of volume if they have a good supply of wooden or clay cubes which they can handle and make into various shapes. They can then go on to making cuboids and gradually begin to see that there are quick ways of finding how many cubes make a particular cuboid.

Through handling and making many cuboids the children find that their quick ways can be used for any cuboid. That is, the children generalize their results and ultimately some children are able to make a general statement using symbols (e.g. $V = lwh$).

This kind of progression in building up mathematical ideas underlies the learning process of every child in a class. But children vary in their natural abilities. Some learn quickly, others take much more time. So we have to find ways of helping **each** child according to his ability and his rate of learning. We know that if we teach the class as a whole then some children will soon be left behind the others. If we try to help these children by going more slowly then the brighter children quickly become bored and do not make the progress of which they are capable. To try and deal with these problems in class teaching we usually tend to teach the middle ability range in the class. The special needs of the less able and the very able are, however, still not fully met.

One way of dealing with this problem is to organize the mathematical work on an individual basis. That is, the teacher arranges the work for each child according to the child's ability and aptitude.

This means, of course, that instead of dealing with one class the teacher is, in effect, organizing the work of thirty or more classes (with one child in each) all at the same time. This method demands much detailed preparation and very careful organization and keeps the teacher fully occupied all the time. For each child it has obvious advantages but at the same time it has disadvantages. The teacher cannot deal with each of thirty or more children all at the same time so there is a danger that if a child meets a difficulty he may have to wait, doing nothing, for some time before the teacher is free to help him. Another disadvantage is that a child is involved in much less discussion—both with the teacher and with other children—than when he is working with other children. This is a serious disadvantage. For discussion, which involves asking questions and answering questions, is essential for most of us when we are sorting out our ideas about new topics. Any system which may limit the amount of discussion needs to be looked at very critically.

Another aspect of teaching which needs to be considered when thinking about individual organization is the motivation which is often stimulated by a child wanting to do as well as, or better than, the other children. This is a feeling that many children have and it often prompts them to work harder than they otherwise might. There is a danger that this kind of motivation may be lost if a child is working entirely on his or her own.

These disadvantages need to be remembered when considering an individual method of organization. It is not suggested, however, that the method should be rejected because of them. Used in a sensible way the method has many advantages and can be of real help to children.

There are various ways of organizing an individual system. One way is for each child to use a textbook and work through it page by page at his own speed. This is not a very satisfactory system as it depends so much upon the book used. Some teachers try to overcome this by using a variety of books. Then for each child a book can be used which is appropriate to his knowledge and ability.

Another way is for the teacher to break down each topic into a set of steps. For each of these the teacher prepares one or more workcards. These are numbered and graded (some are for the able children only). Each child then works through the workcards, one by one, in order, until he has completed the set. (The last one or two cards aim at testing whether the topic is understood.) The child then goes on to the cards for the next topic. After a time the children in a class are working on various topics and are using the various cards within a topic.

The preparation and organization of this system demands much time and effort on the part of the teacher, but some teachers find it rewarding.

Most teachers, however, find it more satisfactory to use workcards as part of another way of organizing the children's work. This is a kind of middle way between class and individual organization. The children are arranged in three or more groups according to their abilities. The work for each group is then related to its average ability. There are still differences between the abilities of the able and the less able in each group but these are much less than the differences for the class as a whole. The children in the less able groups have an opportunity to enjoy success (even if it is at a lower level) while the able students can be stretched more. The teacher has to prepare carefully the work for each group but can more easily attend to the needs of each group than if he were dealing with the children on an individual basis. The children have adequate opportunities for discussion (among themselves and with the teacher) and there can be a competitive aspect within each group.

If a group organization is used a teacher has to decide whether each group is to be a unit on its own (following its own course at its own speed), or whether the groups should be linked together in some way. This decision cannot usually be made by an individual teacher for it is affected by the general policy of the school. If all the children in a particular class are expected to have been introduced to the same topics during a year then there must be some link between the work in the various groups.

In these circumstances it is probably best to make use of class, group, and individual organizations as each becomes appropriate. For example, when the children have reached the stage where they can start to think about ways of finding the area of a rectangle their work can be organized as below. (For illustration, there are three groups: A = less able, B = average, C = able.)

Group work	**Groups A, B, and C**
	1 The children have a supply of paper or cardboard squares. With these they make various rectangles and find, by counting or other means, how many squares are needed for each.
Class discussion	Ways in which the number of squares was found are discussed. That is, by counting them one by one and/or by using 'number in a row' and 'number of rows'.
Group work	**Groups A, B, C**
	2 By using the grid lines on 1 cm graph paper the children draw various rectangles and find the number of squares enclosed by each. They write a statement about the method they used.
Class discussion	The statements are discussed. The idea and use of 1 cm^2 is introduced and discussed.
Group work	**Group A**
	3 More practice is provided in Activity 2 together with the use of cm^2. The teacher discusses and checks their results.
	Group B
	3 As for A3.
	4 Duplicated sheets are provided on which rectangles are drawn on 1 cm square grid. The children find the area of each.

5 Duplicated grids are provided on which rectangles are drawn (without a grid). The dimensions are shown. The children find the area of each rectangle. The teacher discusses and checks their results.

Group C

3 As for B3.

4 As for B4.

5 As for B5.

6 Duplicated sheets are provided on which rectangles are drawn, with no dimensions shown. The children find the area of each. The teacher discusses and checks their results.

The teacher discusses what the children have done so far and gets them to say how they can quickly find the area of a rectangle.

Group work

Group A

4 As for B4 above.

5 As for B5 above.

6 As for C6 above.

Group B

6 As for C6 above.

·7 On a 1 cm grid the children draw as many different rectangles as they can with an area of 24 cm².
They show their results by a graph.
They repeat for other areas such as 30 cm², 20 cm², 36 cm², etc.

Group C

7 As for B7.

8 On a 1 cm grid the children draw as many different rectangles as they can with a perimeter of 14 cm. They find the area of each and show the results by a graph. They repeat for other perimeters such as 20 cm, 30 cm, etc.

9 The children draw squares of edge-length 1 cm, 2 cm, 3 cm, 4 cm, 5 cm, etc. They find the area of each and draw a graph to show their results. They write statements about what they notice.

10 If the children have been introduced to the idea of using letters for numbers they can discuss how the area of any rectangle can be shown.

Individual
assessment   A written assessment test is answered by each child. The questions should be such that the less able can enjoy some success. At the same time there should be one or two questions which stretch the able children.

This short example indicates how a mixture of class, group, and individual methods can be used in developing a topic. It enables a teacher to introduce the topic to all the children and then develop it according to their abilities. The teacher is kept busy dealing with the various groups but, with careful preparation, most teachers find that they can cope with this kind of organization. In a lot of small schools teachers have been using this method for many years.

A teacher who has previously used only class teaching may, at first, find many problems in using together some form of group and individual organization and, at times, may experience failure. This is not unusual (it happens, too, in class teaching!) and, in fact, can be of real value if the cause of the failure can be discovered. The same kind of failure can then be avoided in the future. A teacher who is interested in mathematics and is keen to help the children in their learning will quickly overcome the initial difficulties.

Over a period of time it is the attitude of the teacher and children to mathematics which is most important. If a teacher enjoys and obtains satisfaction from his or her work and if the children welcome mathematics lessons and come to them with a desire to take a full part in all the activities, then the teacher is succeeding and the children will make good progress.

Index

List of apparatus

WHERE TO FIND A TOPIC

WHERE TO FIND A TOPIC

PUTTING THE TOPICS IN ORDER IN A SCHEME OF WORK

NUMBERS	OPERATIONS				FRACTIONS			SHAPES
	ADDITION	SUBTRAC-TION	MULTIPLI-CATION	DIVISION	COMMON	DECIMAL	PERCENTAGE	
Sorting Comparing Matching Numbers: 1– 5 1–10 1–20	Totals to 5 Totals to 10 Totals to 18	From ≤ 5 From ≤ 10 From ≤ 18			Idea and notation $(\frac{1}{2}, \frac{1}{4})$			Handling 3-D and 2-D shapes
Place-value					Idea of a mixed number			Sorting them
Numbers to 100	TU + TU (totals <100)	TU − TU	First ideas		$\frac{1}{2}, \frac{1}{4}, \frac{1}{8}$			Naming common 3-D and 2-D shapes
			Totals: to 24 to 48	First ideas	First ideas of equivalence			
Numbers to 200	TU + TU (totals to 199)	HTU − TU (H = 1)	to 81	Division: of 24 or less of 48 or less of 81 or less	+ and − of $\frac{1}{2}$'s and $\frac{1}{4}$'s			Finding some of their properties
					Fractions of objects			
Numbers to 1000	HTU + HTU (Totals <1000)	HTU − HTU	Multiplying TU by U	Divisions outside the known facts	Families of fractions: $\frac{1}{2}, \frac{1}{4}, \frac{1}{8}$ $\frac{1}{3}, \frac{1}{6}, \frac{1}{9}$			Sorting and naming triangles and quadrilaterals
Numbers >1000	Then totals >1000		Multiplying by 10	TU ÷ U (e.g. 54 ÷ 3)	Equivalence			
			Multiplying by numbers from 11 to 19		+ and − of fractions of same kind			
			Multiplying TU by 20, 30, 40, . . . , 90	HTU ÷ U (H = 1) (e.g. 124 ÷ 4)	+ and − when (a) one fraction to be changed			
			Multiplying TU by TU		(b) both			Fitting shapes together
Larger numbers	Adding larger numbers	Subtracting larger numbers	Multiplying by 100, 200, . . . , 900	HTU ÷ U (e.g. 651 ÷ 3)	fractions to be changed	Showing tenths		Line symmetry
Multiples Factors Prime numbers			Multiplying by HTU	'Short' division	Use of equivalence	+ and − of tenths		Sorting and naming polygons
Ratio and proportion	Adding several numbers		Multiplying by larger numbers	Dividing HTU by a number from 11 to 19 (e.g. 254 ÷ 13)	Multiplying by a fraction Multiplying by a mixed number	Showing hundredths ÷ and − (2 places) Showing thousandths		Forming shapes Congruence and similarity
				HTU ÷ TU (e.g. 467 ÷ 34)	Dividing by a fraction and by a mixed number	Multiplying a decimal by: a whole no. a decimal no.		
				Dividing by larger numbers		Decimal answers in divisions		Geometrical constructions
Idea of a negative number						Recurring decimals	Comparing fractions by changing them to hundredths	Drawing and copying shapes
						Changing a common fraction to a decimal Dividing by a decimal	Use of 'percentage' and '%'	

PUTTING THE TOPICS IN ORDER IN A SCHEME OF WORK

MEASURES							GRAPHICAL WORK
LENGTH	AREA	VOLUME CAPACITY	TIME	MASS	ANGLE	MONEY	
Comparing lengths Use of 'natural' measures		Water and sand activities for comparing capacities	Telling the time in hours	Comparing masses		Use of coins in buying. Getting change	Arrow graphs, block graphs, and pictographs should be used whenever possible throughout the course
Use of metres Idea and use of centimetres		Measuring in litres Making shapes with unit cubes	Telling the time in $\frac{1}{2}$ hours	Use of everyday objects for balancing Use of kg and $\frac{1}{2}$ kg, $\frac{1}{4}$ kg		Equivalence of coins Buying. Getting change + and −	
Measuring in m and cm + and − of m and cm Perimeters of simple shapes First ideas of scale Measuring in millimetres	Using grids to compare sizes of shapes (regular and irregular) Use of cm² Area of a rectangle	Making cuboids and cubes with unit cubes Using litres (and $\frac{1}{2}$ l and $\frac{1}{4}$ l) Volumes of cubes and cuboids (whole numbers) Conservation of volume	Idea and use of 'quarter past' and 'quarter to' Use of minutes in telling the time Larger units of time (e.g. days, months, years)		The idea and use of a 'complete turn' Fractions of a turn A right-angle Direction Idea and use of degrees	Equivalence of coins and banknotes Buying and getting change × and ÷ + and − of notes and coins	
Use of kilometres Using scale on maps and plans	Conservation of area	Litres and millilitres	Use of seconds The 24-hour clock		Measuring and drawing angles		Pie-graphs
Showing cm and mm as decimal fractions of 1 m Circumference of a circle	Areas of triangles and parallelograms Ares and hectares Area of a circle	Showing ml as a decimal fraction of 1 l Volume of an irregular object Volumes of cubes and cuboids (use of decimals) Volume of a prism Volume of a cylinder	Tenths and hundredths of a second	Showing grams as a decimal fraction of 1 kg The metric tonne	Acute, obtuse, and reflex angles Angle sum of a triangle	The decimal notation for money Profit and loss × ÷ Profit and loss as a percentage Interest	Use of points on a grid

Oxford University Press, Walton Street, Oxford OX2 6DP

London Glasgow New York Toronto
Delhi Bombay Calcutta Madras Karachi
Nairobi Dar es Salaam Cape Town Salisbury
Kuala Lumpur Singapore Hong Kong Tokyo
Melbourne Auckland

and associate companies in
Beirut Berlin Ibadan Mexico City Nicosia

ISBN 0 19 832539 8

© D. Paling, 1982

Printed in Great Britain by Spottiswoode Ballantyne Ltd, Colchester and London